The Genesis Family Photo Album

The Genesis Family Photo Album

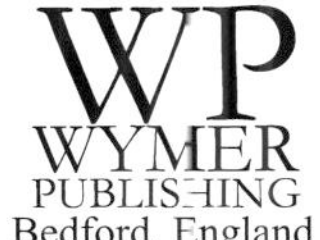

WP
WYMER
PUBLISHING
Bedford, England

First published in Great Britain in 2018
by Wymer Publishing as:
Genesis… Counting Out Time: A Photographic Journey
(ISBN: 978-1-912782-00-0, limited edition hardback)

www.wymerpublishing.co.uk
Tel: 01234 326691
Wymer Publishing is a trading name of Wymer (UK) Ltd

Typeset by The Andys.
Printed and bound in Wales by Cambrian Printers.

A catalogue record for this book is available from the British Library.

Cover design by The Andys.
Front cover photo © Alan Perry

Counting Out Time
6

Better Not Compromise.
It Won't Be Easy
8

Then There Were Four...
46

...And Three...
68

Acknowledgements
127

Counting Out Time

There are very few bands that over the course of a career have produced as much notable work as Genesis. Both collectively and individually. To get one band member who flies solo and has a high level of success is impressive, but to have pretty much all of them achieve such a thing is quite astounding.

This photographic document takes us on that journey from the early days, through the departures of Peter Gabriel and then Steve Hackett, and onwards and upwards as those two individuals' careers blossomed. Not to be outdone, Phil Collins and later Mike Rutherford did likewise.

In between all of this there has been the odd reunion as well as joint collaborations, and we have tried to celebrate as much as possible of the

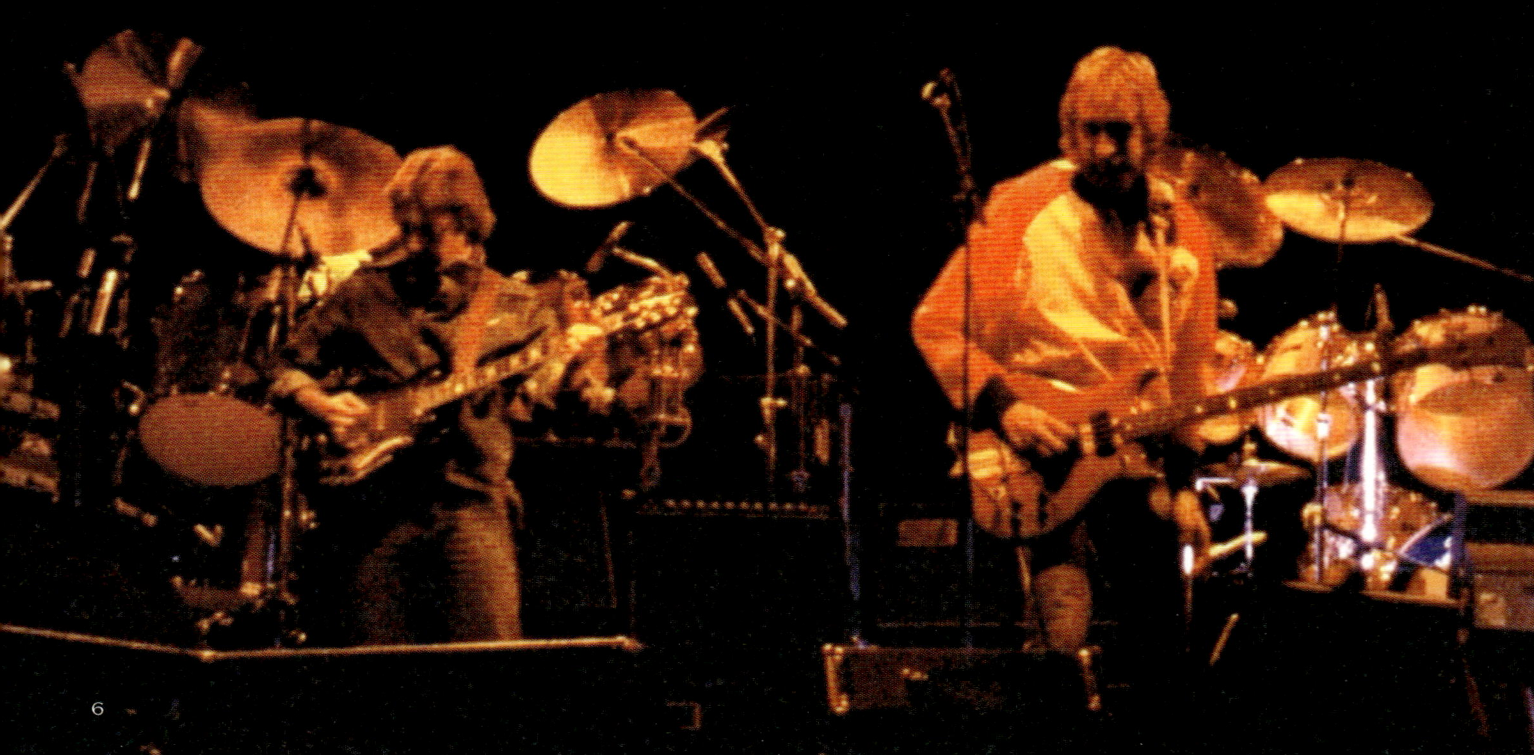

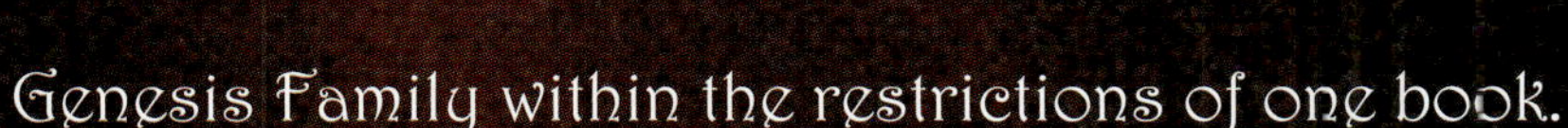

Genesis Family within the restrictions of one book.

We duly acknowledge that there are gaps in this journey that started in 1967. Most notably the absence of any band photos with original guitarist Anthony Phillips. The band's own official publication Chapter & Verse, pretty much captures the majority of photos from those very early days and it seemed pointless to try and replicate them here. Sadly the handful of photos we did manage to unearth were met with huge intransigence from the copyright holder and the aggravation wasn't worth the loss of hair that could have ensued.

Nevertheless, we have tried to compile a book for you to enjoy and hopefully with many photos that you have not seen in print before. A souvenir of "a time of valour and legends born." Harold Demure still might not be sure but if you come away humming your favourite Genesis tunes after absorbing this, it will all have been worthwhile.

William Wright

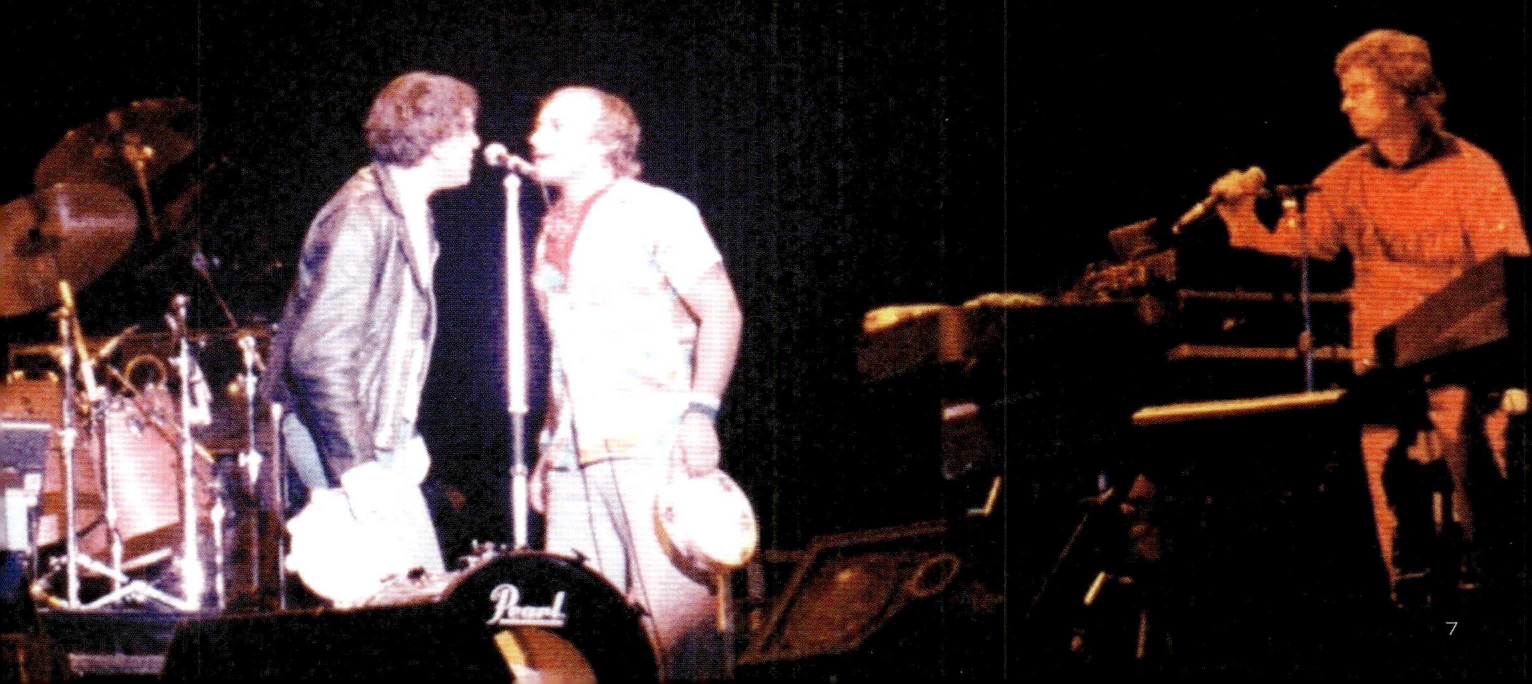

Better Not Compromise. It Won't Be Easy.

Genesis is a unique band in so many ways. Sure, they originated from school bands, like so many others did, but I can't think of too many bands that came from such prestigious backgrounds as Charterhouse, one of the top independent schools in the country.

A good education is no guarantee of success, but in such an environment, the norm would seem to be to prepare pupils for vocations that require first rate degrees. I can't be certain but I would imagine that it has produced more doctors, lawyers and financiers than rock stars.

Still, its just as well that we are not all the same as that would indeed make a dull world. Dull is anything but what Genesis has been over the past fifty years.

Initially, largely thanks to Peter Gabriel's theatrics they stood out from most other bands of the late sixties and early seventies. Taking his inspiration from a variety of sources Gabriel ensured that the band got noticed.

For many the early seventies was a golden era for rock music. The freedom of expression had never been so welcomed and it gave Genesis the room to be far more adventurous than they could have dreamt of. That said they always focused on the music first.

As those immortal lines from 'Supper's Ready' proclaimed, "better not compromise. It won't be easy." But for Genesis who didn't compromise their art, the ease with which it delivered success paid dividends. They soon went from playing clubs and universities to arenas before Peter donned his batwings and flew off to pastures new.

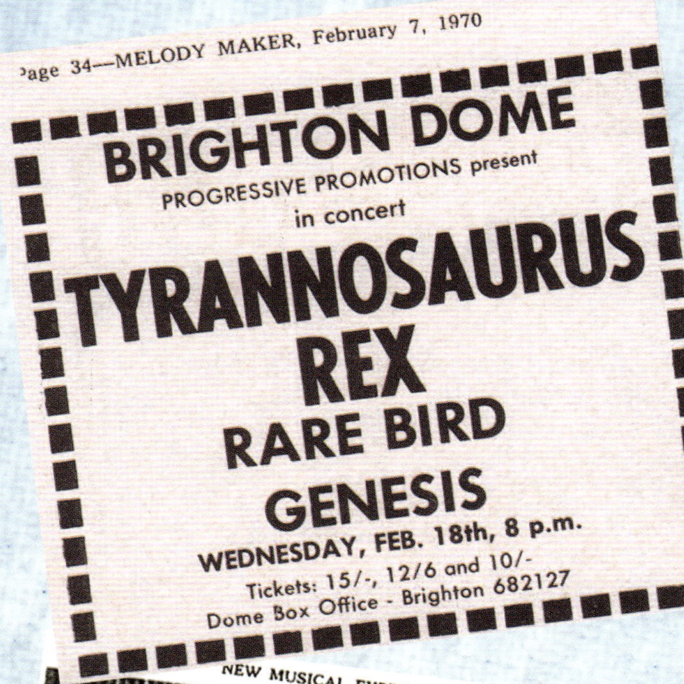

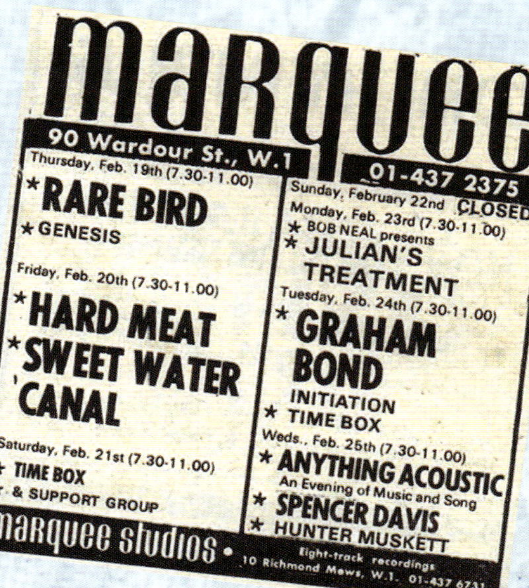

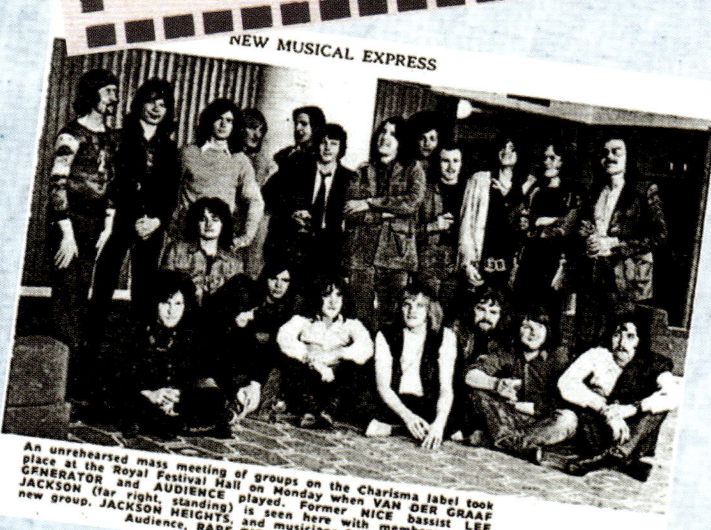

An unrehearsed mass meeting of groups on the Charisma label took place at the Royal Festival Hall on Monday when VAN DER GRAAF GENERATOR and AUDIENCE played. Former NICE bassist LEE JACKSON (far right, standing) is seen here with members of his new group, JACKSON HEIGHTS, and musicians from Van Der Graaf, Audience, RARE BIRD and GENESIS.

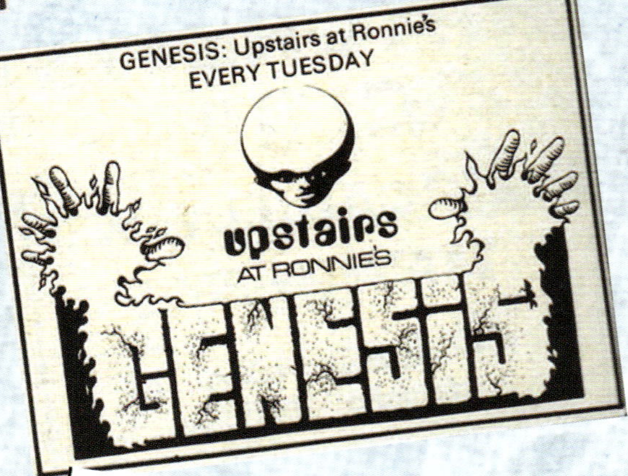

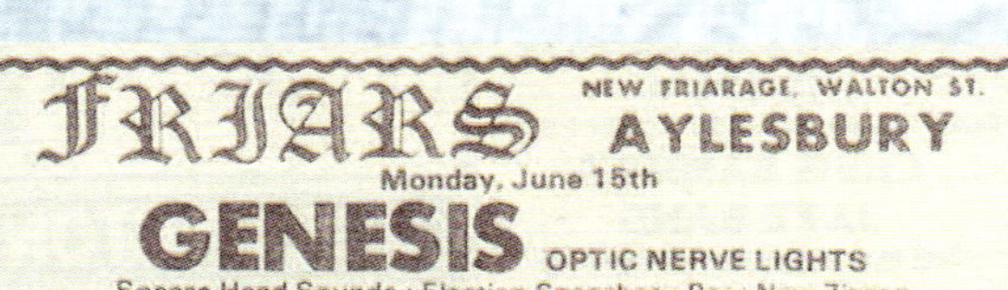

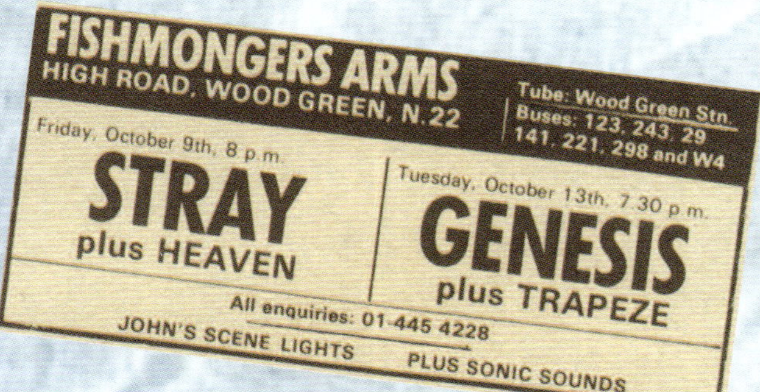

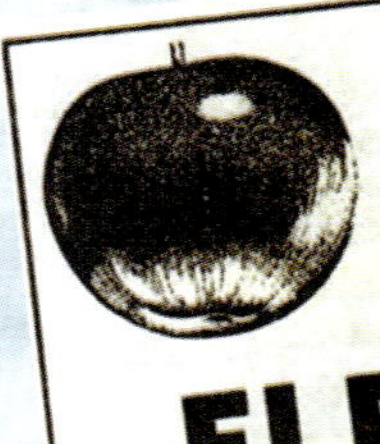

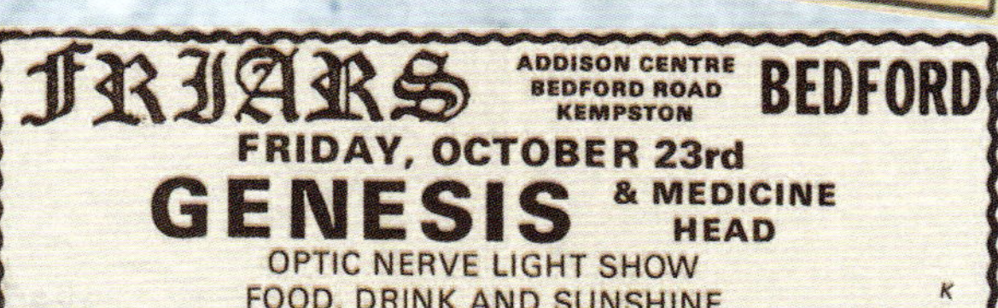

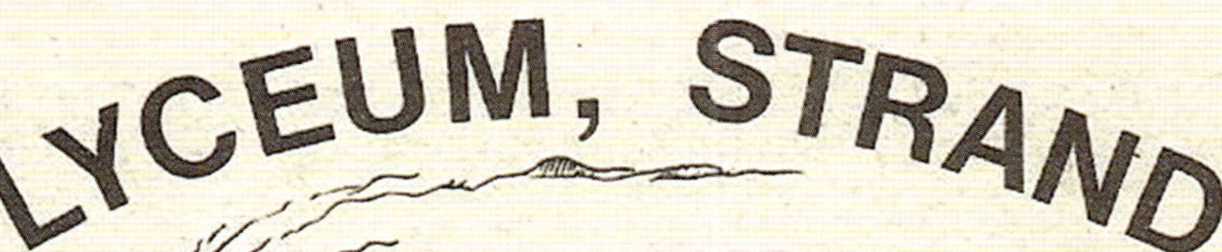

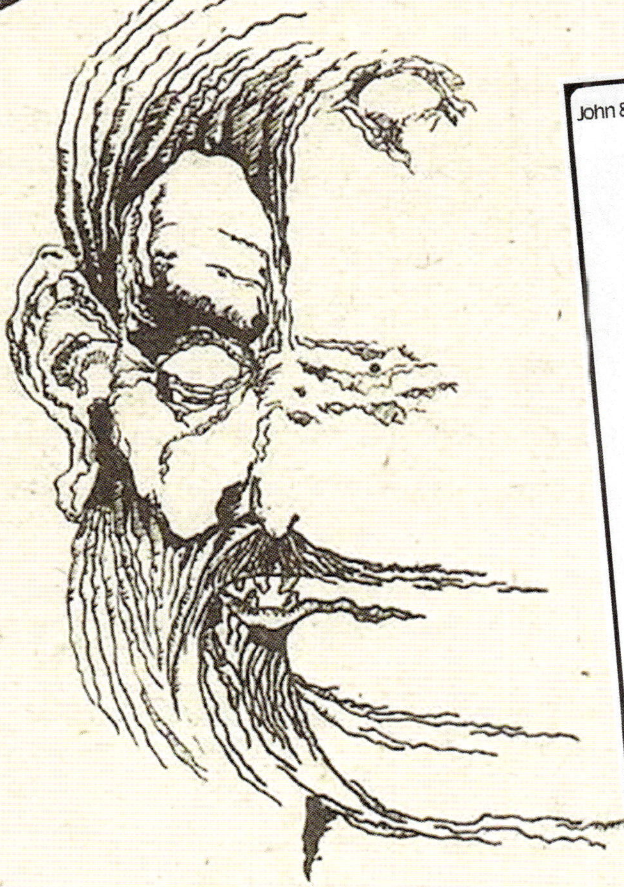

John & Tony Smith in association with Tony Stratton Smith and Terry King

PRESENT

TOGETHER IN CONCERT

on the following dates

January	24th	Lyceum Strand London*
"	25th	Town Hall Birmingham
"	26th	Colston Hall Bristol
"	27th	City Hall Sheffield
"	28th	St. Georges Hall Bradford
"	30th	Free Trade Hall Manchester
"	31st	City Hall Newcastle
February	11th	Dome Brighton
"	13th	Winter Gardens Bournemouth

VAN DER GRAAF GENERATOR

'Van der Graaf's 'The Least We Can Do Is Wave To Each Other' was one of the best debut albums — any, one of the best albums — of 1970, but their new epic 'H to He, Who Am The Only One' threatens to overshadow it to a large extent'
RICHARD WILLIAMS, 'MELODY MAKER' 28.11.70.

LINDISFARNE

'Herald an exciting new band — one of the few to have emerged this year... Their hallmark is strong, clear, straight-ahead songs... Alan Hall and Rod Clements reveal a simplicity and force-fulness of approach reminiscent of Lennon and McCartney in their mid-period'
MICHAEL WATTS, 'MELODY MAKER' 12.12.70.

GENESIS

'This is exactly what Genesis required to compile the beautiful 'Trespass' — The time and patience to achieve perfection... Now, without doubt, they have come of age. At the famous Mothers Club, they are regarded as the best new band to have appeared there'
JEREMY GILBERT, 'SOUNDS' 9.1.71.

ADMISSION ALL SEATS 6/– (30np)

Numbered tickets available in advance from the box office
Admission 9/- this concert only

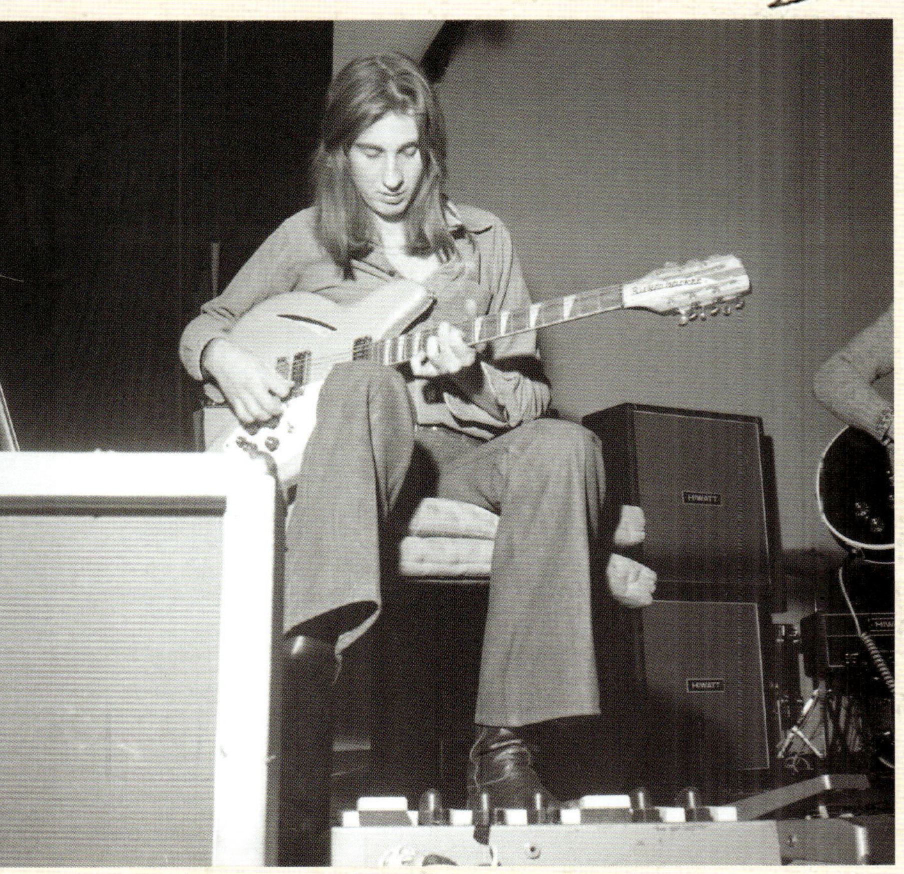

This first set of photos were taken at London's Lyceum on 24th January 1971 by Colin McLeod who explains, "my first job at 16 was as a darkroom assistant on a local paper. They trained me as a photographer and at weekends I'd go to gigs and take photos."

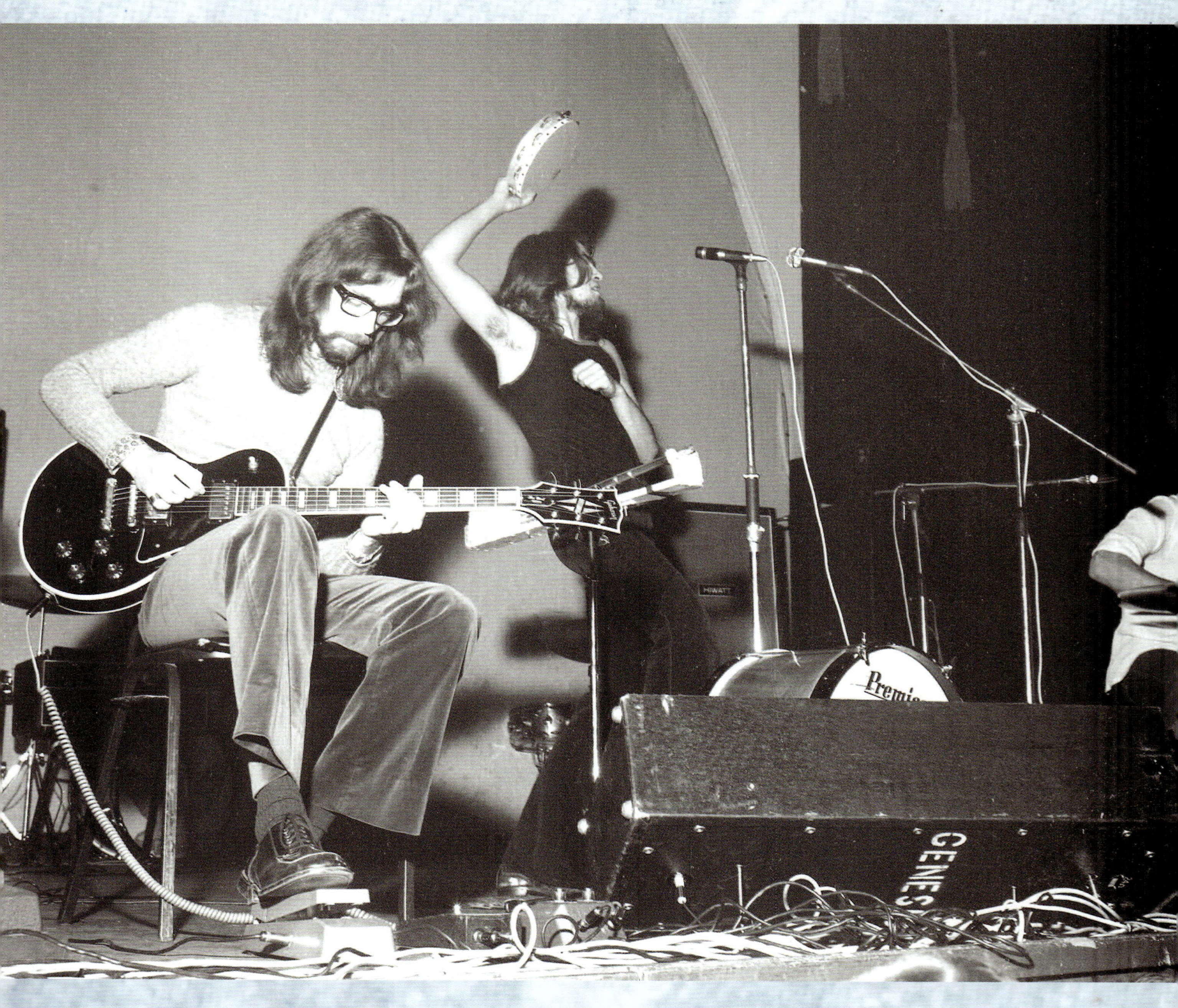

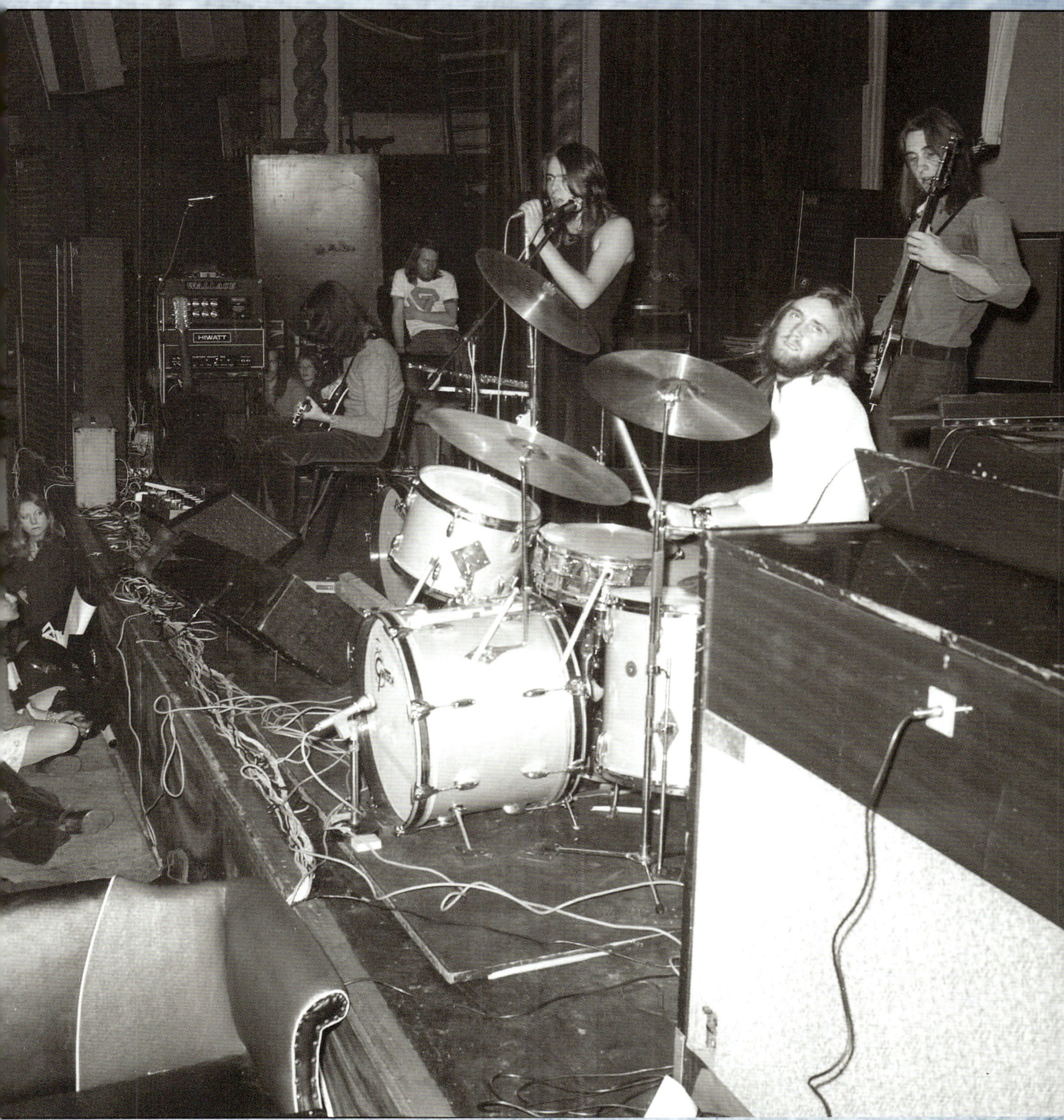

The band has always remarked that in the early days the audience was predominantly male but as this photo shows, there were certainly some attentive girls... at least at this particular gig.

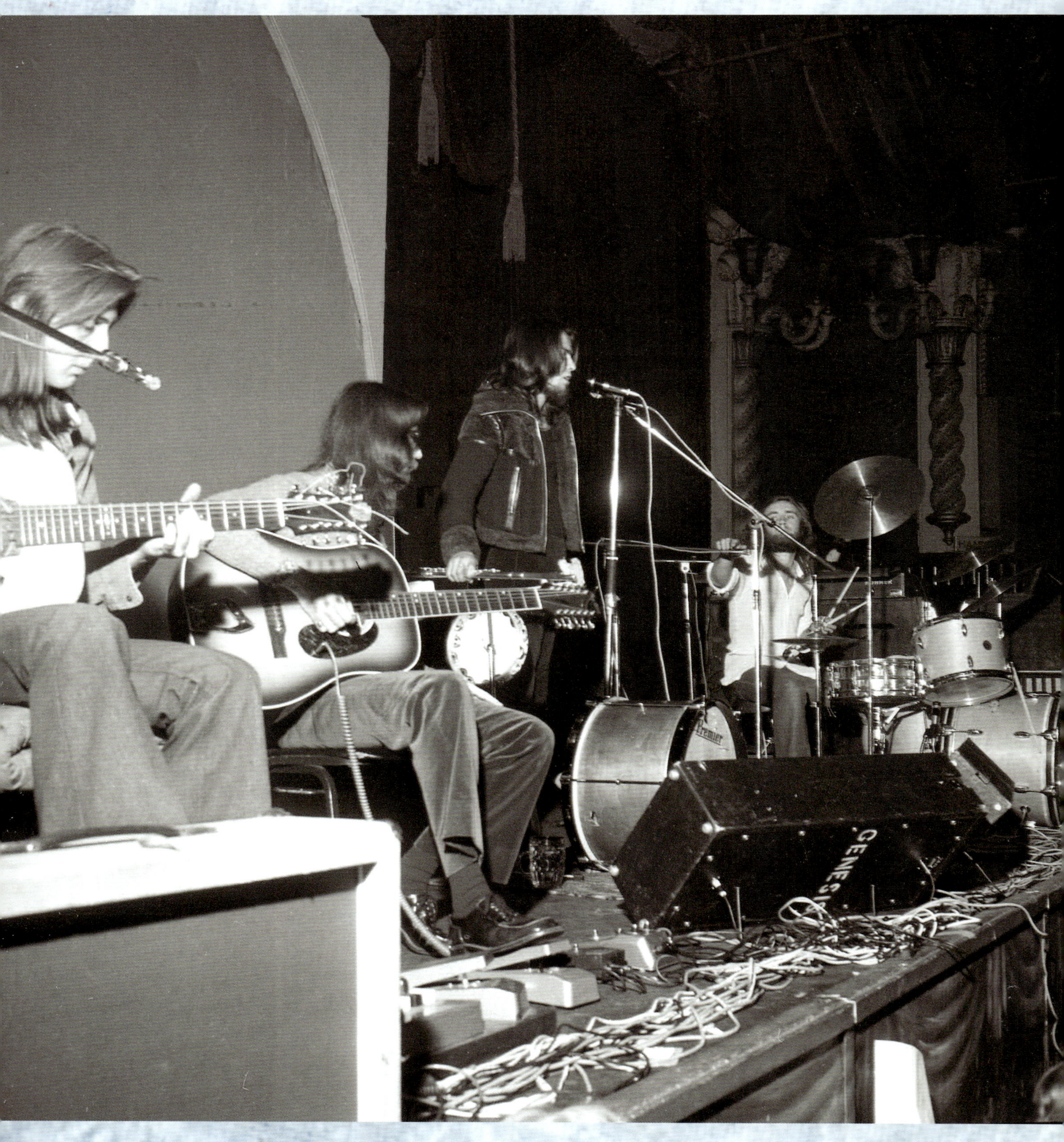

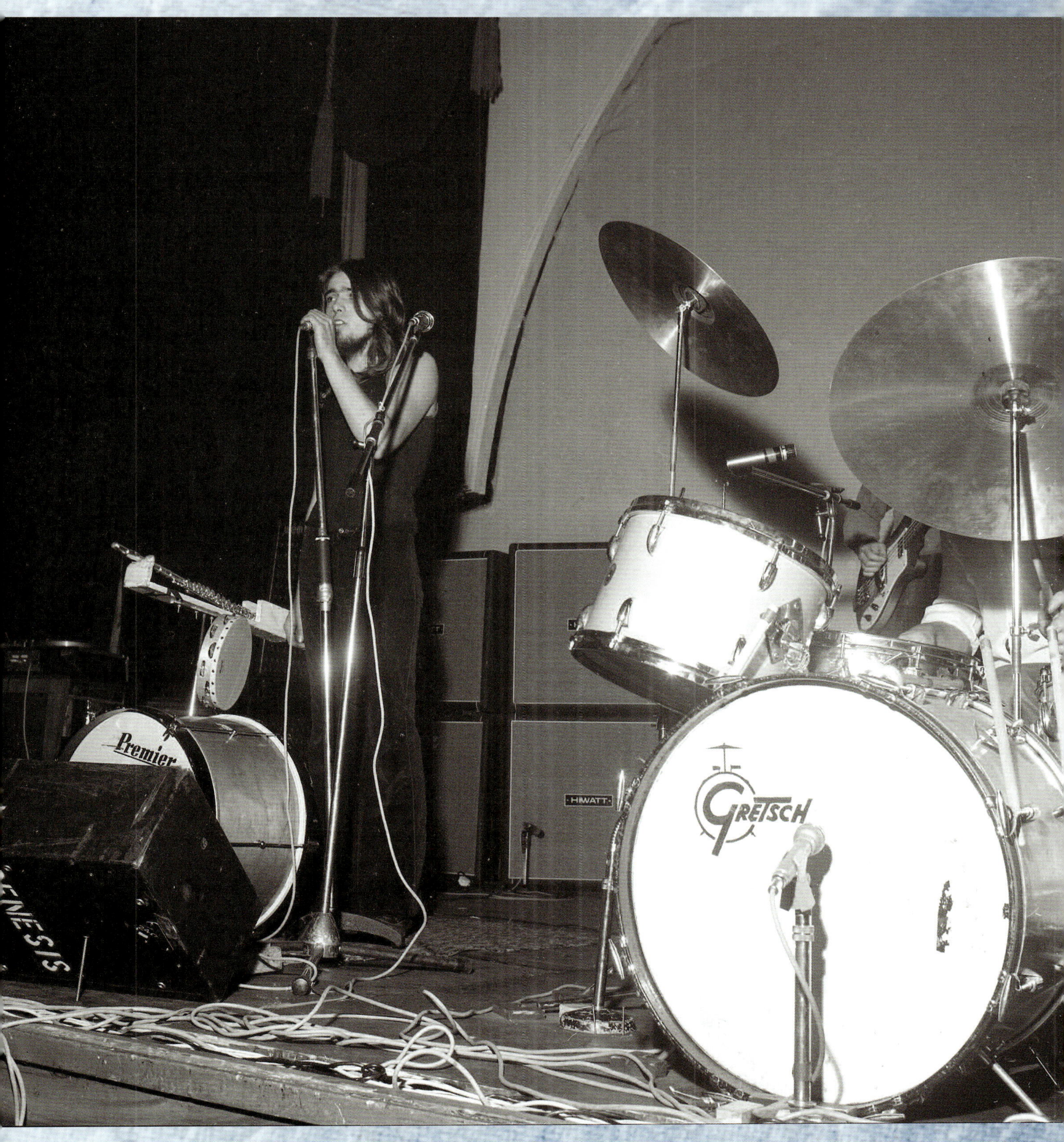
Premier
GRETSCH
GENESIS
HIWATT

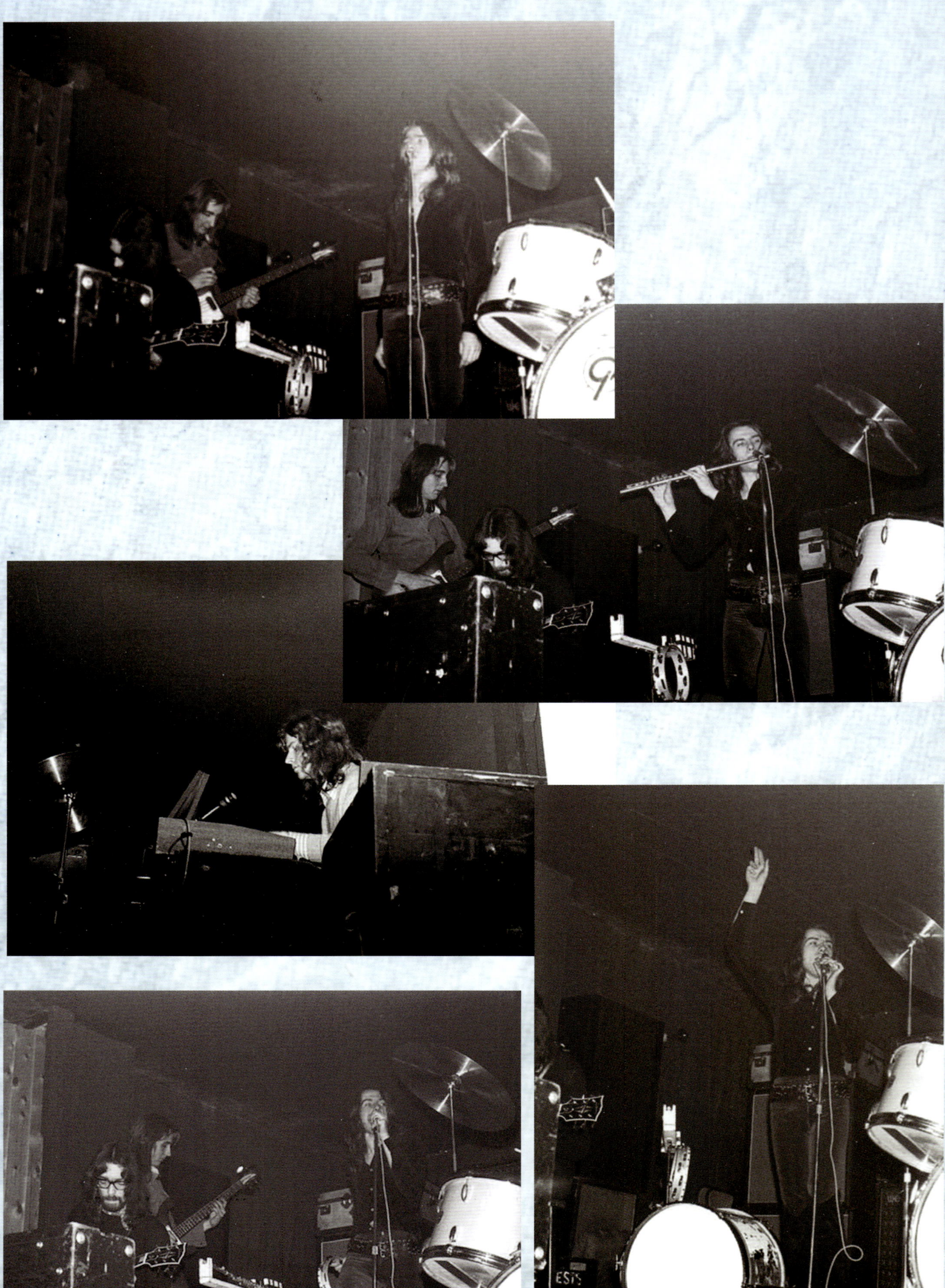

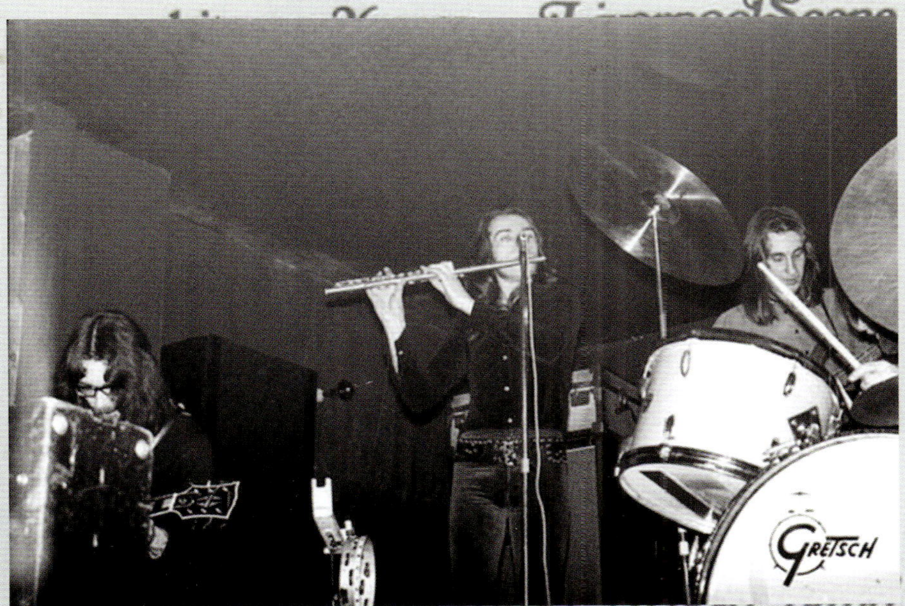
VanDike
Exmouth Road
PLYMOUTH ·· 51326/7

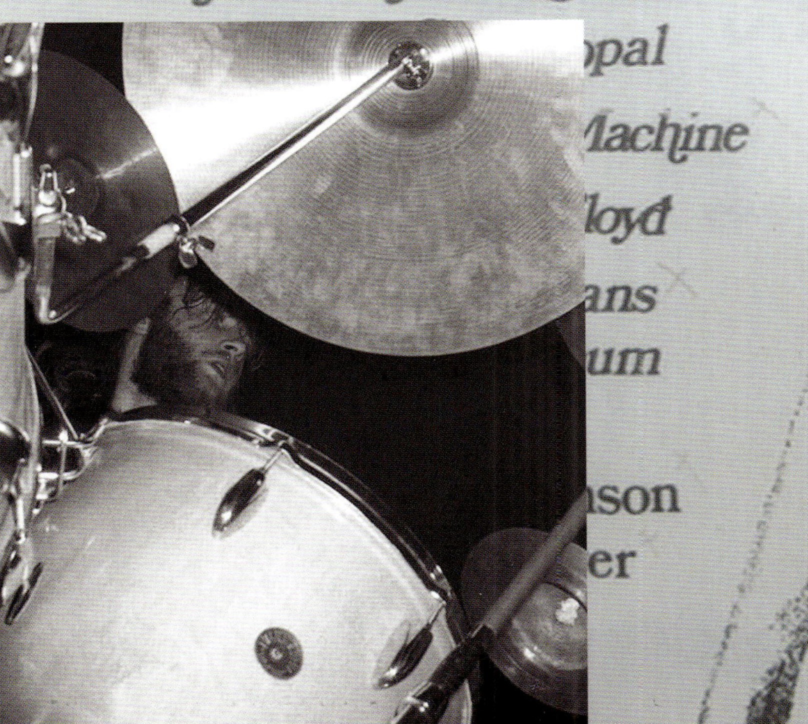

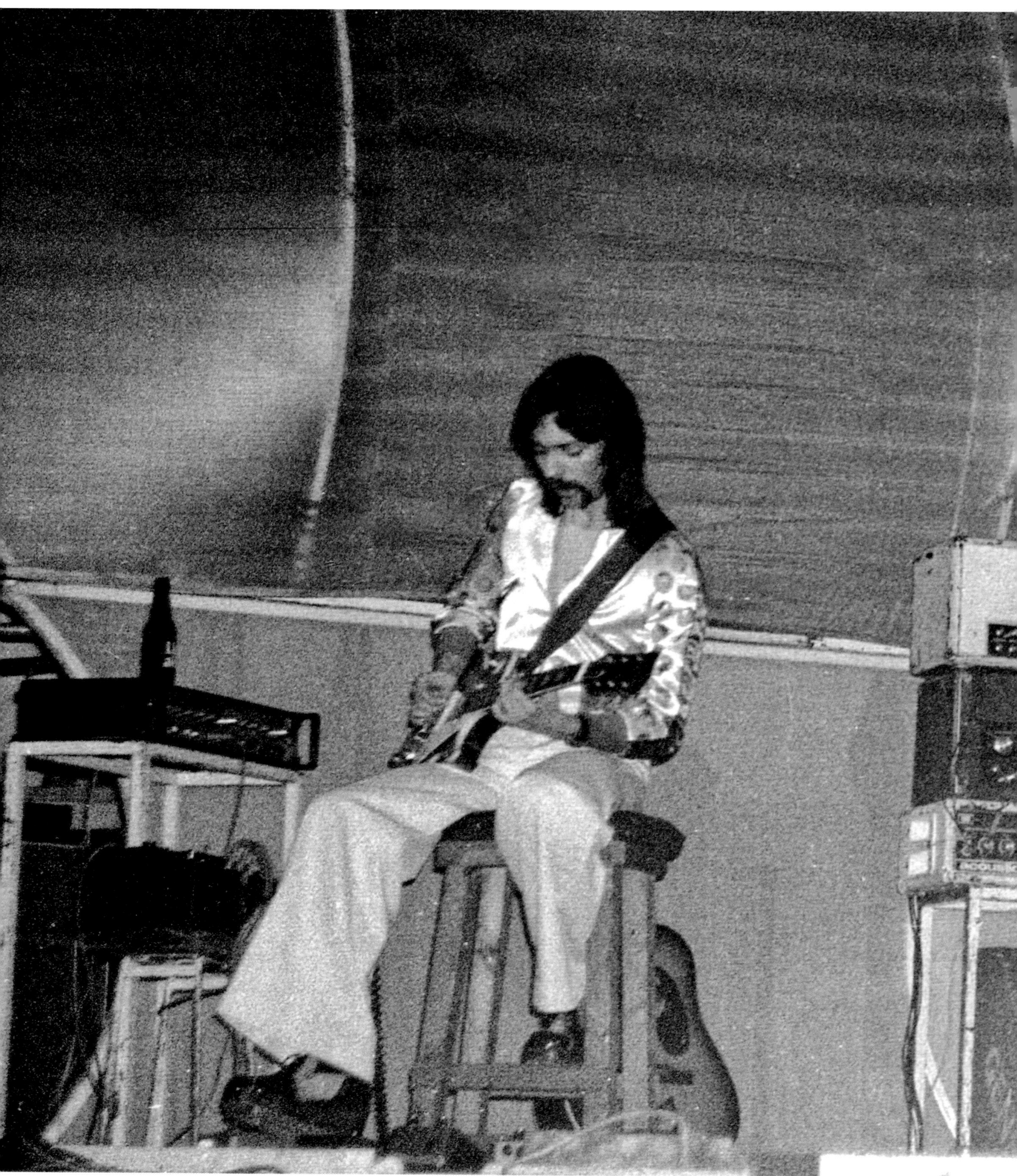

Richard Haines: "Having seen Genesis support Lindisfarne at The Top Rank in Brighton on 27th October 1972 I became a huge Genesis fan. The band was promoting the *Foxtrot* album. I really liked the progressive movement in music and was enjoying King Crimson, Yes and Pink Floyd, but Genesis surpassed these for me. The melodies, the complex instrumentation and Peter Gabriel's stunning stage performances and charisma were outstanding. Peter is the best stage performer and showman I had seen and, for that matter, have ever seen."

"I went to see the band a second time on Tuesday 7th November 1972 at Fairfield Halls Croydon, and to see 'Suppers Ready' played live was just fantastic."

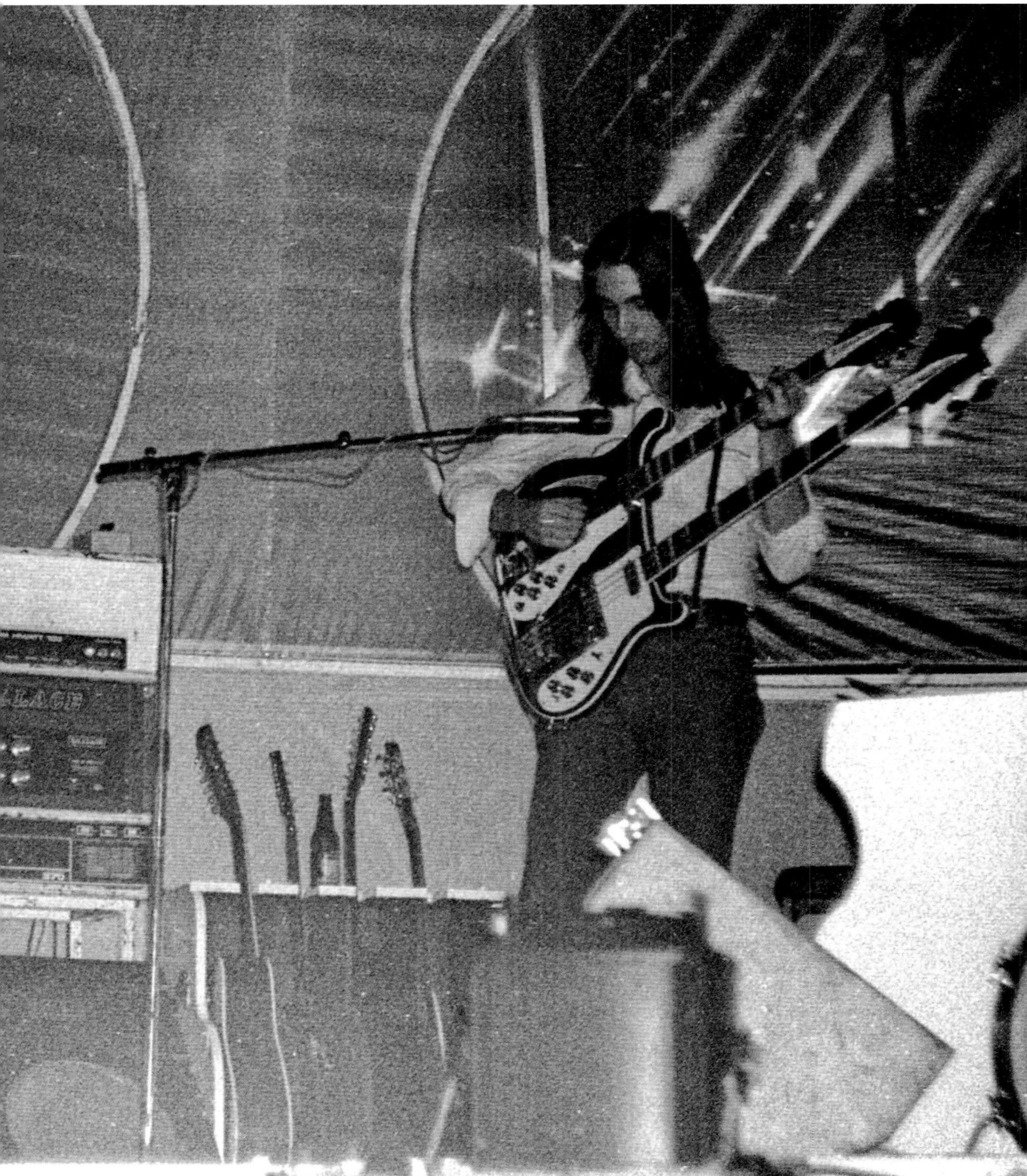

"The encore was usually 'The Knife' which created a brilliant atmosphere. Peter Gabriel's storytelling and vocals were very original, Phil Collins inventive complex drumming, Tony Banks soaring melodies and keyboard gymnastics, Mike Rutherford's dramatic bass and Steve Hackett's inimitable guitar parts."

"It's hard to describe the excitement at hearing this music. I immediately bought *Nursery Cryme*, *Trespass* and *Genesis to Revelation* and listened to them constantly until *Selling England by The Pound* was released."

"I also went to see the band live whenever they were anywhere near. The ticket price was 12s 6d old money relating to about 62p now!"

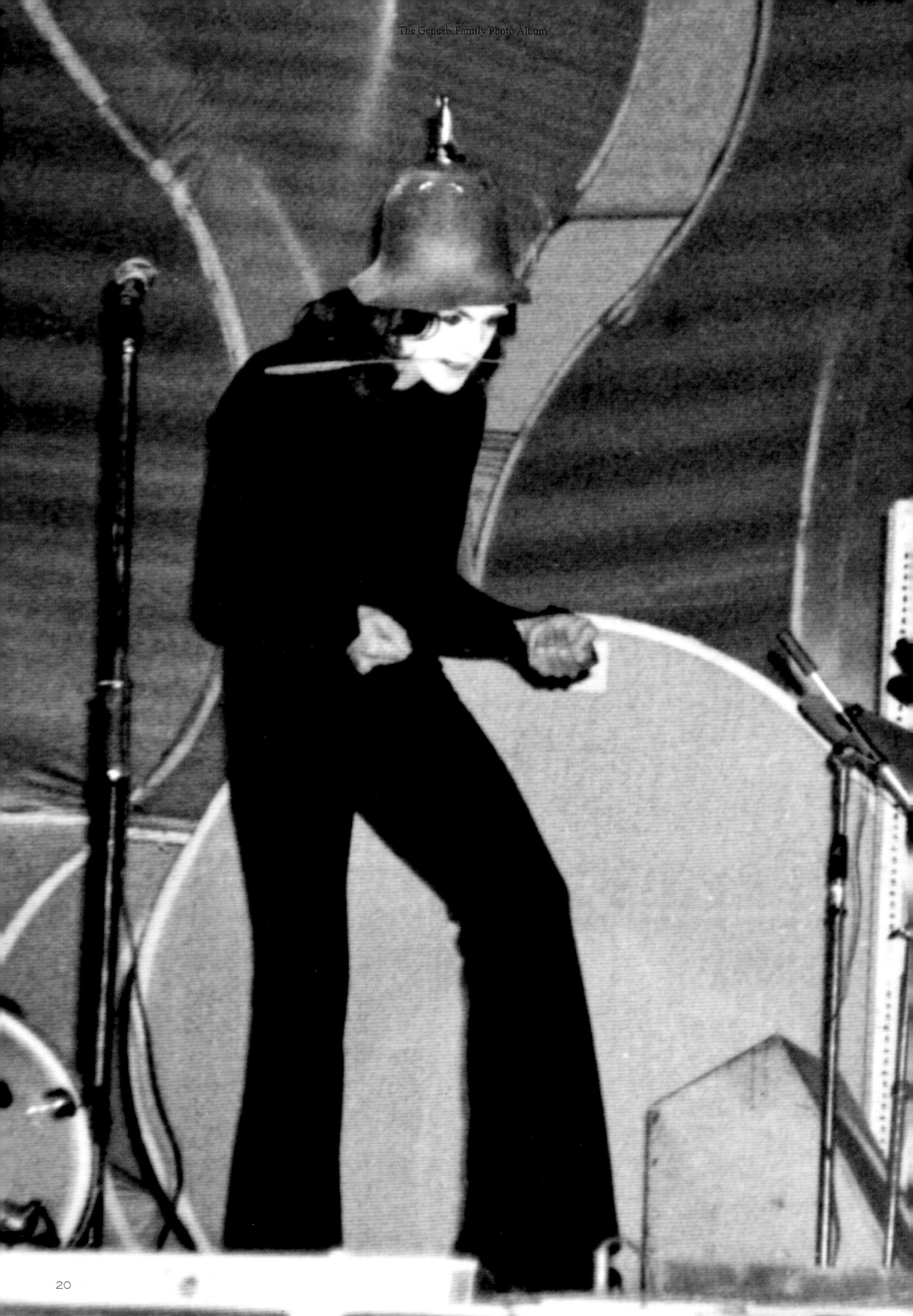

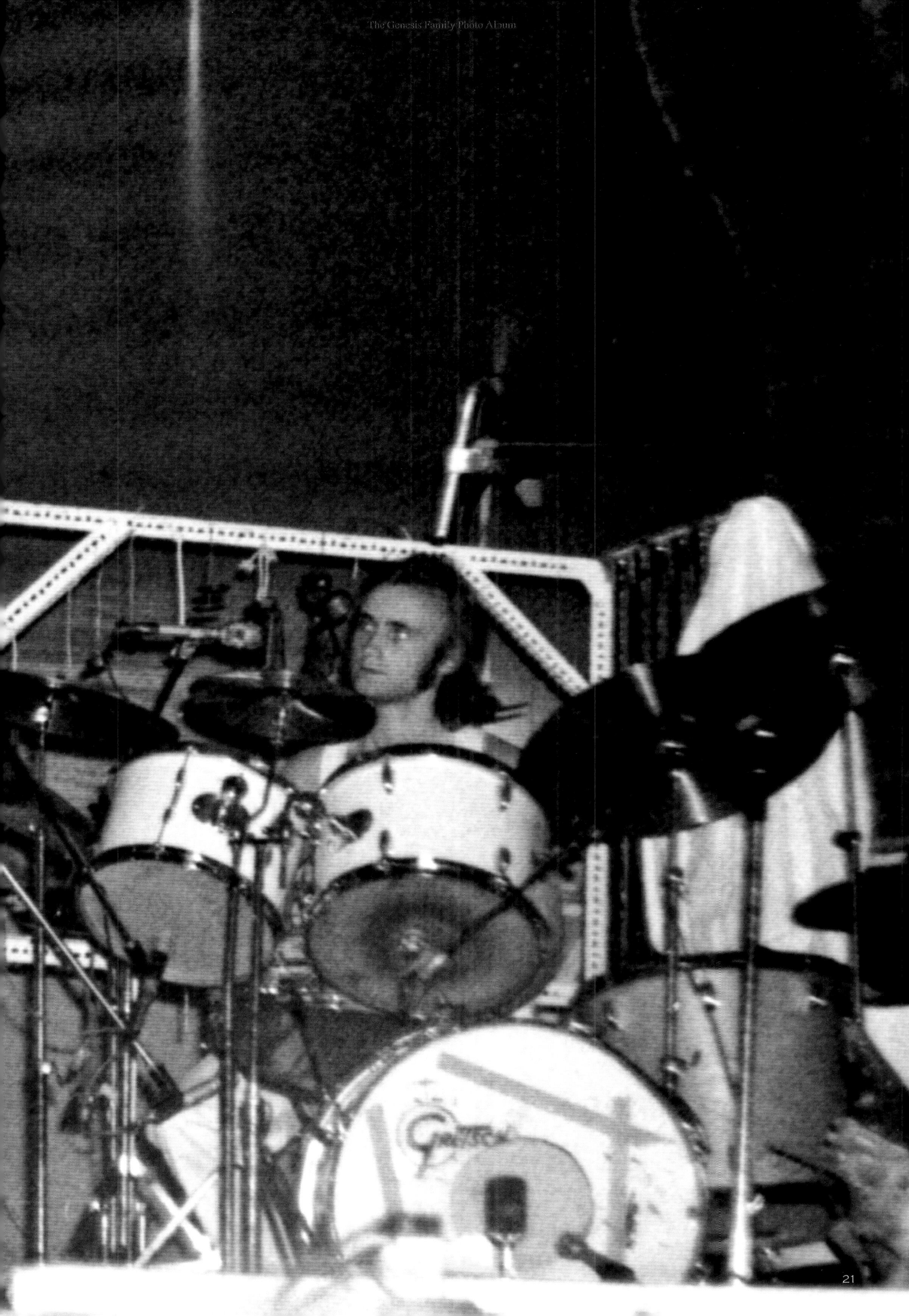

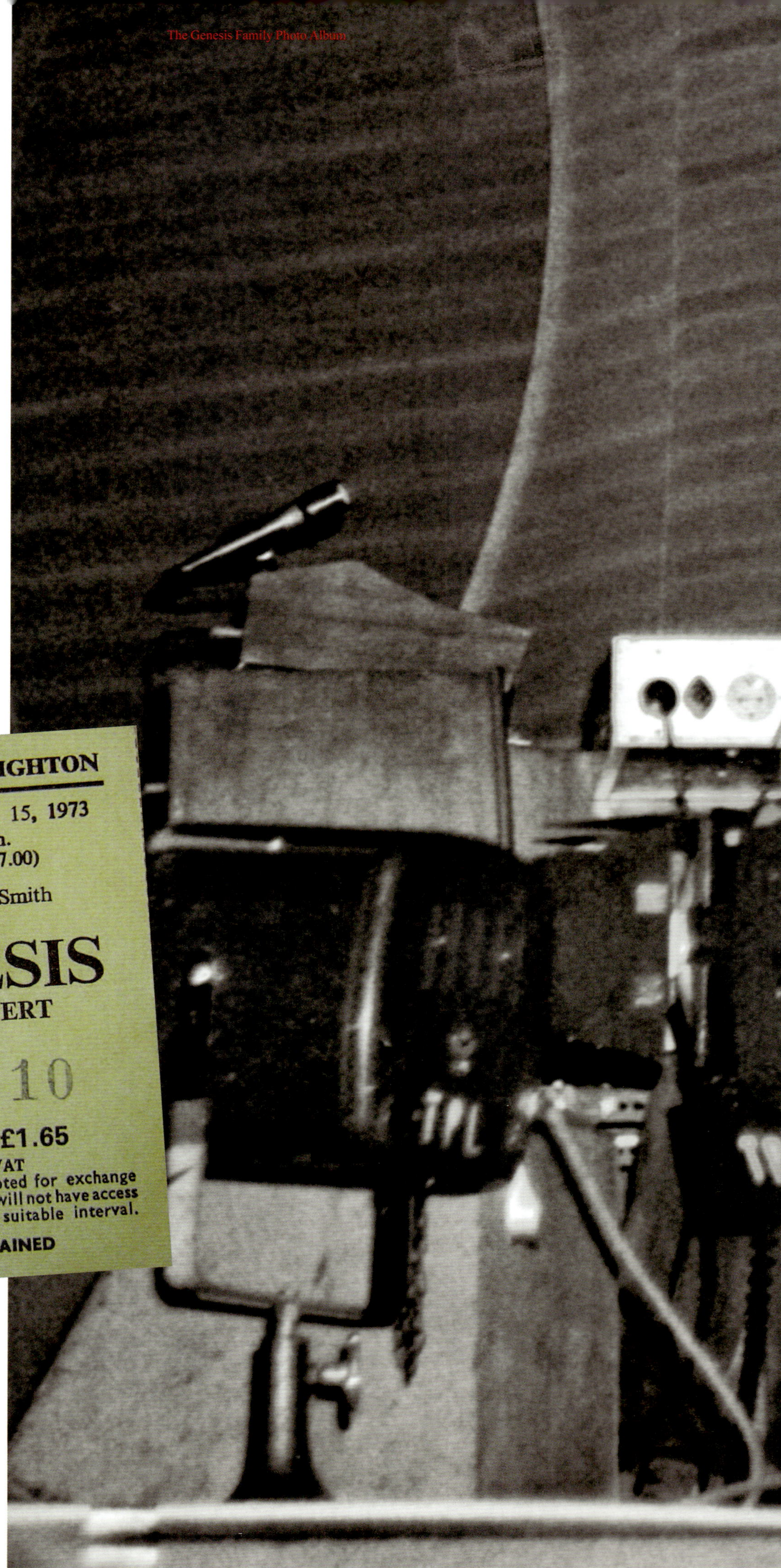
THE DOME, BRIGHTON
MON., OCTOBER 15, 1973
at 7.30 p.m.
(Doors open 7.00)
John & Tony Smith
present
GENESIS
IN CONCERT
ROW
C 10
STALLS £1.65
Including VAT
Tickets cannot be accepted for exchange
or refund. Latecomers will not have access
to their seats until a suitable interval.
TO BE RETAINED

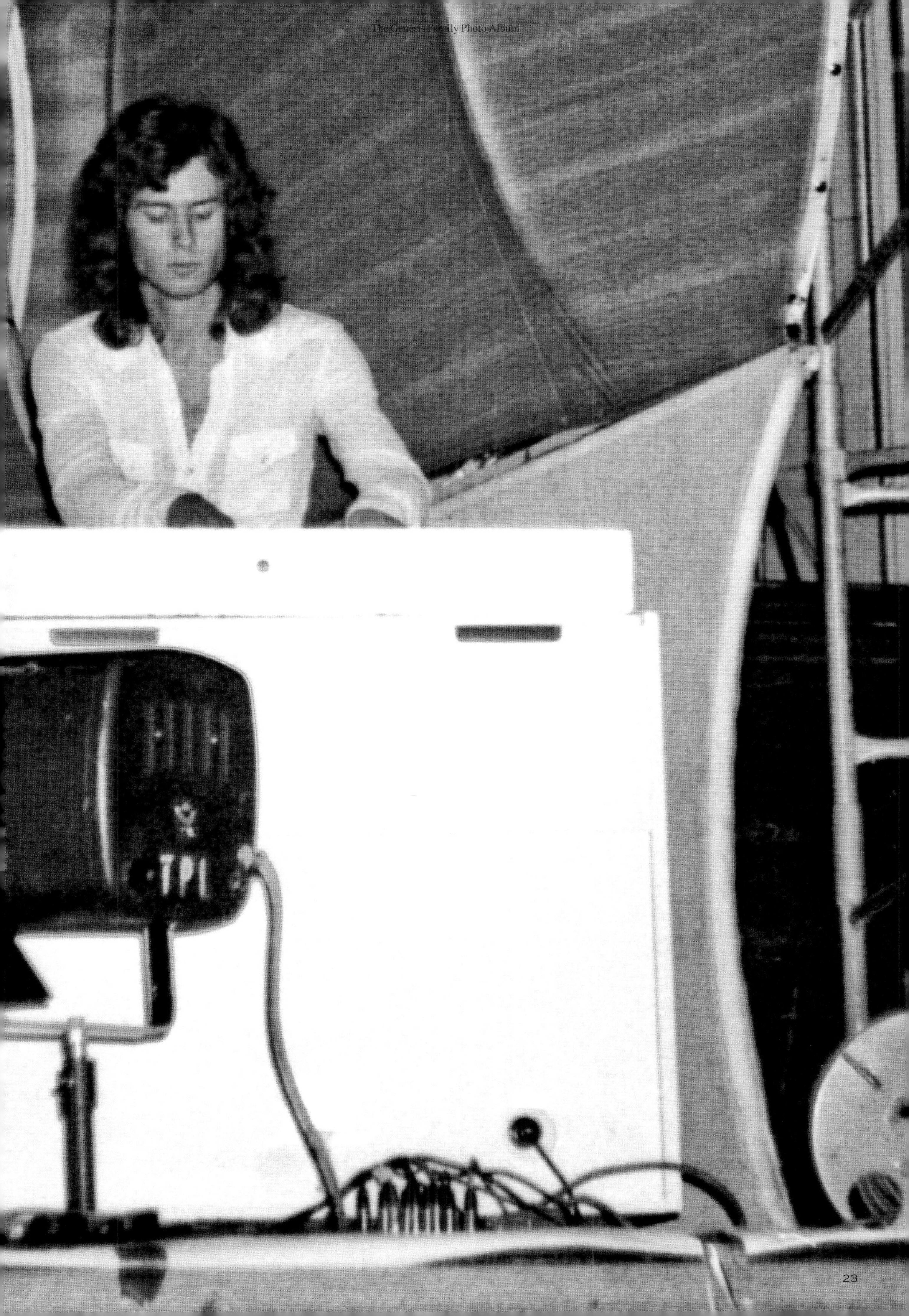

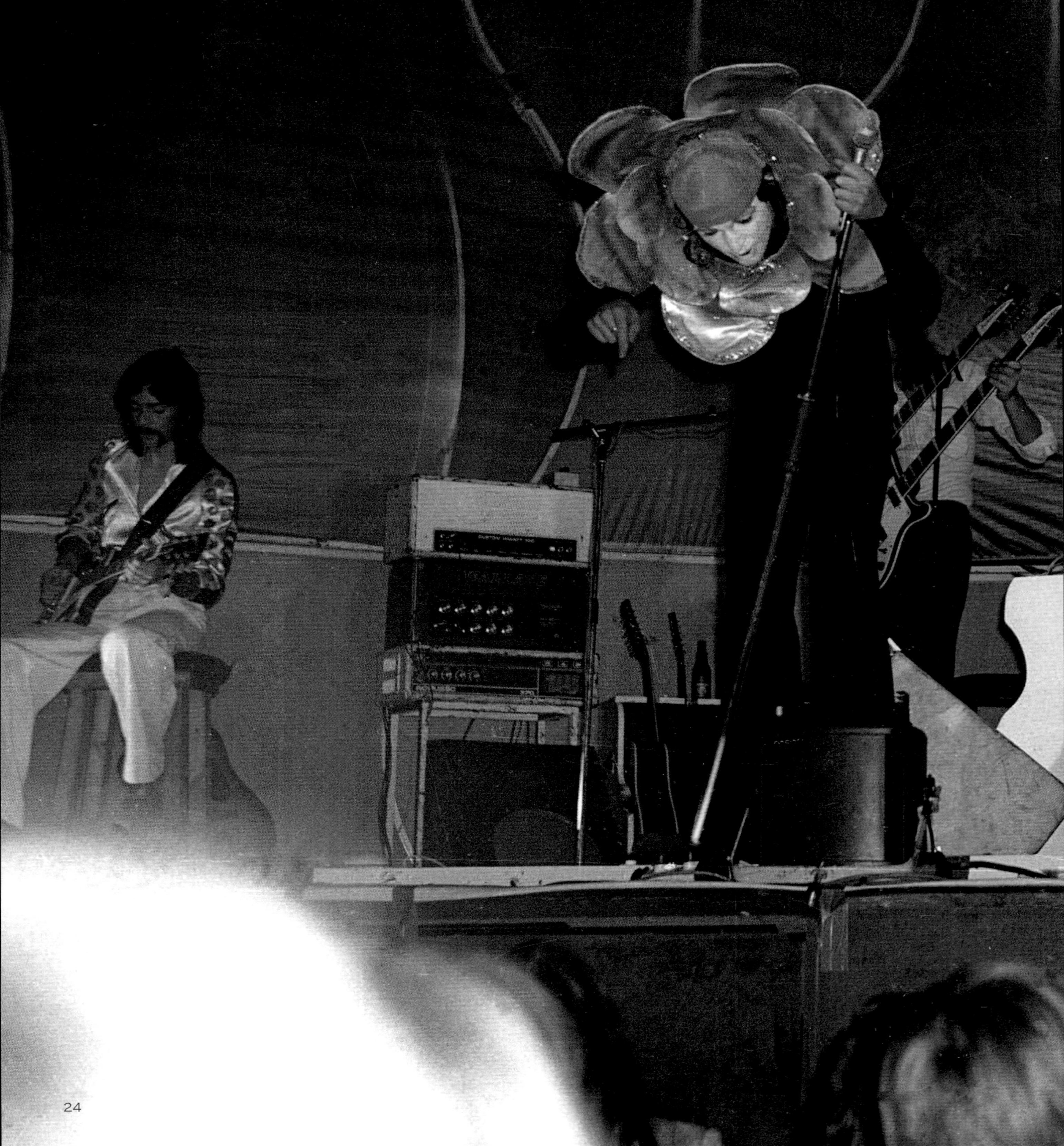

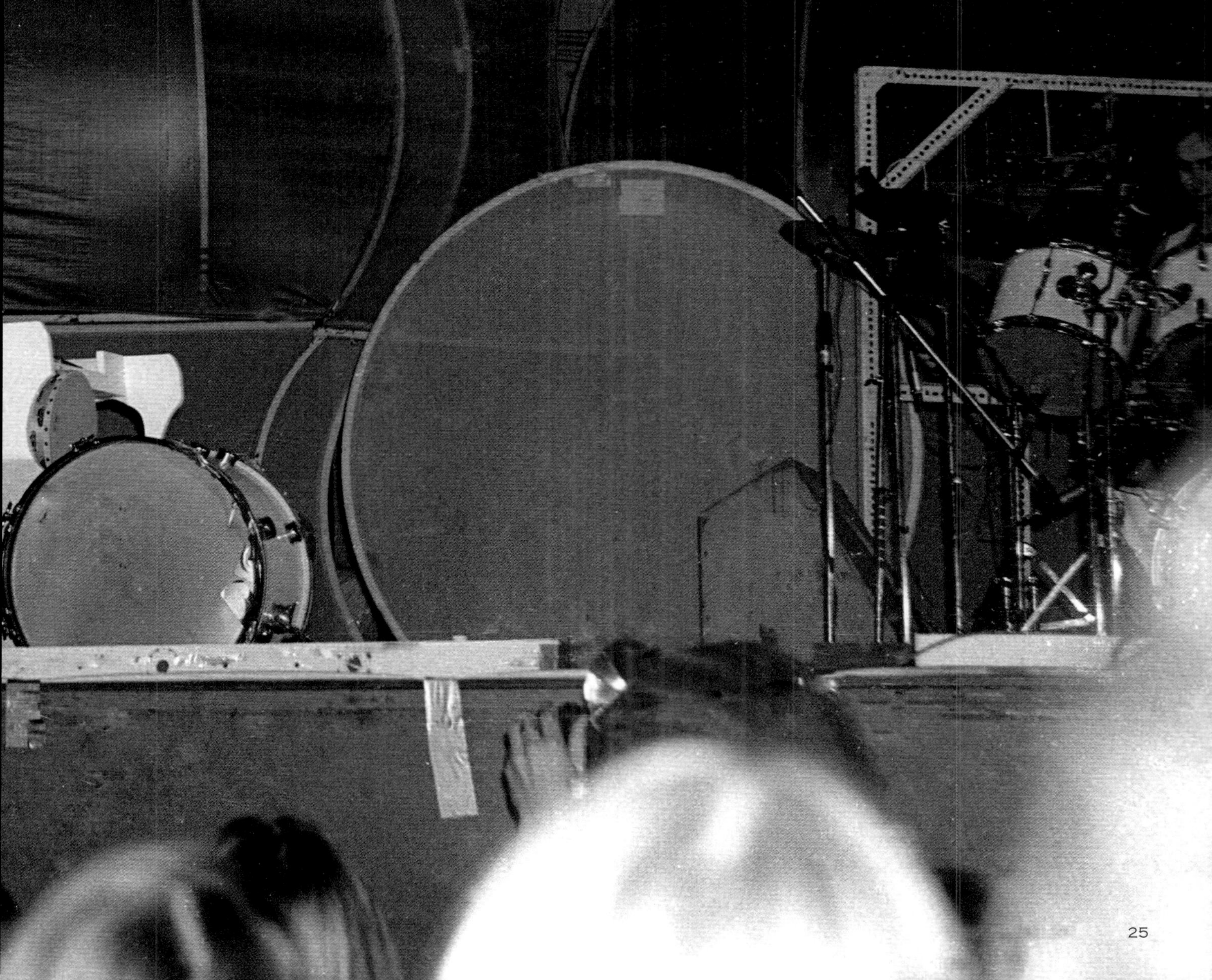

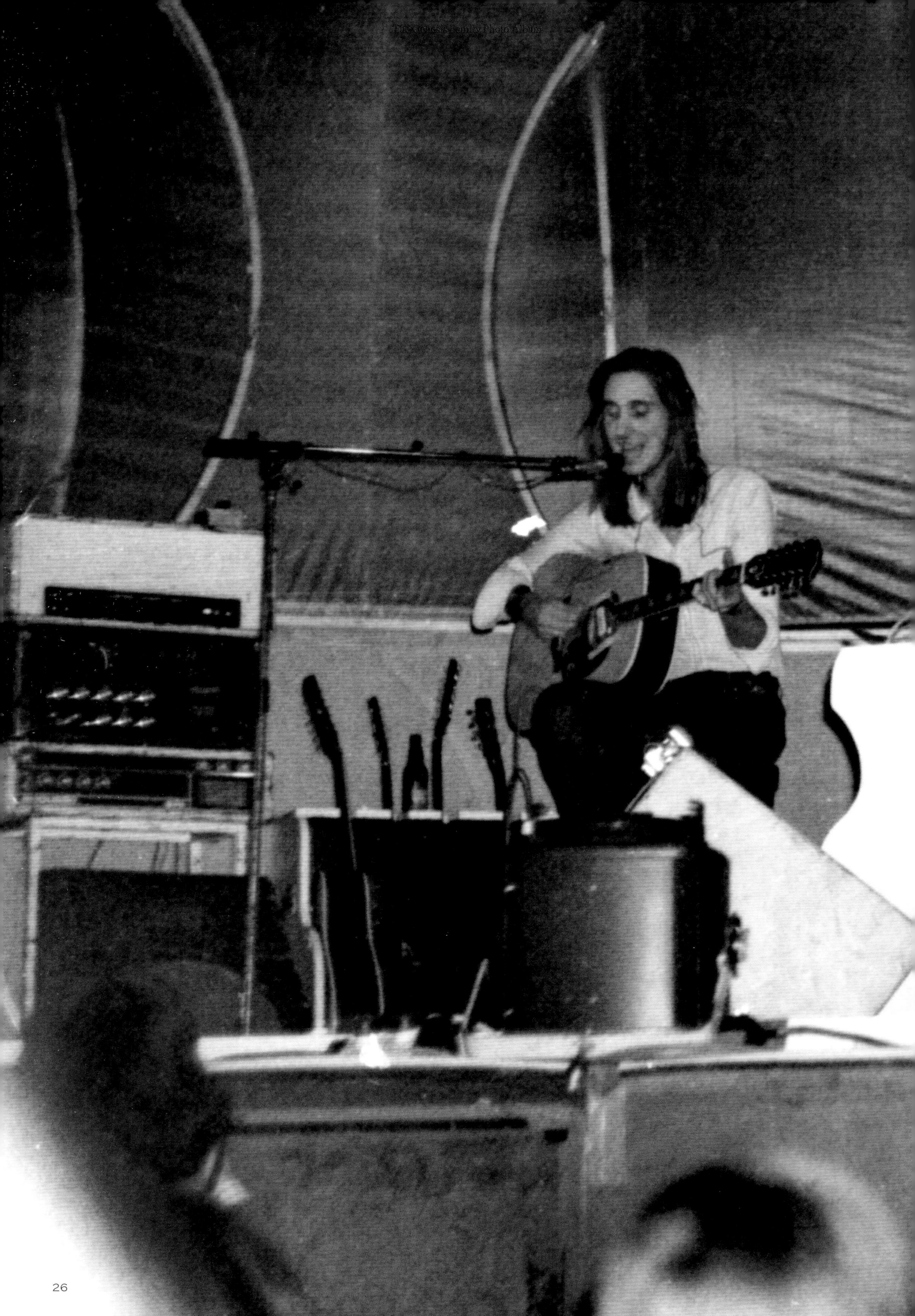

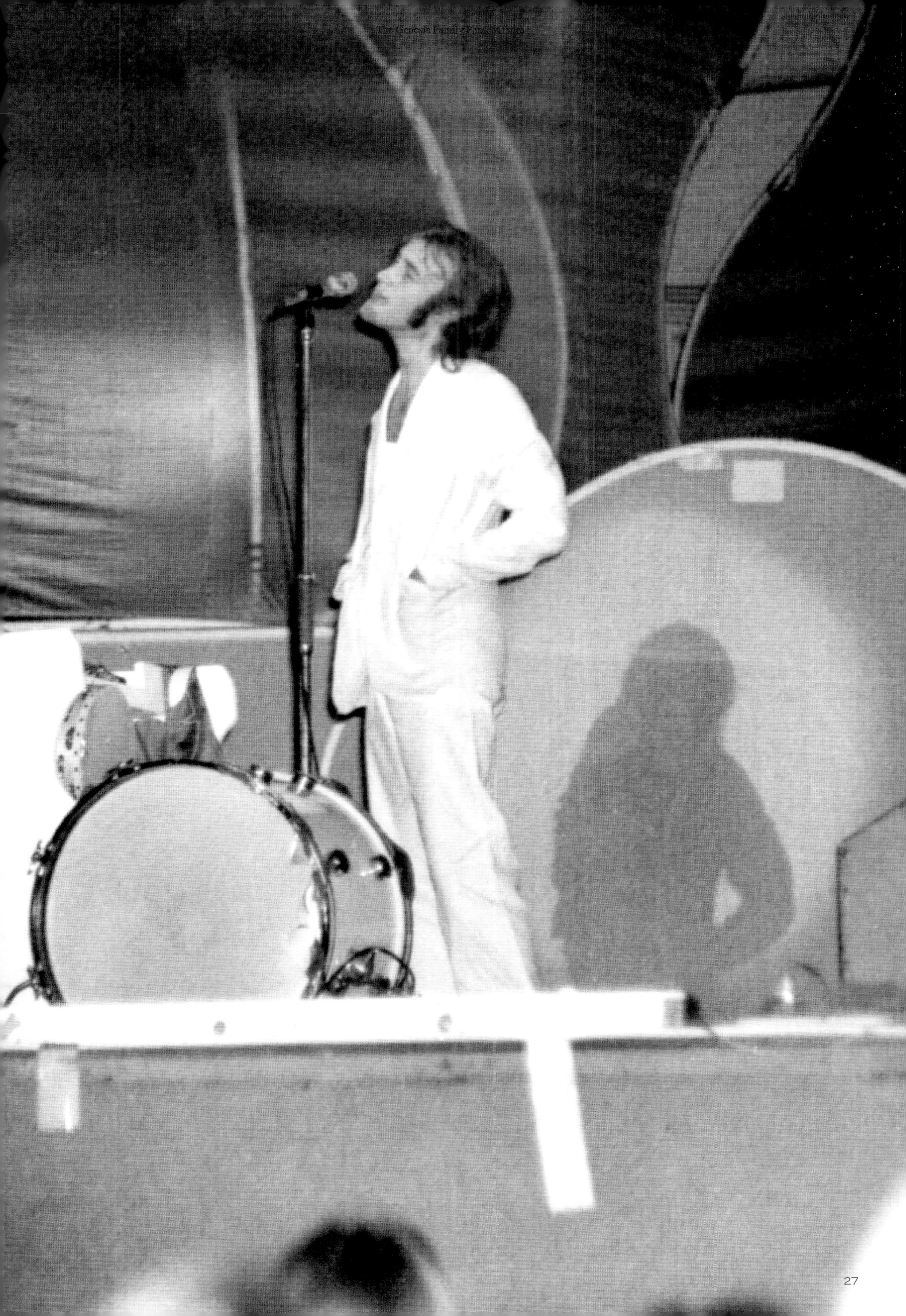

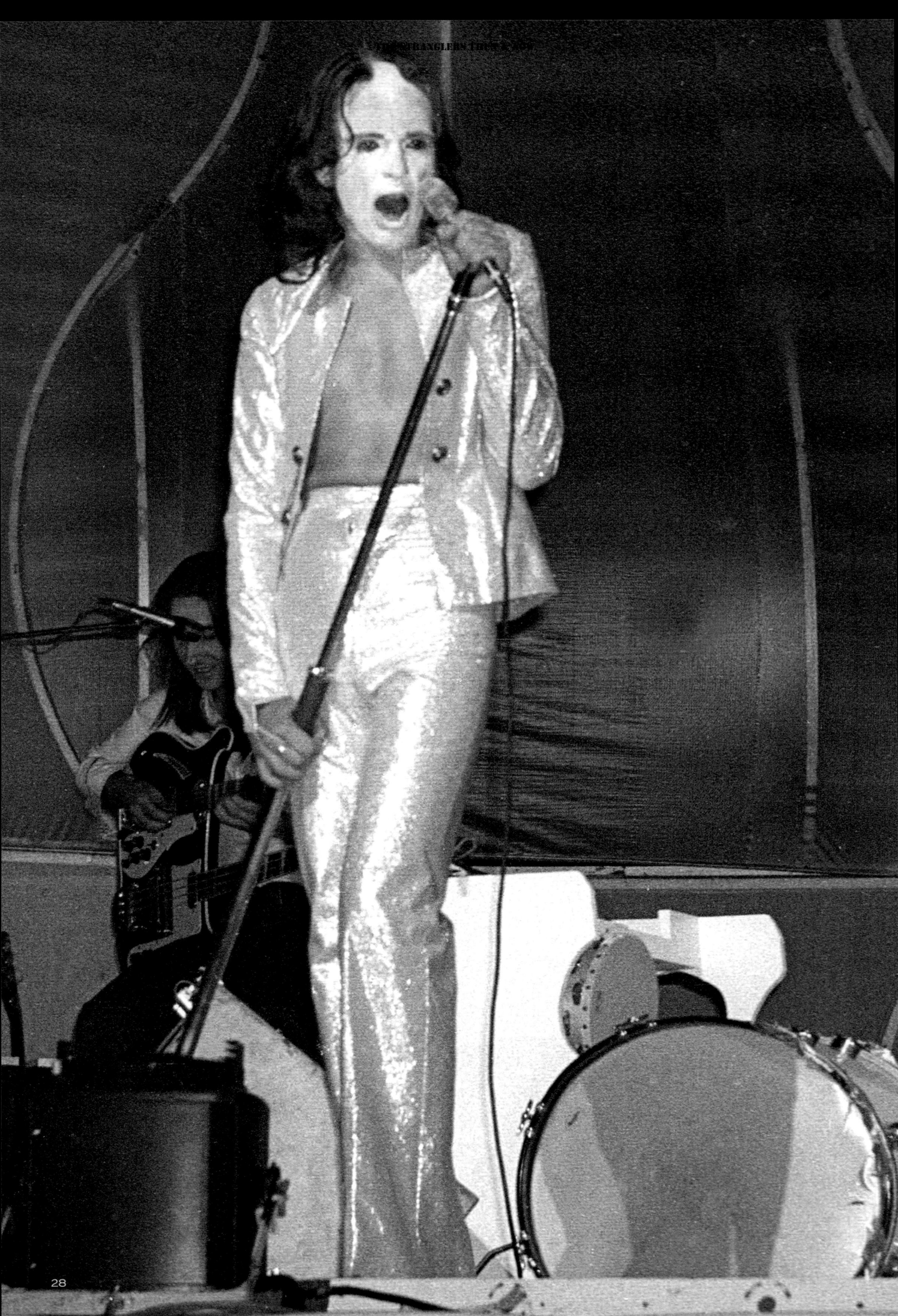

LIVE SOUNDS

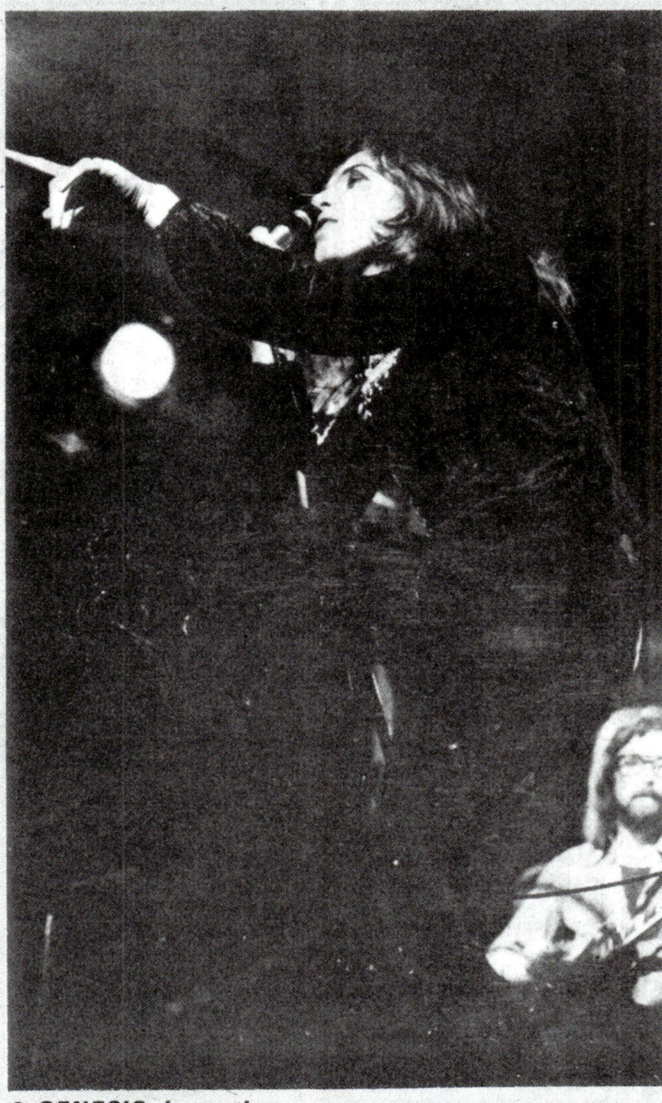

● GENESIS: *innorative*

Genesis

THERE WAS a moment in the past when Genesis, transformed from promising hopefuls into concerned stars seemed to run out of momentum. Their innovative emphasis on the visual areas of performance seemed in danger of overbalancing the musical aspects, and the ever younger and more enthusiastic audiences seemed to encourage this tendency.

In the light of the most recent concert I've seen, however, at the Colston Hall, Bristol last week, I am delighted to announce that all has been put right — or alternatively, that there was never anything at all wrong. It was just something I ate.

The white envelope of the stage now forms the screen for back projected slides, and a highlighting colour backdrop to the mood of the music. Peter Gabriel's red herrings of introductions now challenge the audience to recognise the clues to the next song and his use of costume changes and effects is shorter, slicker and sometimes stunningly superb. But all this would still be an excess of overlaid gilt were the musical quality not equally excellent.

The instrumental sections — and those not playing now swiftly rid the stage of their unwanted presence — are freer, more interesting, more clearly audible.

Tony Banks' keyboard deserves special mention; much of Genesis' style rests on his section, and consequently much of their present brilliance rests on his, too. When the show closed, to the strains of the riotuously popular "Supper's Ready", the applause continued loud and long for an encore. None came but no-one cared — we all knew the band had given their best, which was more than adequate. — HOWARD FIELDING.

The review is from the Colston Hall, Bristol show and the photos on the preceding pages are from the previous night's gig at the Dome, Brighton during the *Selling England By The Pound* Tour.

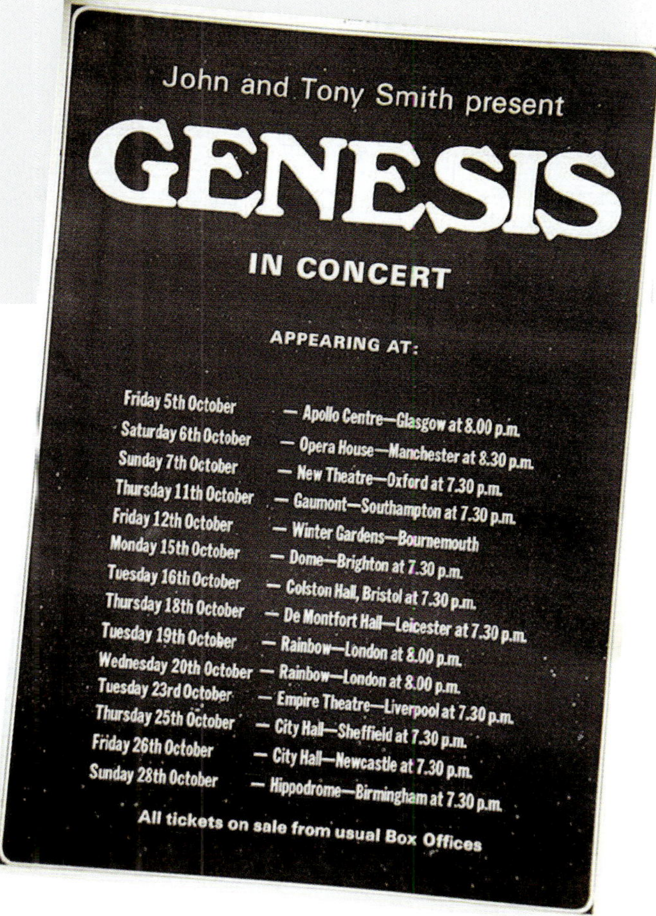

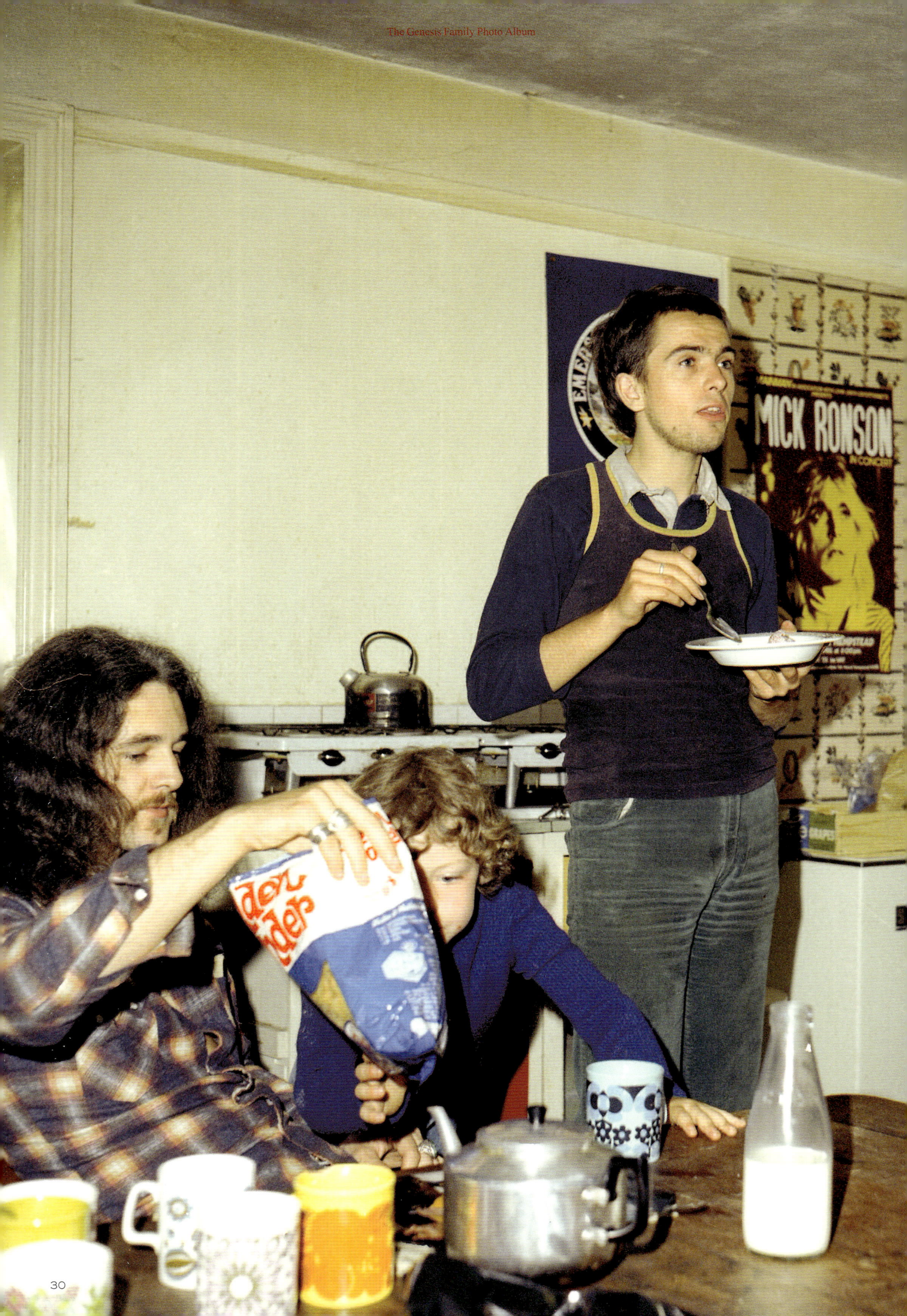
MICK RONSON
IN CONCERT

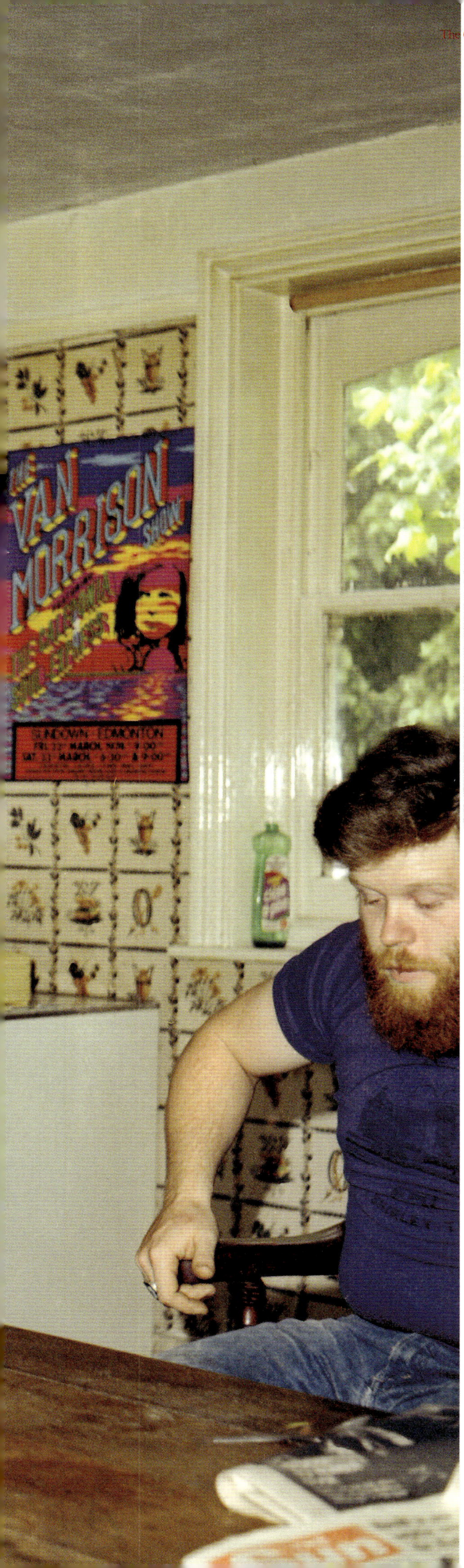

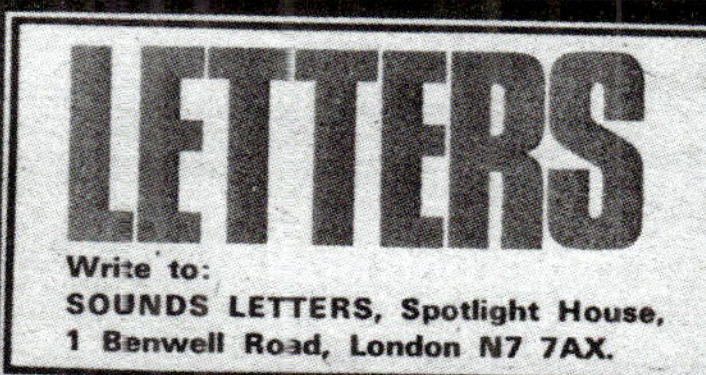

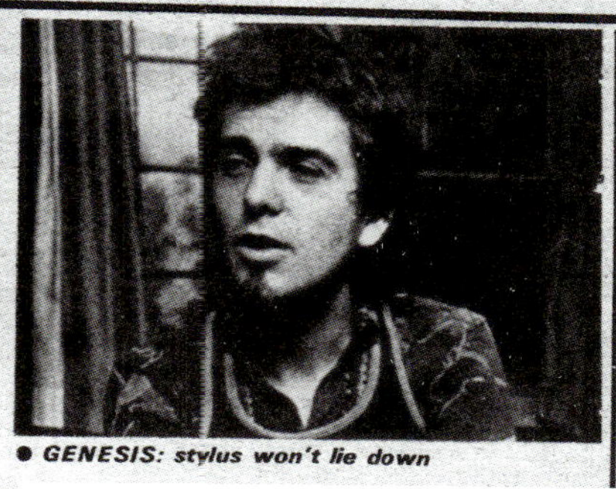
● GENESIS: stylus won't lie down

GIVE THE PUBLIC A BETTER DEAL

CAN I suggest that Charisma Records get their finger out. I've just bought my sixth copy of Genesis's new album "The Lamb Lies Down On Broadway". The previous five had numerous jumps and annoying surface noises.

The sixth copy still has a few jumps on it, but I decided to keep this because I was sick and tired of going back to the record shop.

Don't say it must be my record player because the record shop in Edinburgh informed me they had to return sixty copies to Charisma.

Come on record companies, give the public a better deal for the outrageous prices we have to pay! — Angus Gollan, Edinburgh.

● A spokesman for Charisma Records said that the company were aware of the fault, but unfortunately it is out of their hands. The actual pressing of the albums took place at EMI's plant in Middlesex. Charisma suggest that you send your copy to: The Manager, Customer Service Dept., EMI Records, 1-3 Uxbridge Road, Hayes, Middx.

GENESIS REPLY

I AM writing to you with reference to the letter "Will Genesis Go Back On Their Word?" from Genesis Freak in Greenock, printed in SOUNDS November 9 issue. There are two main reasons why Genesis were not playing at the Apollo Centre in Glasgow during their cancelled tour. When the tour was being planned, there was no available date at the Apollo Centre and as the new Genesis stage show production was in the throes of being constructed we were not sure of the stage size it would require. However, on completion it was discovered that the minimum stage size required for the production was far in excess of that abailable at the Apollo Centre.

May I assure the writer in question that Genesis do stand by their original principles—it s only due to the fact that they wish to present to their audience the best possible show under the best possible conditions that they will not compromise on their minimum production requirements.

PETER THOMPSON
(Press Agent for Genesis)
● Splendid sentiments, but no solace for the fans in Glasgow -Ed

The following sequence of photos were taken in July 1974 during the writing and rehearsing of *The Lamb Lies Down On Broadway* at Headley Grange in Hampshire.

Built in 1795 Headley Grange was a former poorhouse that had been converted to a private residence in 1870.

The 1970s saw several bands use it as a studio with the aid of a mobile recording truck. Most notably Led Zeppelin, who had already made three albums there before Genesis moved in, as well as Bad Company who recorded its debut album there in November 1973.

Richard Haines had already captured Genesis in concert as the photos from Brighton on the preceeding pages demonstrate. As Richard recalls, "I sent one of the live photographs to the band at Charisma records as a Christmas card and shortly after received a call from Tony Smith asking if I would like to take photographs of the band at Headley Grange where they were working on *The Lamb Lies Down on Broadway*."

"I was taken to Headley Grange in Tony Smith's speedy Bentley where I took a series of both colour and black and white photographs on my Rolleiflex 6cm x 6cm format camera."

Richard cannot recall who the other two chaps are that flank Peter on either side but the young boy is Tony Smith's son Chris.

As it was the height of summer, strawberries were the dish of the day as these photos aptly illustrate.

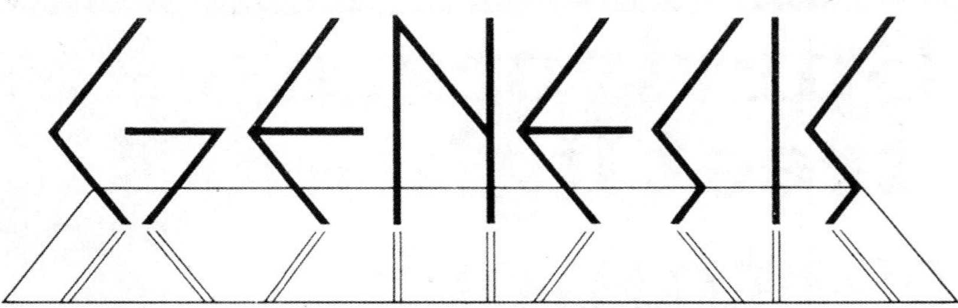

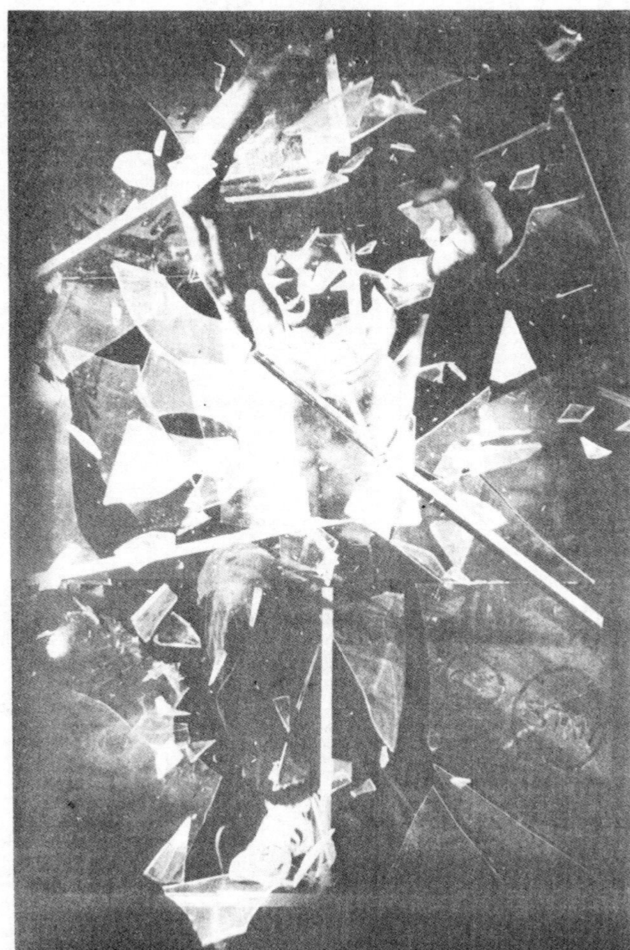

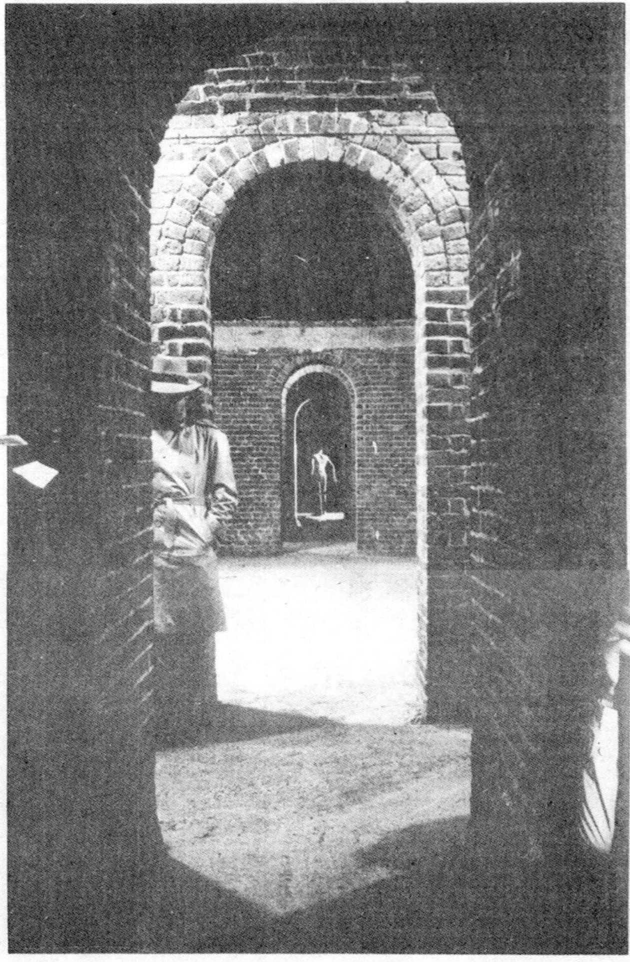

NEW DOUBLE ALBUM
ON CHARISMA CGS 101

OUT NOW!
GENESIS NEW SINGLE CB 238
COUNTING OUT TIME

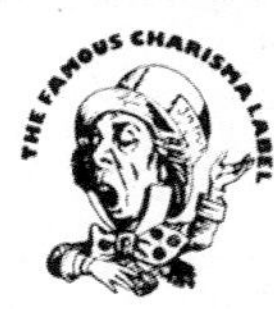

MARKETED BY B&C RECORDS LTD., 37 SOHO SQUARE, LONDON W1

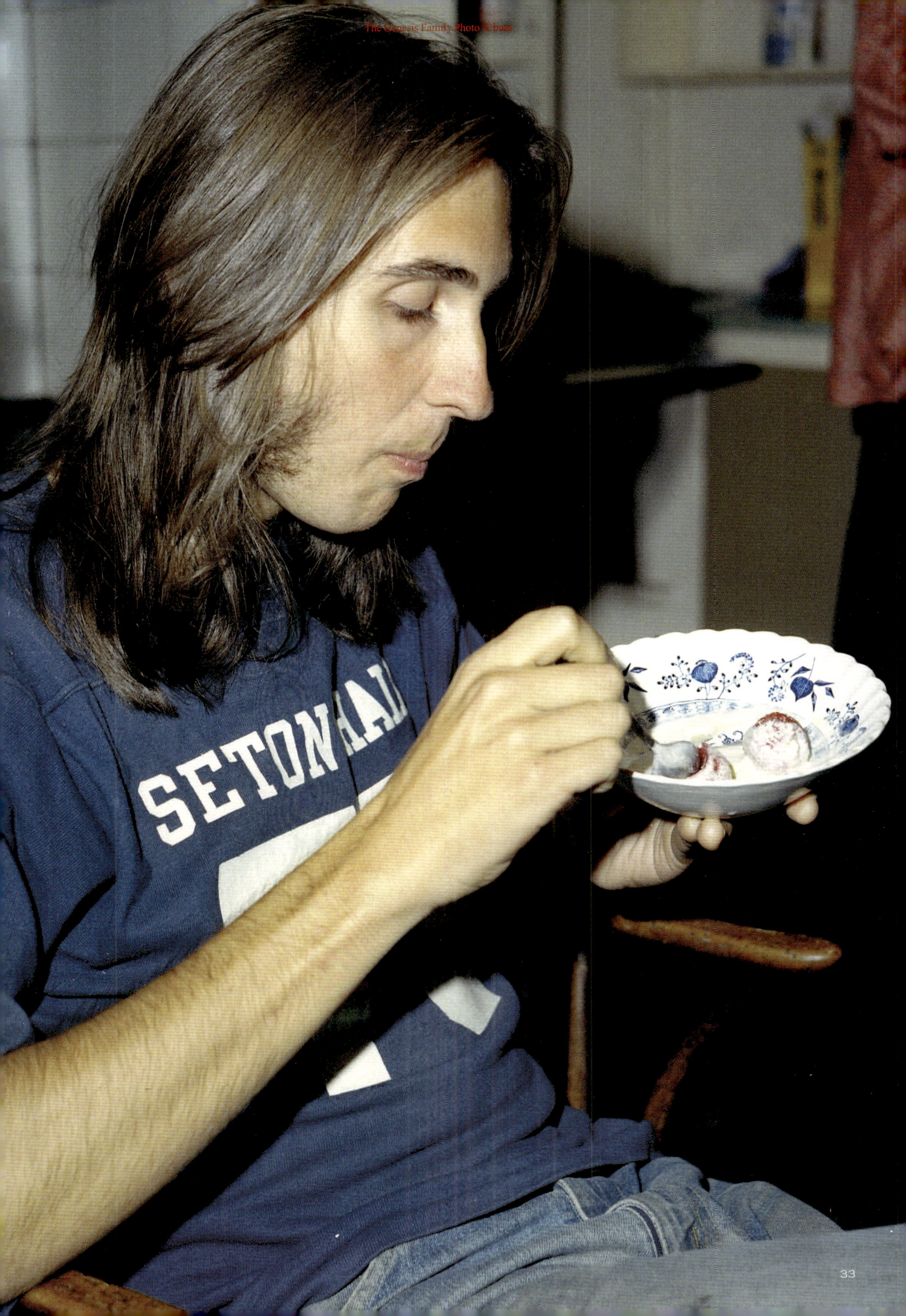

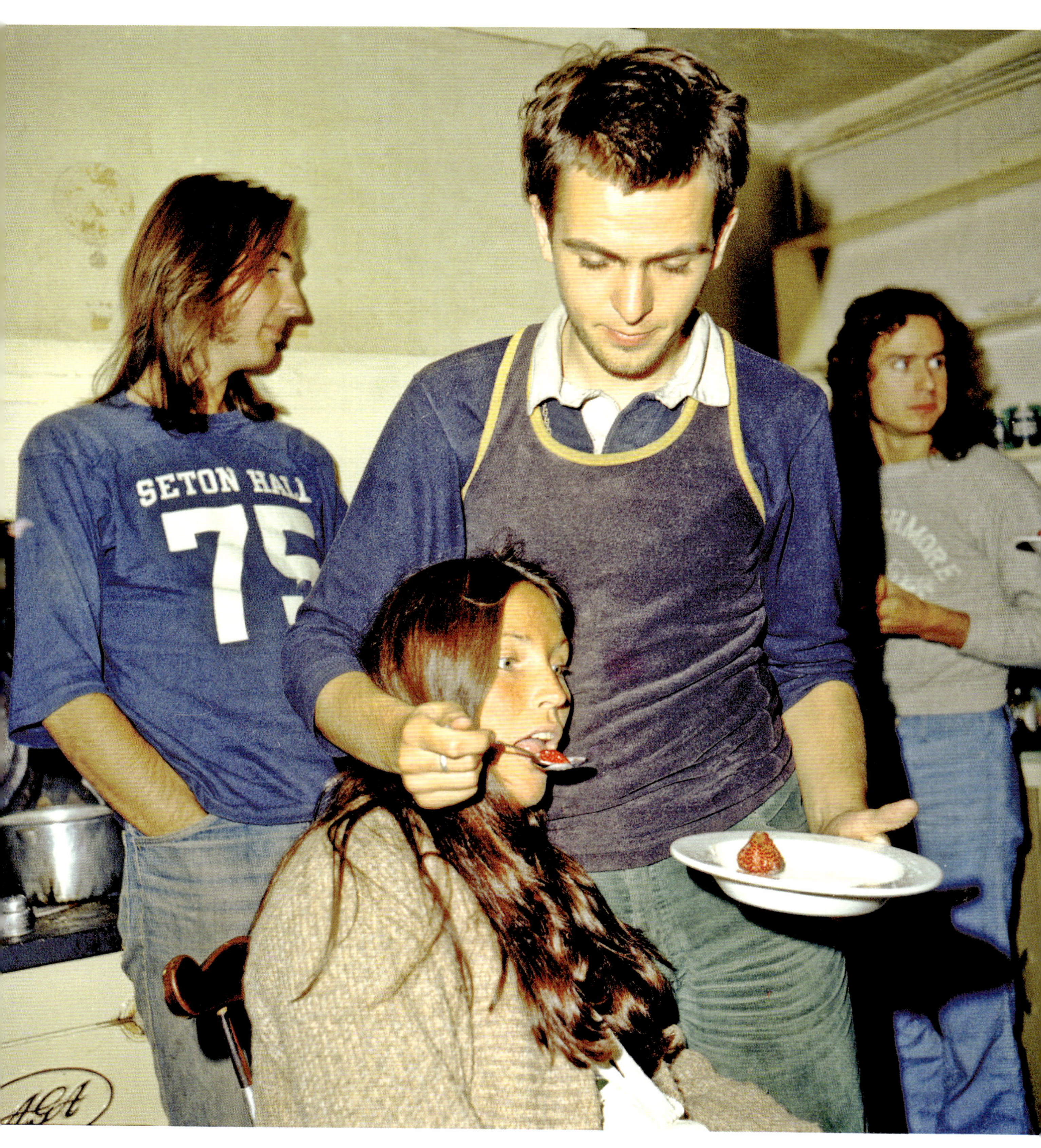

Peter feeding strawberries to his then wife Jill.
Mike is wearing a Seton Hall University jersey that he also wore
for the 'A Trick Of The Tail' video released in 1976.

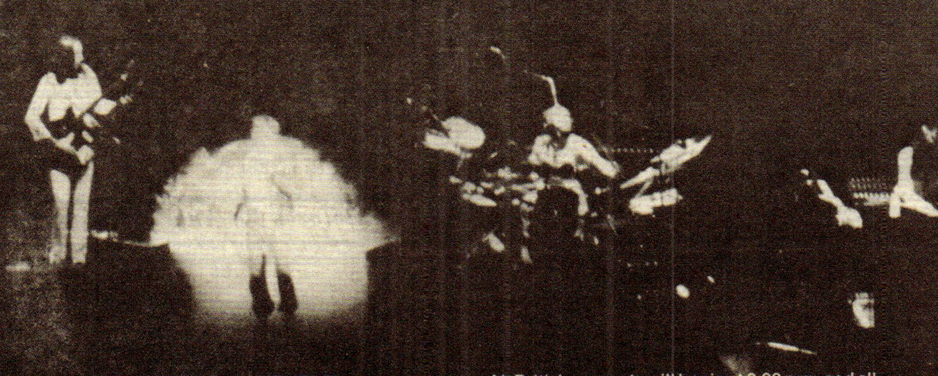

14 APRIL	EMPIRE POOL	WEMBLEY
15 APRIL	EMPIRE POOL	WEMBLEY
16 APRIL	GAUMONT THEATRE	SOUTHAMPTON
18 APRIL	EMPIRE THEATRE	LIVERPOOL
19 APRIL	EMPIRE THEATRE	LIVERPOOL
22 APRIL	USHER HALL	EDINBURGH
23 APRIL	USHER HALL	EDINBURGH
24 APRIL	CITY HALL	NEWCASTLE
25 APRIL	CITY HALL	NEWCASTLE
27 APRIL	PALACE THEATRE	MANCHESTER
28 APRIL	PALACE THEATRE	MANCHESTER
29 APRIL	COLSTON HALL	BRISTOL
30 APRIL	COLSTON HALL	BRISTOL
1 MAY	HIPPODROME	BIRMINGHAM
2 MAY	HIPPODROME	BIRMINGHAM

All British concerts will begin at 8.00 p.m. and all tickets will go on sale on Monday 10 March except at Bristol where the tickets will go on sale on 8 April. In the case of Wembley 14 April concert, tickets originally issued for 4 November 1974 will be valid, and for Edinburgh tickets originally issued for 6 and 7 November and then validated for 24 and 25 April respectively will now be validated for 22 and 23 April respectively. Ticket prices at all British dates except Wembley, Bristol and Southampton will be £2.00, £1.75, £1.50 and £1.20. At Wembley and Bristol tickets will be £2.00 and £1.50 and at Southampton £2.00, £1.75, £1.50, £1.00 and 80p.

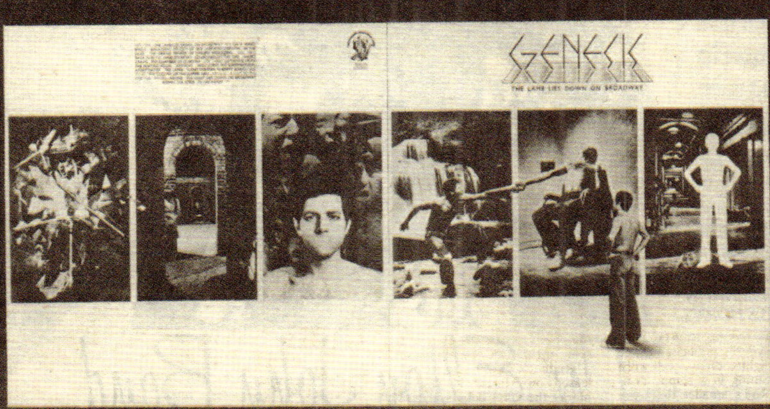

CGS101

MARKETED BY B&C RECORDS LTD., 37 SOHO SQUARE, LONDON W1

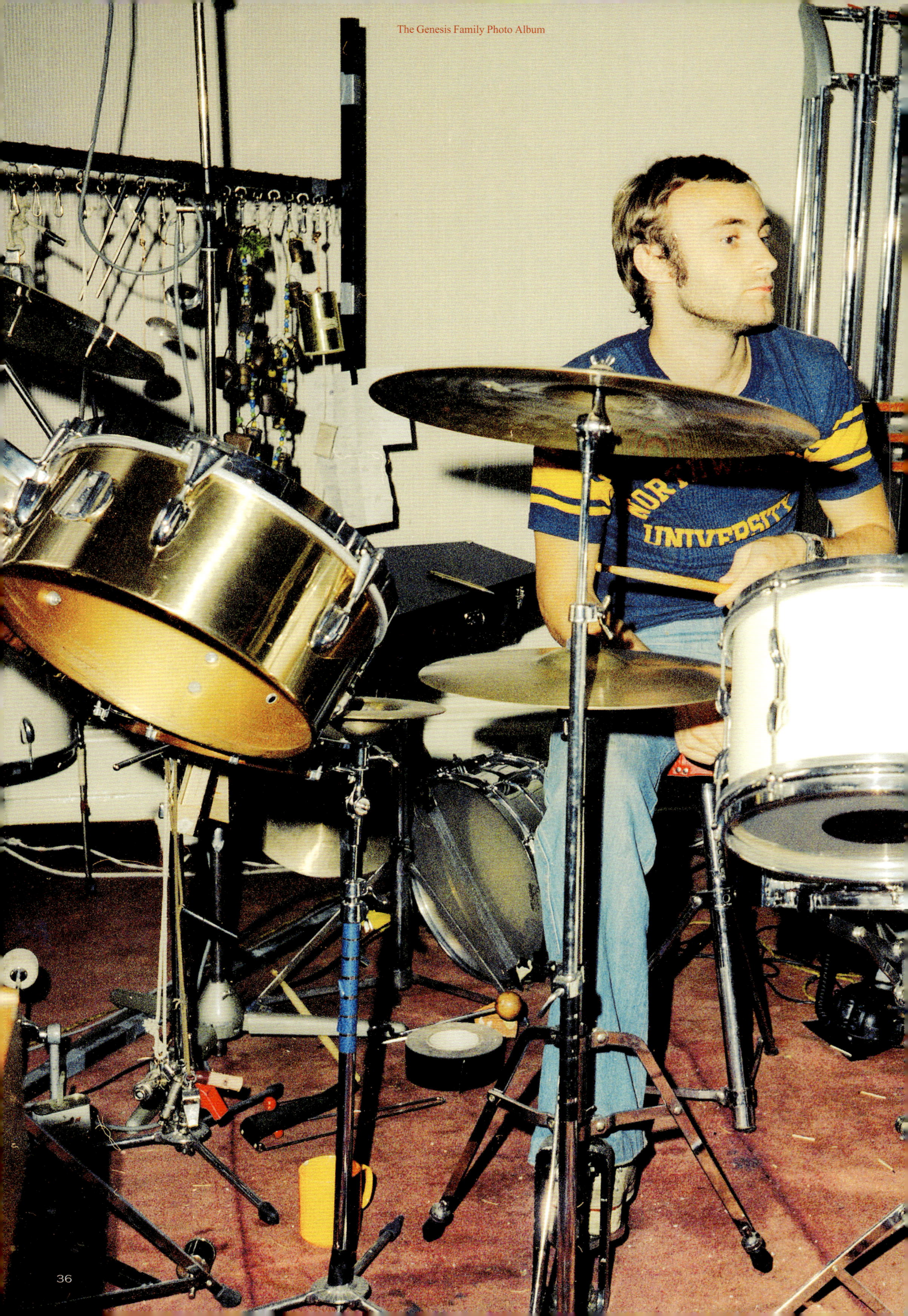

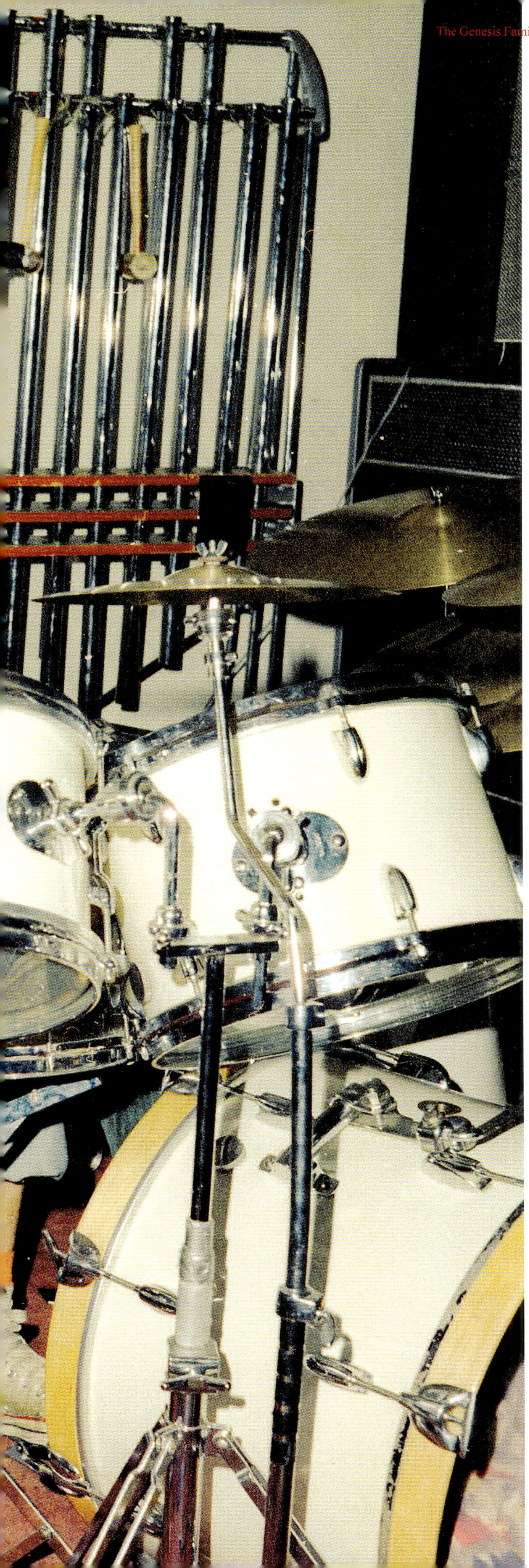

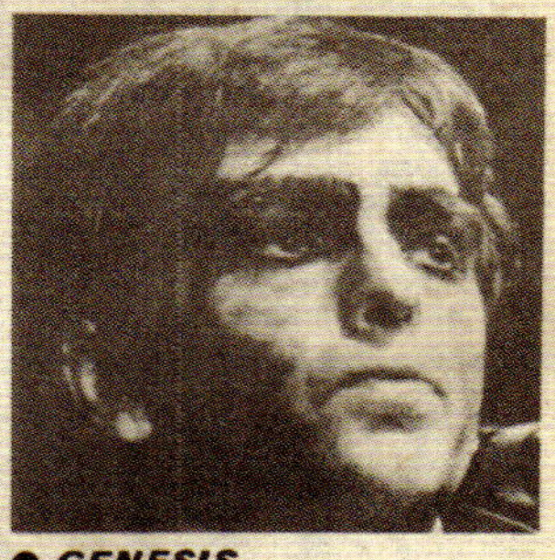

● GENESIS

Genesis single

CHARISMA RELEASE a new Genesis single 'The Carpet Crawlers' on April 4 to coincide with their up-coming British tour. Also set for release in April is a special limited edition compilation called 'The Genesis Collection'.

The compilation, which will be in two volumes, will consist of a repackaging of 'Trespass' and 'Nursery Cryme' as volume one, another double set with 'Foxtrot' and 'Selling England By The Pound' as volume two. Also included in each package is a specially designed poster. The sets will retail at £4.49 each. Genesis have added a date to their tour which has sold out all dates at Liverpool Empire on April 20.

It wasn't all strawberries at Headley Grange and work on the album began in ernest as this shot of Phil testifies.

As with Mike, it would appear that Phil had acquired his shirt in the USA. The band first ventured there in December '72 for a few shows but did their first extensive American tour throughout November and December '73.

With the completion of the *Lamb Lies Down On Broadway* the album was released in November '74. Genesis embarked on their biggest US tour to date and went right through to early February.

The album was performed in its entirety, but it would prove to be the last US tour with Peter who departed after the conclusion of the European Tour in May '75.

The press announcement was made in August.

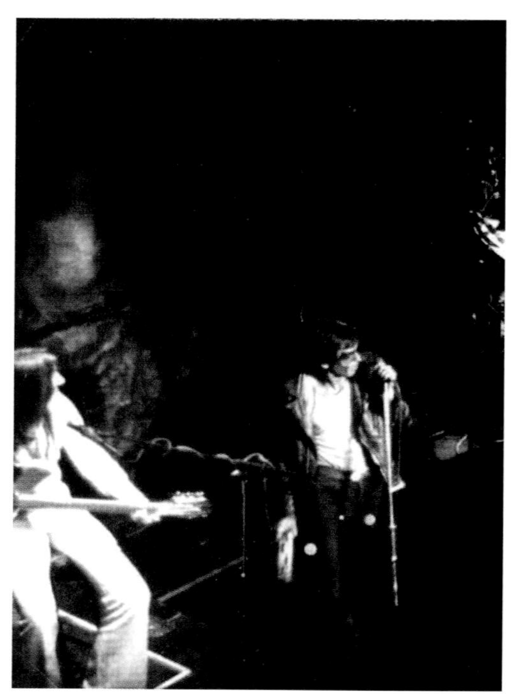

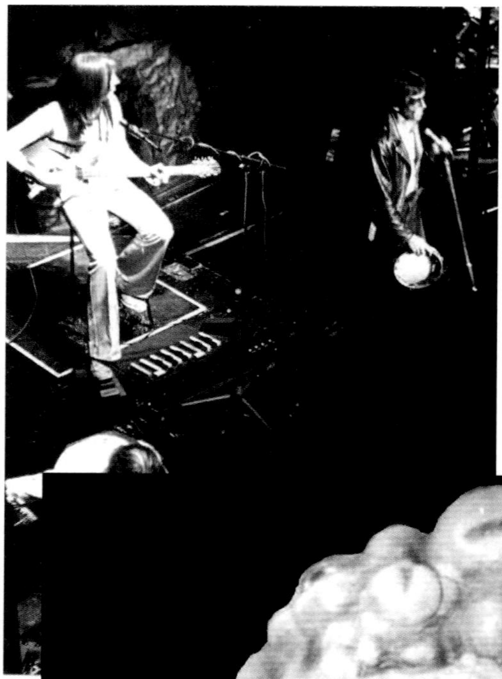

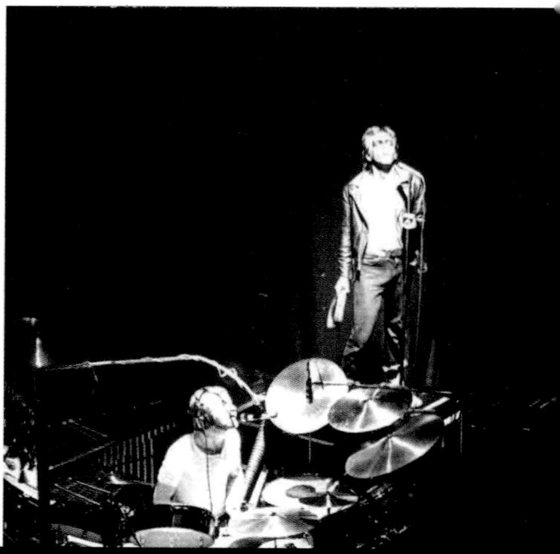

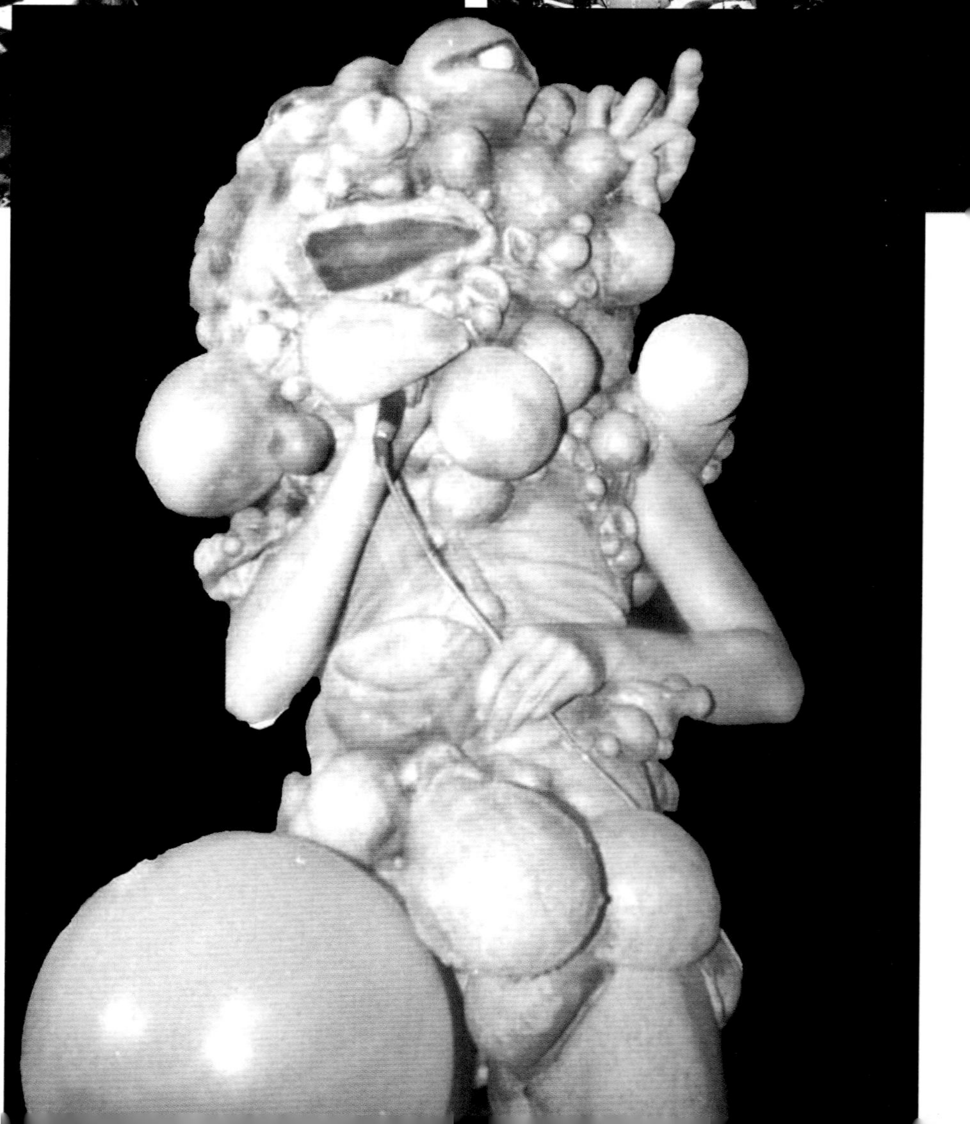

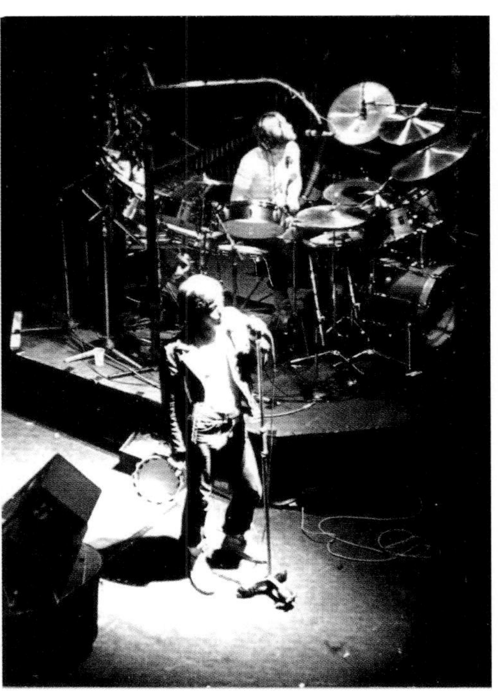 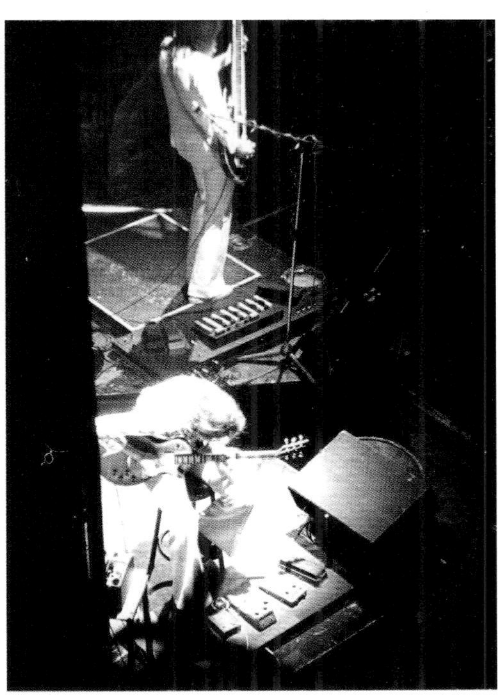 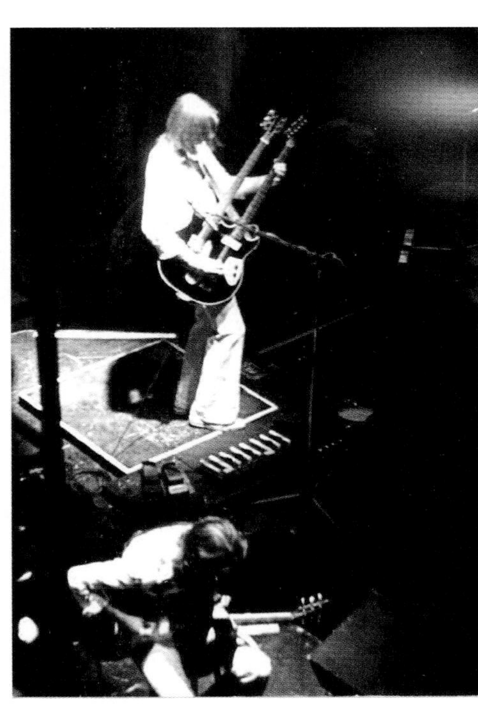

Liverpool 18th April 1975.

Liverpool did not figure when the original tour dates for The Lamb Lies Down On Broadway tour were announced for November 1974. Steve Hackett cut his hand on a glass, and the tour had to be postponed. I queued all night for tickets for extra shows at Liverpool Empire in 1975. I went twice to that tour, the first night on the middle of the front row. This was first time that I took a camera to a concert. Why do I have no photos of that night? The first thing that I did was to wind the film on so vigorously that the sprockets ripped the film and rendered the camera useless!

The group stayed at the Adelphi Hotel, just around the corner from The Empire Theatre and so most of them walked to the concert. On the 18th I met the group outside the stage-door before the concert — they all autographed my album covers. First I spotted Phil walking up Lord Nelson Street towards the stage door. I went up to him and asked him to sign an album cover, which he did. My brother then took the photograph of me and Phil. Everyone else seemed dumbstruck, so I asked him to sign the rest of my album covers, which he did. Tony Banks was in more of a hurry — he asked me where the stage-door was and I was the only one to get his autograph. Jill Gabriel arrived with their daughter Anna (who was then a babe in arms). Steve and Mike drove up in a Range Rover. At 7.00pm the roadies were pacing up and down Lord Nelson Street, agitated because Peter had not yet arrived and it was time for the sound-check. When he did turn up he appeared to be drunk. He signed my album cover, and was then engaged in conversation with a fan who explained that he had a recurring dream in which he was Peter Gabriel — of course Peter found this fascinating, and spent several minutes in conversation, causing the roadies to come close to exploding!

There are some things worthy of mentioning: Unlike earlier concerts on the tour when Peter introduced Rael in the third person, by the Liverpool concerts Peter was Rael. On the first night Peter's first words to the audience after side one of The Lamb Lies Down On Broadway were "Welcome to Liverpool". Scousers have good memories, and on the second night they repeated this line, so Peter changed his introduction to: "We are, we are... Thank you very much. Welcome to Genesis." Which was greeted by rapturous applause.

[Voice from the audience] "Brilliant."

"We are in the panacea of youth. My name is Real, and I am stuck underneath New York City, really a reconstruction of the City, and I remember my very first romantic adventures when I wandered out with tremendous courage clutching this book entitled Erogenous Zones And Difficulties In Overcoming Finding Them."

[Voice from the audience] "Come on Peter."

'This... tremendously... and after many months of continuous study I went home,

opposite number to be, and we went and performed the complete outfit, the complete routine from motion number one to motion number sixty-nine in an entire seventy-eight seconds. And dare I say it myself this magnificent feat of masculinity left my opposite number a little less than satisfied."

[Voice from the audience] "Are you still knackered?"

"Yes. I was cuddling this prickly porcupine on the soft thick, carpeted corridor made of lambs wool — by Cyril Lord, at prices you can afford. This led to this spiral staircase which led up to this strange chamber with 32 doors, none of which led anywhere at all."

[Voice from the audience] "Knock three times and ask for Lil."

Peter, or should I say Rael, continued his dialogue after side two: "Thank you. Thank you very much. So here I was in this big black tunnel, when a blind lady comes up to me and she says Hello. How could I resist an offer like that? So I grabbed her hand and she took me over right across some strange oval course until we came out of the tunnel where she left me sitting on this cold wet stone throne. And I heard this strange whirling sound coming in from my left, and then these two white golden

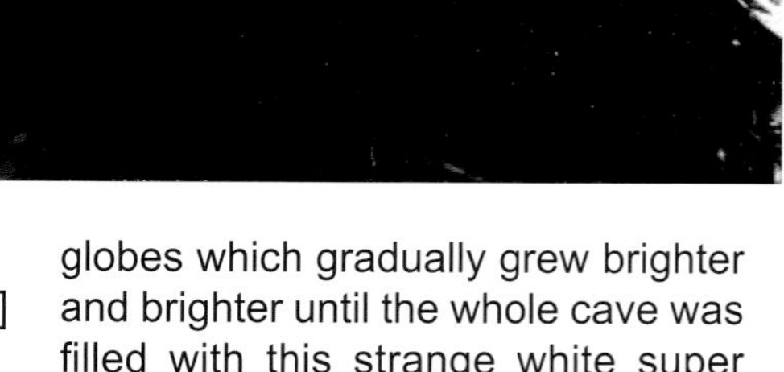

globes which gradually grew brighter and brighter until the whole cave was filled with this strange white super bright light. I was really amazed at the whiteness — Mrs JH of Sunderland. Thank you. So I picked up this stone because it was getting so overwhelmingly bright, I was really frightened. And there was a big crash as it landed in the centre of these...

and the ceiling fell on top of my head. This was a little painful, but like a true hero I was... only to be, only to be discovered by... personally better known to all of us here tonight, your friend and mine, the sensational human inspector called Death. Let's hear it for D E A T H Death. He was wearing one of his delightful costumes, and in particular there was this snuff-puff costume, such a wonderful collection of gas, what a gas, one little puff and you'll snuff it. Three half woman-half snake creatures... my body with their soft hands... which gave them a random attack of indigestion. Rennies bring express relief... in time because they shrivelled up and died. And I eat what was left of their bodies, which in turn turned me into an ugly humpy lumpy bumpy species of humanity, not altogether dissimilar to Mr Stephen Hackett on my right. Those of you who are familiar with the problems of lead guitarists will perhaps realize anyway the only way Steve... Slippermen could get rid of the lumps and bumps was the removal of the sexual organs. This was painful too. But Dr Diper, reformed sniper, for a very small fee offered to remove our very own windscreen wiper — thank you. And he... two fully stabilised yellow plastic tubes, very clean, very, very clean. And a big black bird came out of the sky, flying very low, and grabbing the plastic tube containing my deceased sexual organ. Then he flew off with this. This alarmed me. I recovered very quickly. But alas not in time, because just as I had come through the tunnel which the bird had flown through I noticed he had dropped it into a large

area of gushing water which was called ravine in big blue watery letters. And in this water where my deceased Sexual organ was floating in the yellow plastic tube I also saw my drowning brother John. Oh no, I thought.'

The above comments were transcribed from the original tape. Some parts are so distorted that I gave up trying, so they are represented by ...

For those of you reading this who were not around in the UK in 1975, and old enough to remember, I will add some explanation to some of the above: Rennies are indigestion tablets, and the catchphrase on the TV advert was "Rennies bring express relief". There was also a carpet advertisement on the TV with the catchphrase "carpets by Cyril Lord at prices you can afford". There was a soap-powder advert with the catchphrase "I was amazed at the whiteness said Mrs JH of wherever" (Peter also referred to Mrs JH as coming from Bournemouth on this tour).

The set lists for the three nights were as follows: 18th & 20th: The Lamb Lies Down On Broadway, The Musical Box, Watcher of the Skies.
19th: The Lamb Lies Down On Broadway, The Musical Box, The Knife.

This text is written and transcribed by photographer Alan Perry whose photo with Phil Collins is overleaf.

WP Marketed by Wymer (UK) Ltd, Bedford, England. Manufactured by Harrier LLC and distributed by Wymer Publishing.

Peter wowed the audience by appearing for The Knife wearing a silver lurex suit with no shirt and a v-shaped cutaway in the fly of his trousers!

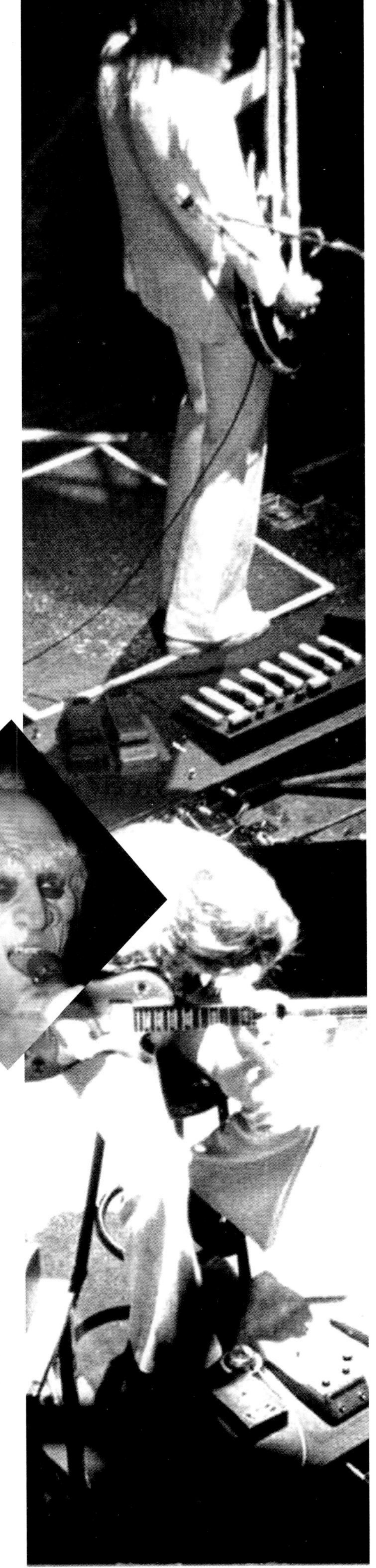

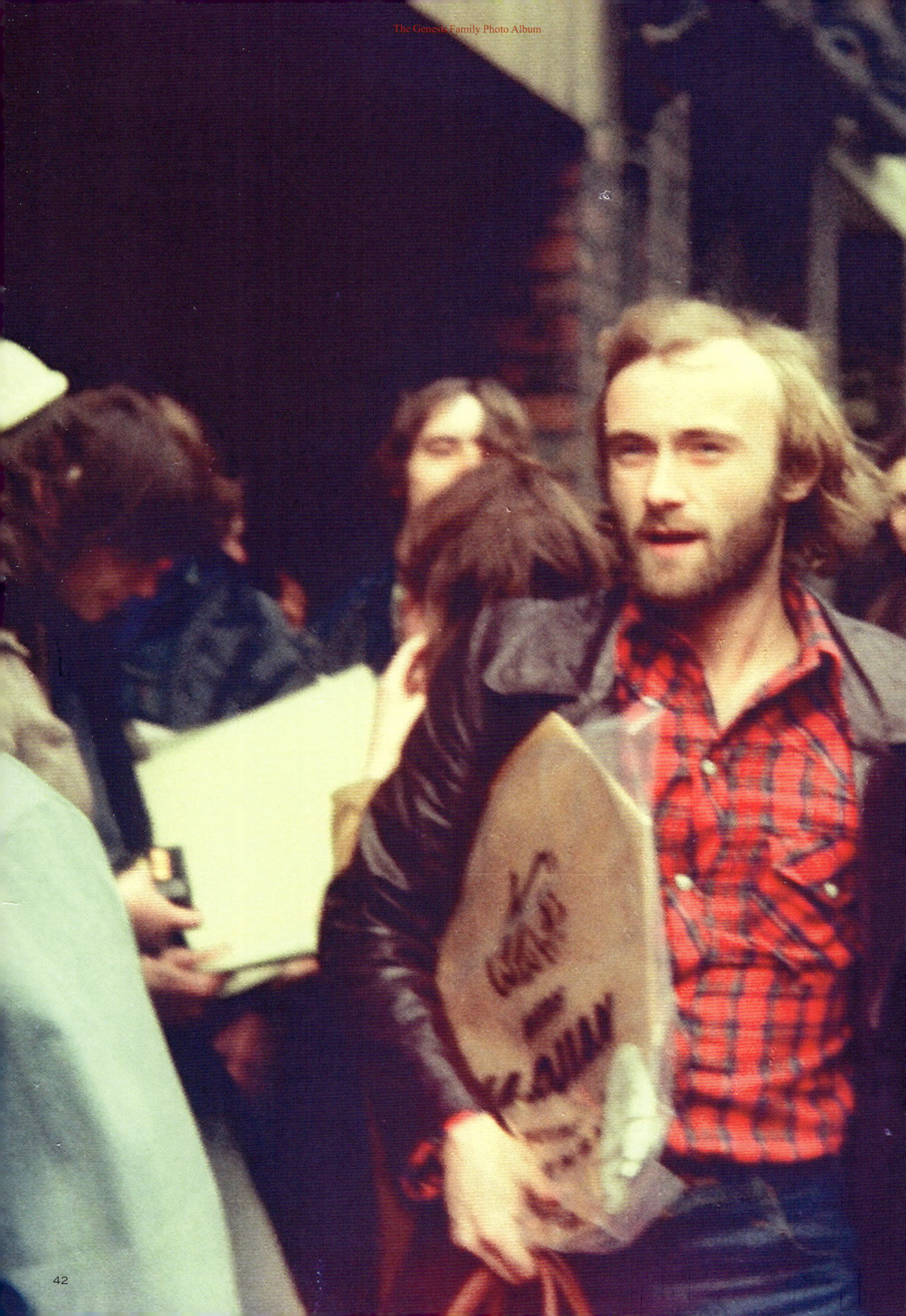

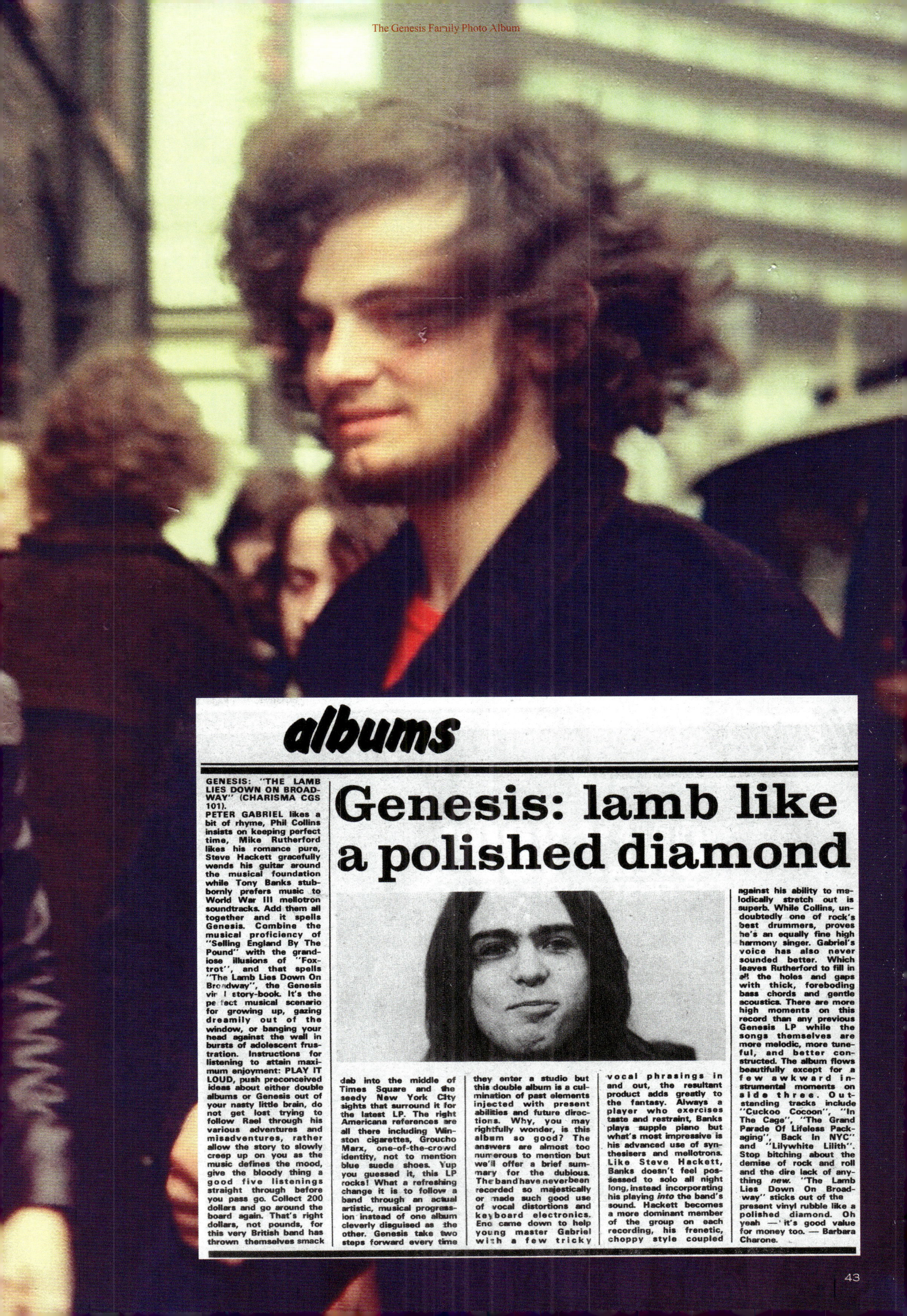

albums

GENESIS: "THE LAMB LIES DOWN ON BROADWAY" (CHARISMA CGS 101).

PETER GABRIEL likes a bit of rhyme, Phil Collins insists on keeping perfect time, Mike Rutherford likes his romance pure, Steve Hackett gracefully wends his guitar around the musical foundation while Tony Banks stubbornly prefers music to World War III mellotron soundtracks. Add them all together and it spells Genesis. Combine the musical proficiency of "Selling England By The Pound" with the grandiose illusions of "Foxtrot", and that spells "The Lamb Lies Down On Broadway", the Genesis virtual story-book. It's the perfect musical scenario for growing up, gazing dreamily out of the window, or banging your head against the wall in bursts of adolescent frustration. Instructions for listening to attain maximum enjoyment: PLAY IT LOUD, push preconceived ideas about either double albums or Genesis out of your nasty little brain, do not get lost trying to follow Rael through his various adventures and misadventures, rather allow the story to slowly creep up on you as the music defines the mood, give the bloody thing a good five listenings straight through before you pass go. Collect 200 dollars and go around the board again. That's right dollars, not pounds, for this very British band has thrown themselves smack

Genesis: lamb like a polished diamond

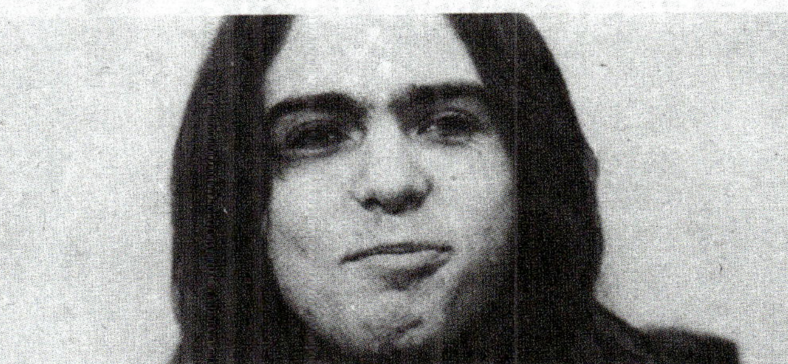

dab into the middle of Times Square and the seedy New York City sights that surround it for the latest LP. The right Americana references are all there including Winston cigarettes, Groucho Marx, one-of-the-crowd identity, not to mention blue suede shoes. Yup you guessed it, this LP rocks! What a refreshing change it is to follow a band through an actual artistic, musical progression instead of one album cleverly disguised as the other. Genesis take two steps forward every time

they enter a studio but this double album is a culmination of past elements injected with present abilities and future directions. Why, you may rightfully wonder, is this album so good? The answers are almost too numerous to mention but we'll offer a brief summary for the dubious. The band have never been recorded so majestically or made such good use of vocal distortions and keyboard electronics. Eno came down to help young master Gabriel with a few tricky

vocal phrasings in and out, the resultant product adds greatly to the fantasy. Always a player who exercises taste and restraint, Banks plays supple piano but what's most impressive is his advanced use of synthesisers and mellotrons. Like Steve Hackett, Banks doesn't feel possessed to solo all night long, instead incorporating his playing *into* the band's sound. Hackett becomes a more dominant member of the group on each recording, his frenetic, choppy style coupled

against his ability to melodically stretch out is superb. While Collins, undoubtedly one of rock's best drummers, proves he's an equally fine high harmony singer. Gabriel's voice has also never sounded better. Which leaves Rutherford to fill in all the holes and gaps with thick, foreboding bass chords and gentle acoustics. There are more high moments on this record than any previous Genesis LP while the songs themselves are more melodic, more tuneful, and better constructed. The album flows beautifully except for a few awkward instrumental moments on side three. Outstanding tracks include "Cuckoo Cocoon", "In The Cage", "The Grand Parade Of Lifeless Packaging", Back In NYC" and "Lilywhite Lilith". Stop bitching about the demise of rock and roll and the dire lack of anything *new*. "The Lamb Lies Down On Broadway" sticks out of the present vinyl rubble like a polished diamond. Oh yeah — it's good value for money too. — Barbara Charone.

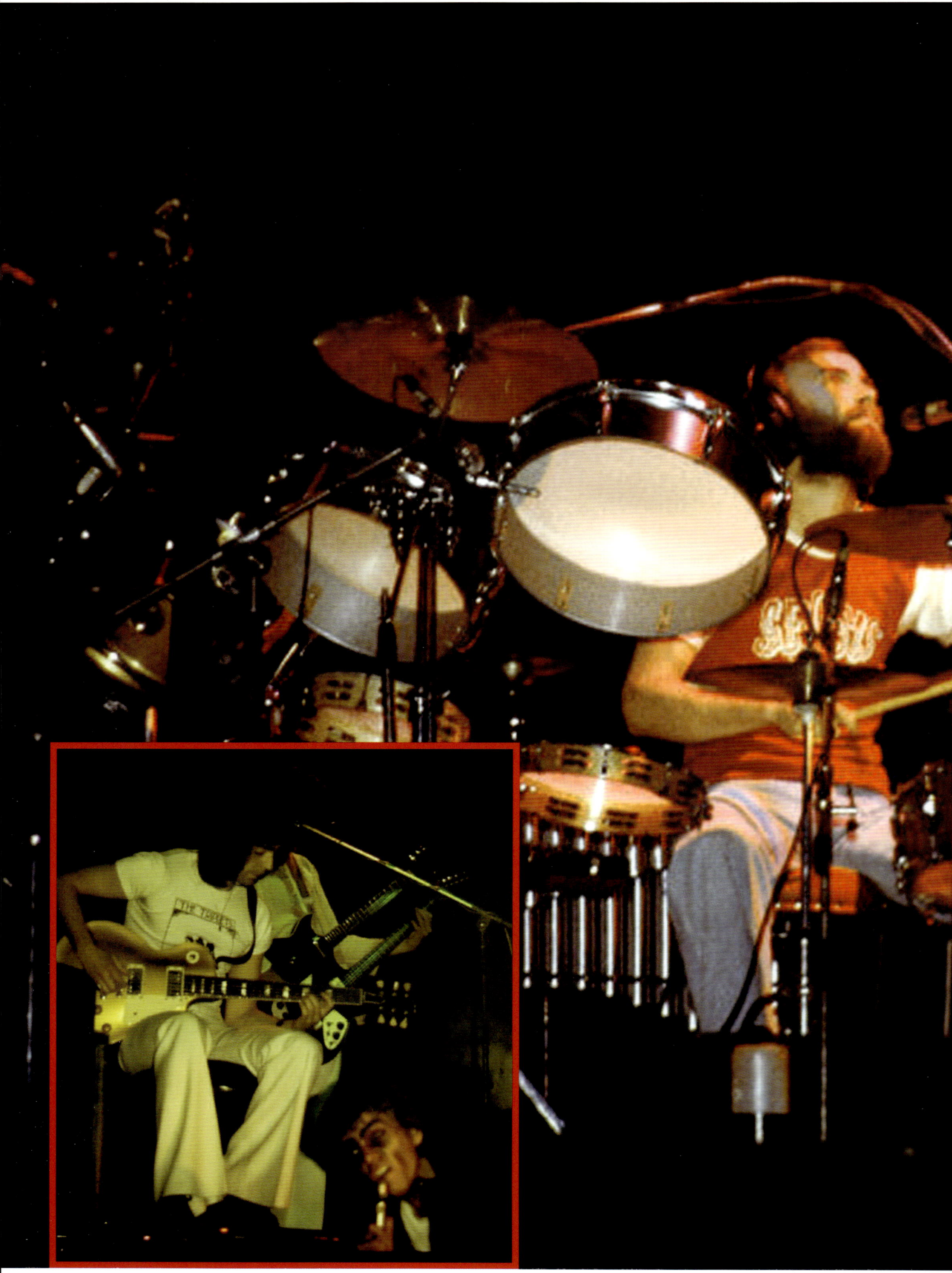

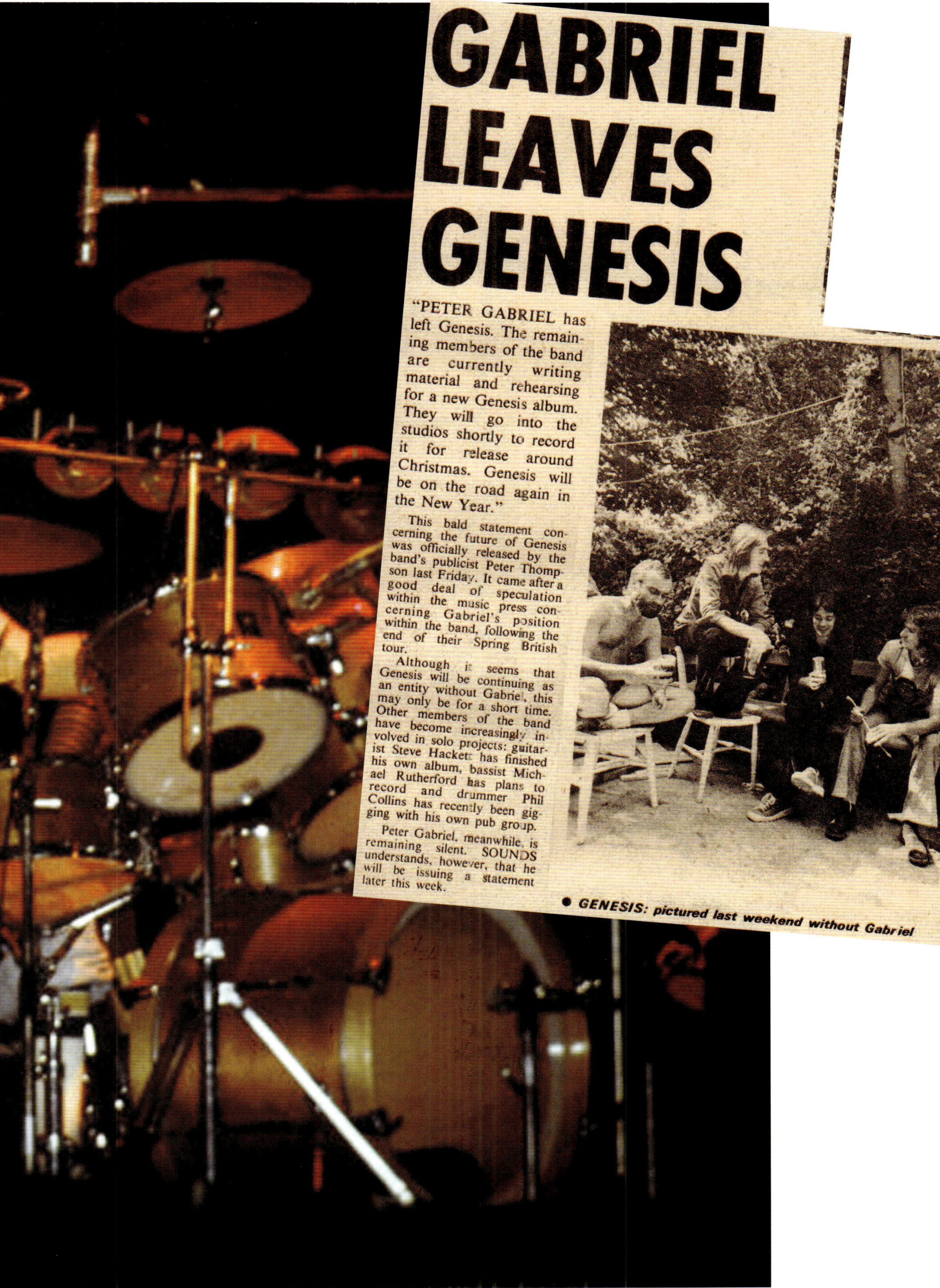

GABRIEL LEAVES GENESIS

"PETER GABRIEL has left Genesis. The remaining members of the band are currently writing material and rehearsing for a new Genesis album. They will go into the studios shortly to record it for release around Christmas. Genesis will be on the road again in the New Year."

This bald statement concerning the future of Genesis was officially released by the band's publicist Peter Thompson last Friday. It came after a good deal of speculation within the music press concerning Gabriel's position within the band, following the end of their Spring British tour.

Although it seems that Genesis will be continuing as an entity without Gabriel, this may only be for a short time. Other members of the band have become increasingly involved in solo projects: guitarist Steve Hackett has finished his own album, bassist Michael Rutherford has plans to record and drummer Phil Collins has recently been gigging with his own pub group.

Peter Gabriel, meanwhile, is remaining silent. SOUNDS understands, however, that he will be issuing a statement later this week.

● **GENESIS: pictured last weekend without Gabriel**

Then There Were Four...

Genesis fans around the world still pontificate to this day about the departure of Peter Gabriel in 1975 but whatever individuals' opinions might be concerning this part of the band's history, it gave fans twice as much music.

The next few pages focus on this initial period with photos that have never seen the light of day before and were unearthed specifically for this book. Record Mirror photographer Steve Emberton shot Genesis twice, and Peter Gabriel once over a ten month period between June 1976 and April 1977.

Steve's archive logs documented that he took photos of Genesis at the Hammersmith Odeon and the Rainbow Theatre. Unfortunately they do not indicate which of the six nights at Hammersmith he was in attendance. Also for the Rainbow gig his archive had the year listed as 1978, which is clearly not the case, so assuming the venue is correct then they will have been from January 1977. Once again the actual date cannot be confirmed.

Steve returned to Hammersmith in April 1977 to capture Peter Gabriel's debut tour as a solo artist. Like most press photographers of the time, all his images are in black and white. Not only was it cheaper than colour film, but for the vast majority of cases, it was all that was required for the papers they were destined to be published in.

However Alan Perry pretty much mirrored Steve Emberton's sojourns and captured the band in colour at Hammersmith in '76 and on the 9th January '77 at the Empire Theatre in Liverpool. He also captured Peter Gabriel at the same venue on 28th April '77, which followed on from the shows at Hammersmith.

Genesis fans were rewarded with further delights during this period. Gabriel had launched his solo career in February with the release of his first album and the following month original guitarist Anthony Phillips did likewise with his *The Geese & the Ghost* album.

Gabriel returned to UK concert venues later the same year with a more extensive tour. Once again Alan Perry captured the Liverpool show at the Empire Theatre on the 23rd September.

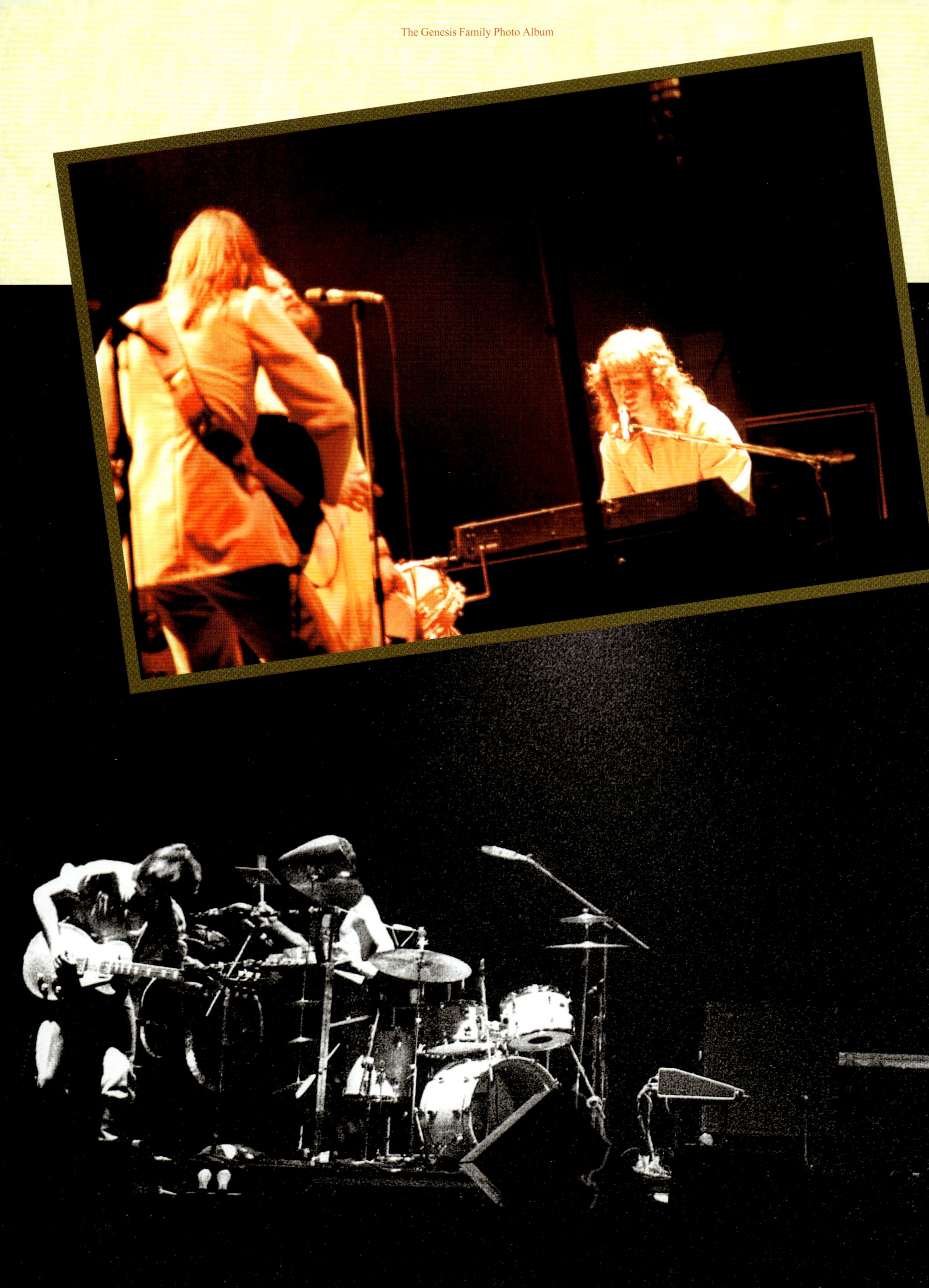

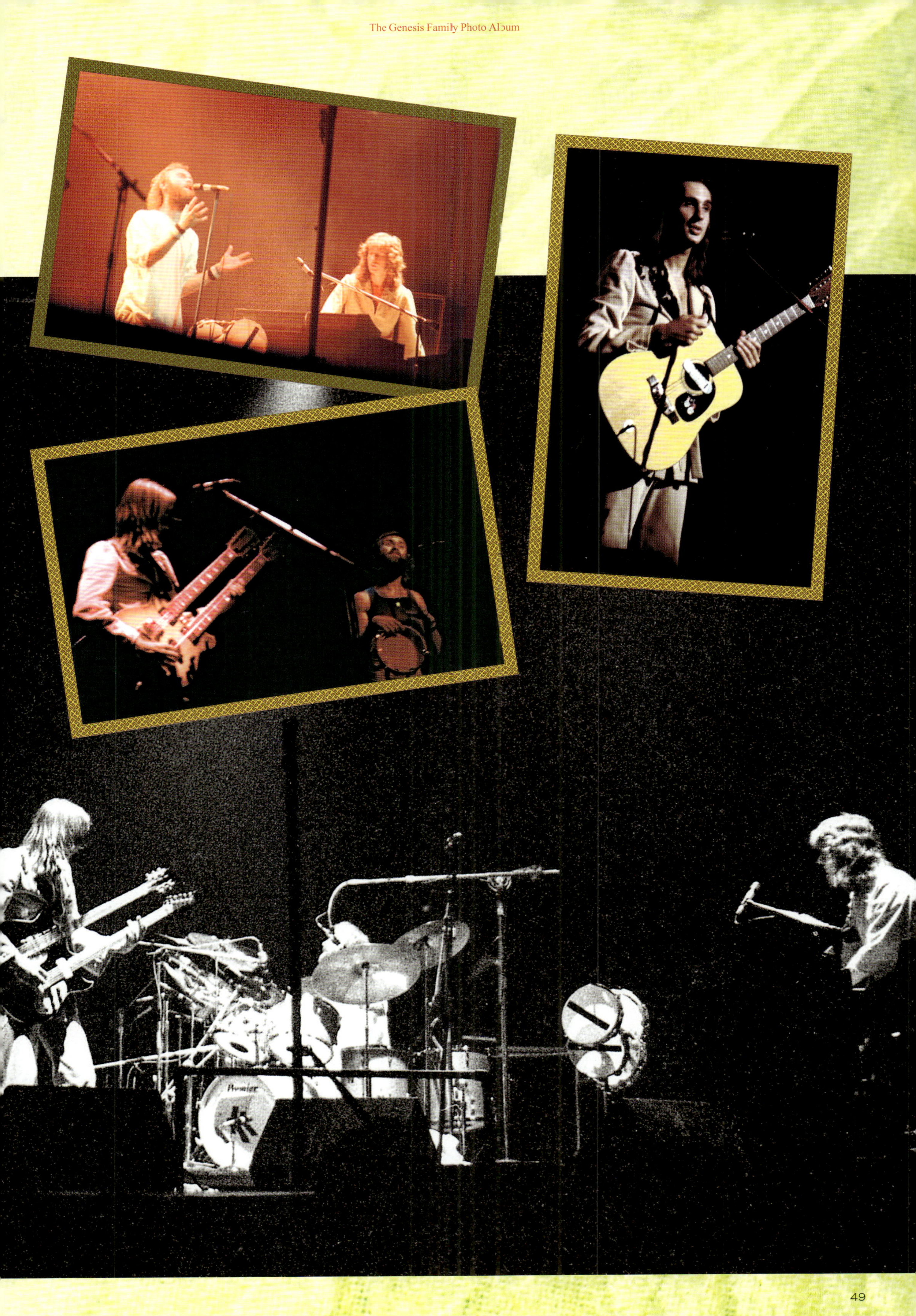

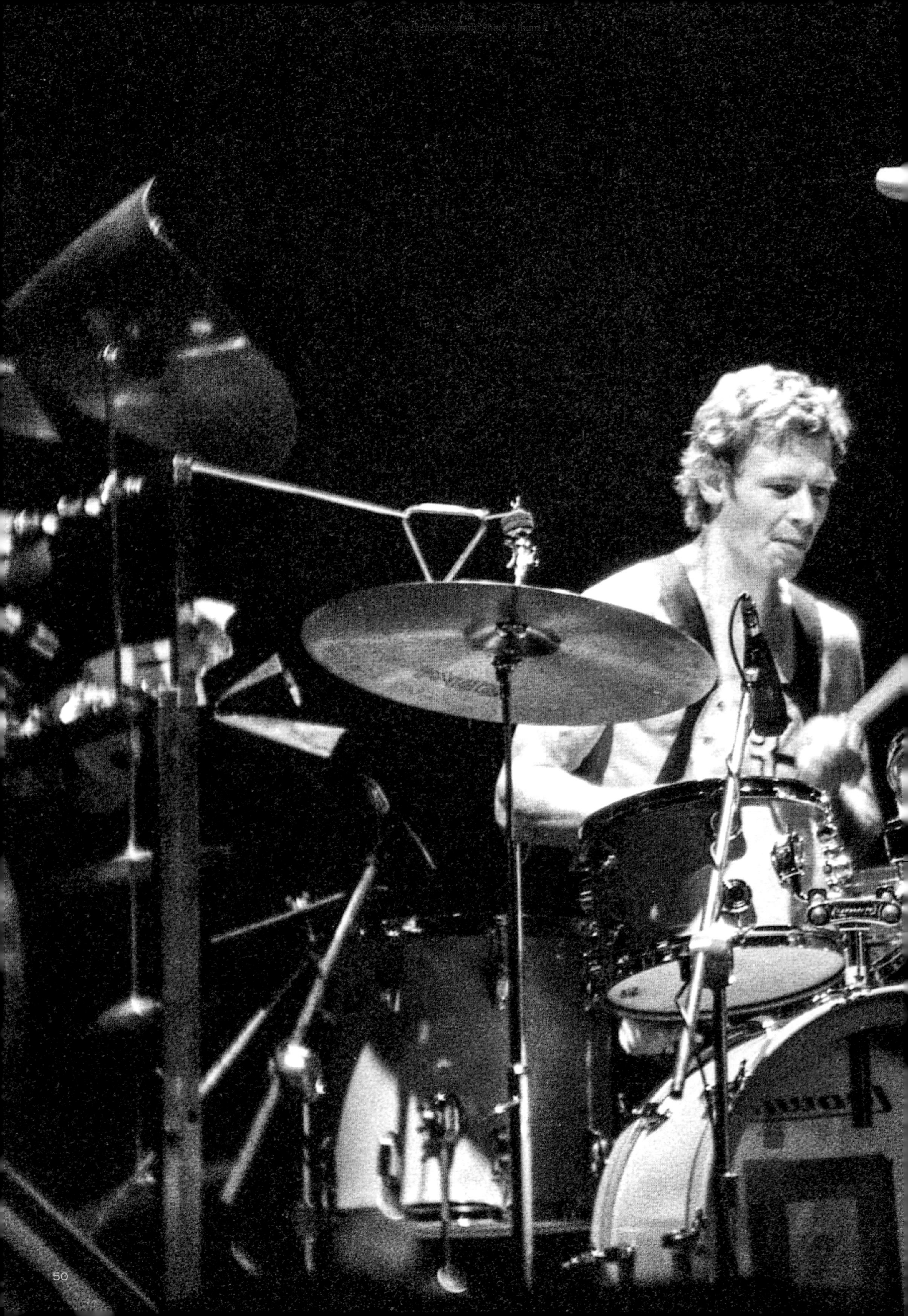

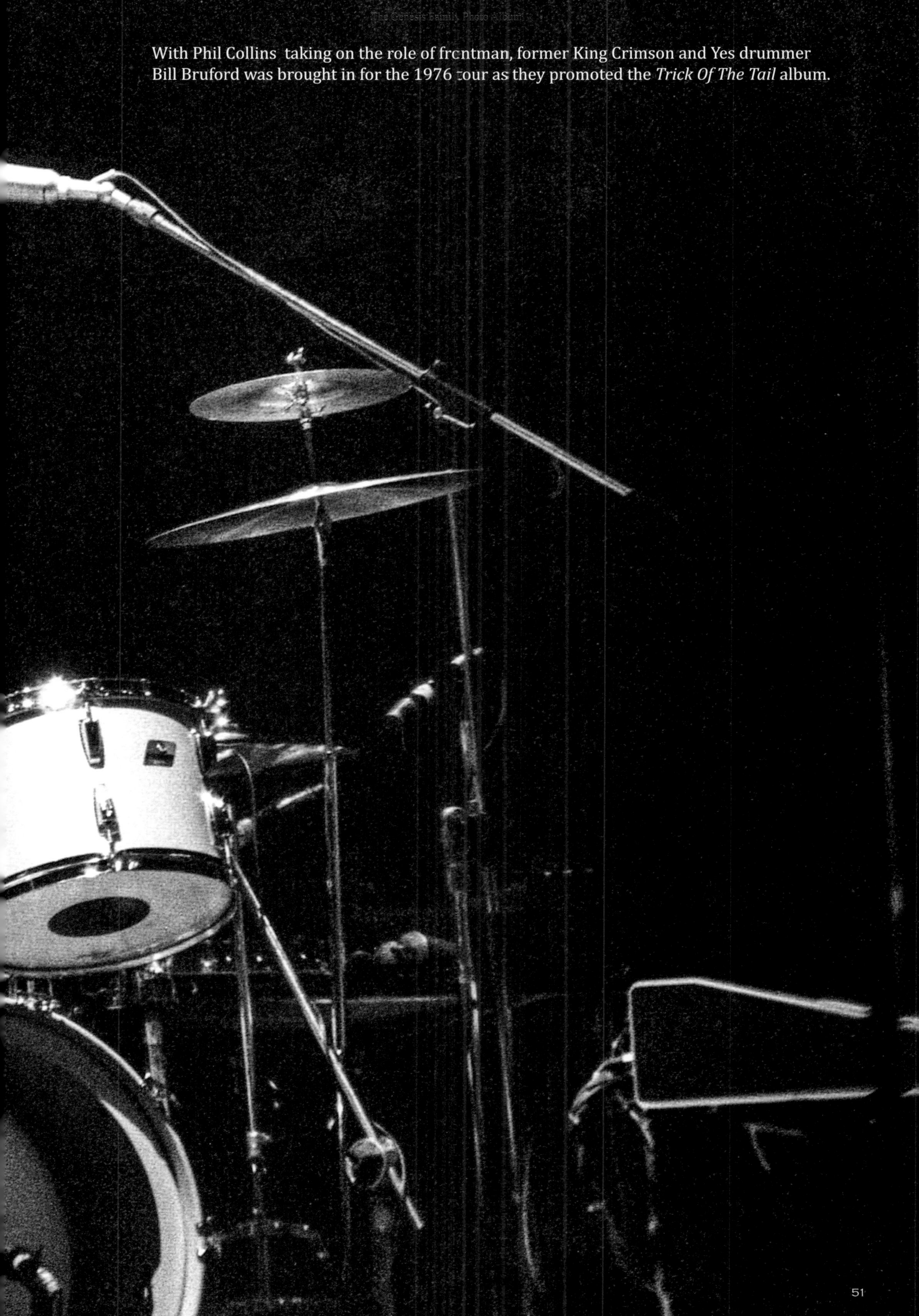

With Phil Collins taking on the role of frontman, former King Crimson and Yes drummer
Bill Bruford was brought in for the 1976 tour as they promoted the *Trick Of The Tail* album.

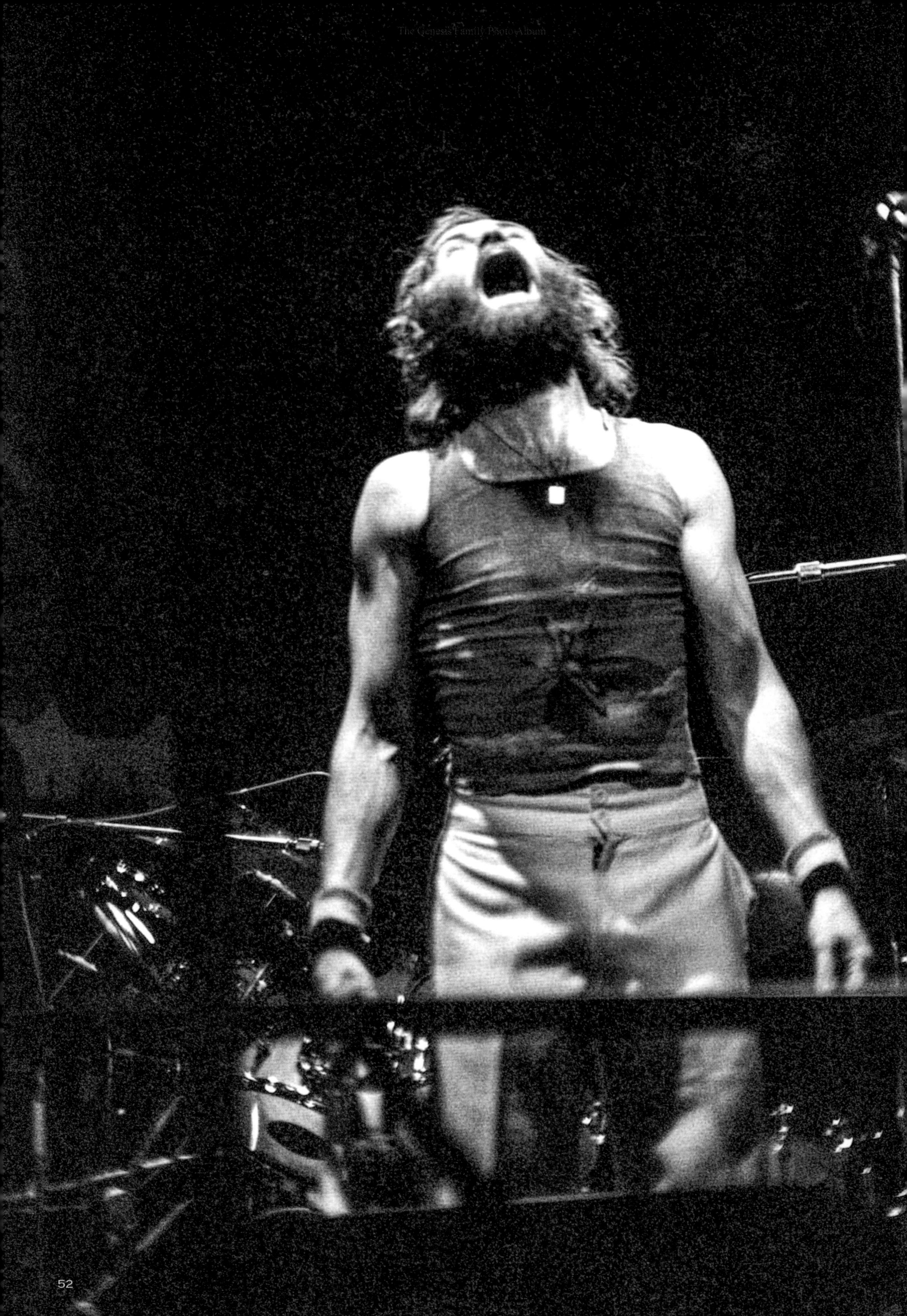

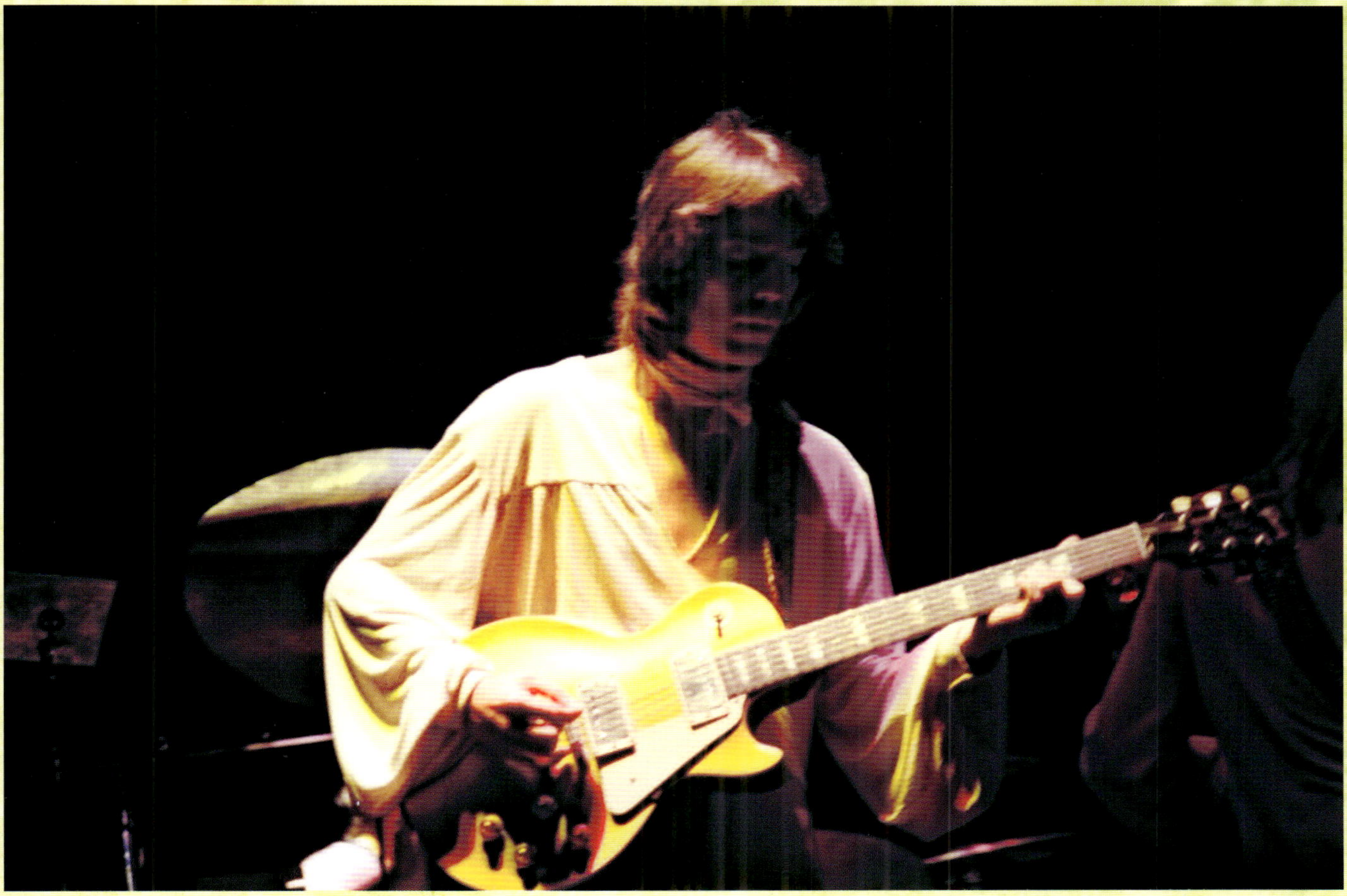

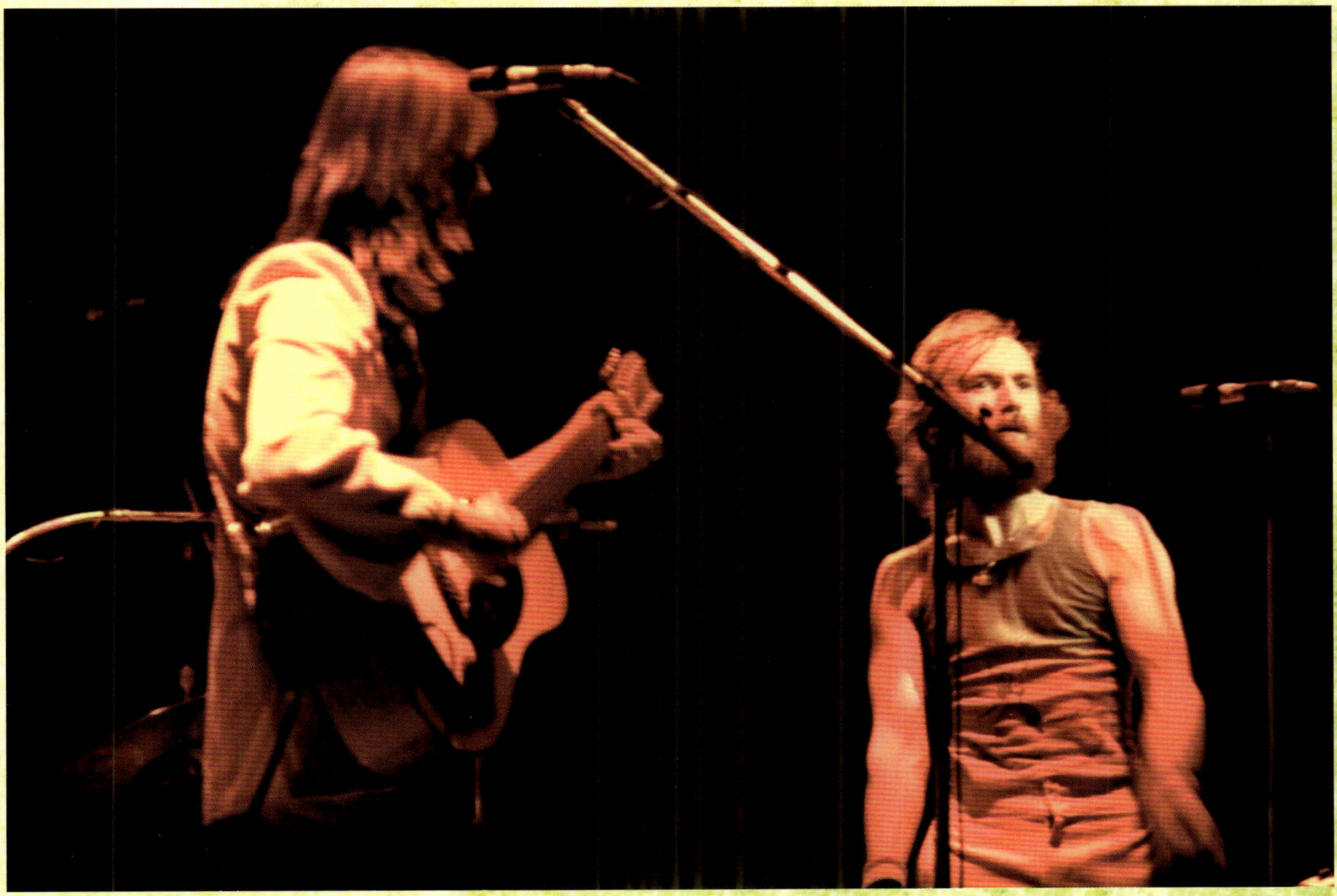

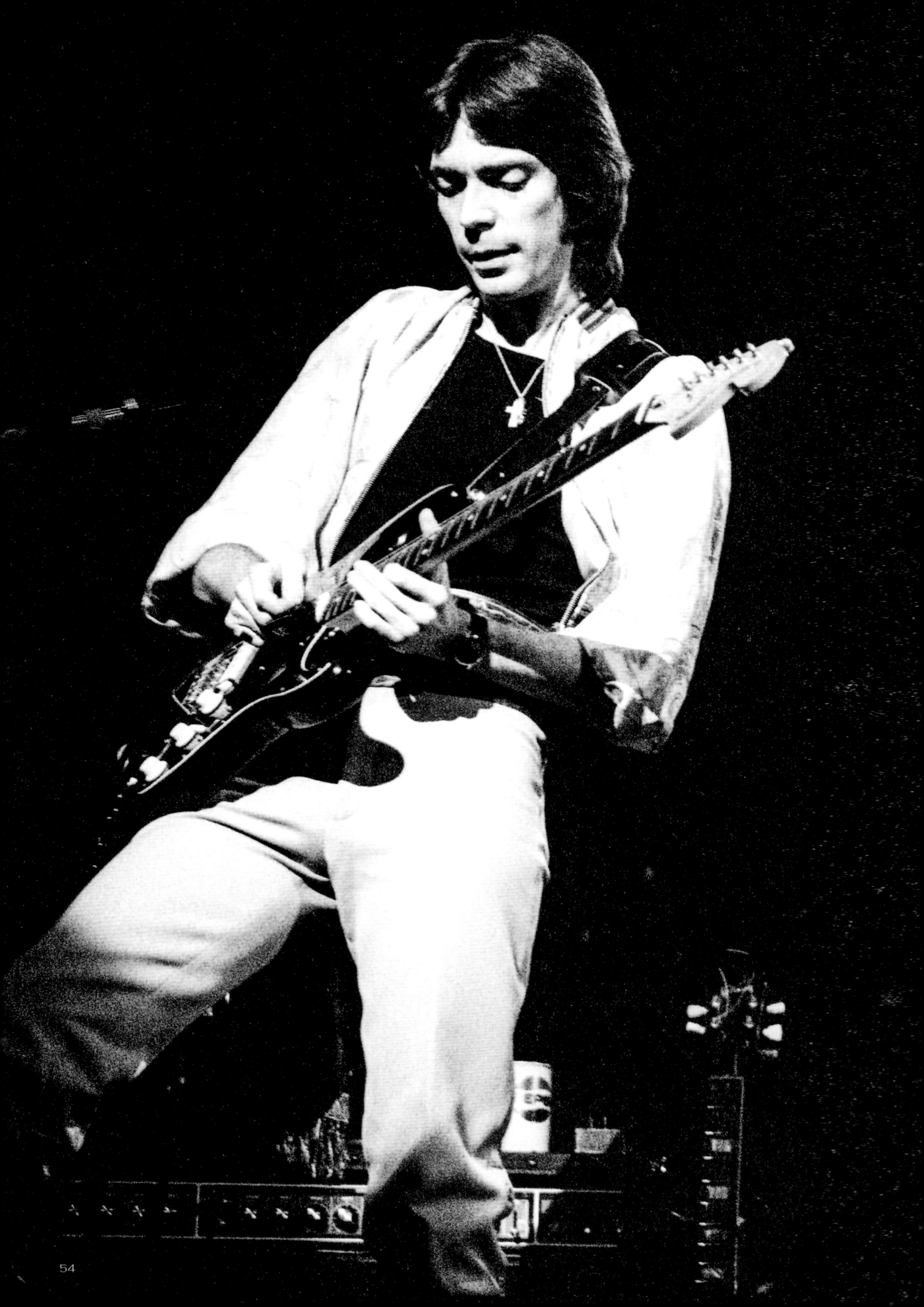

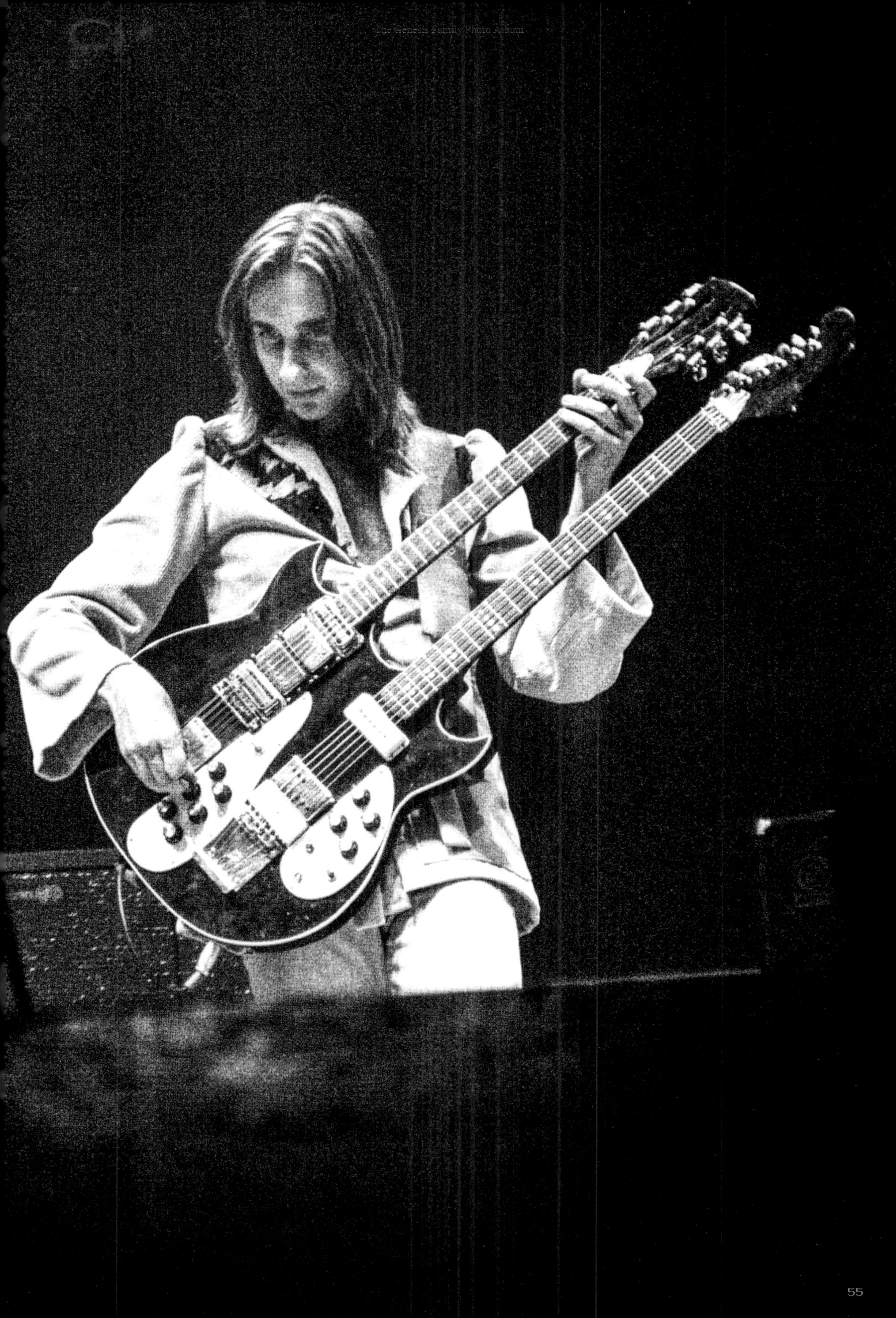

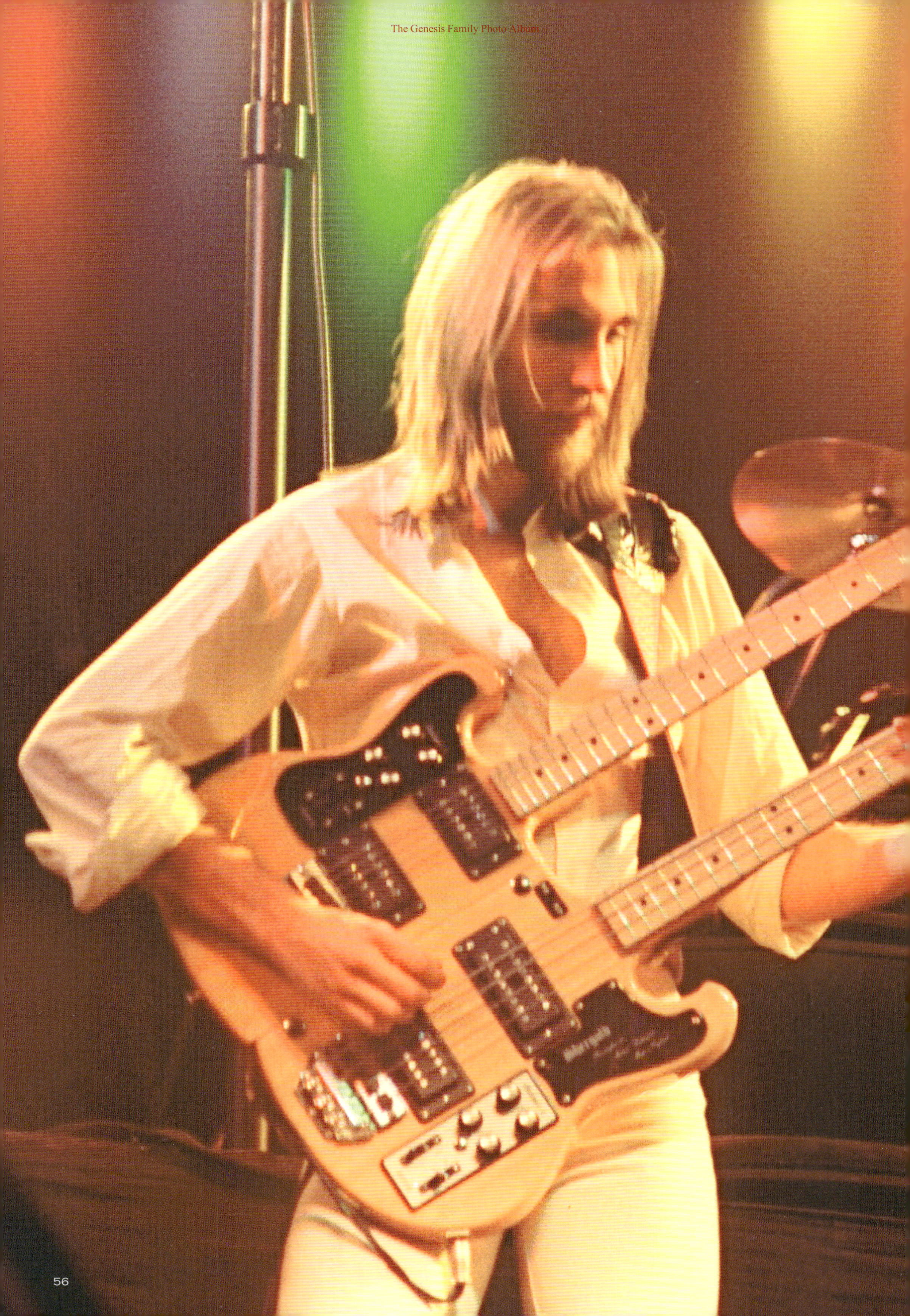

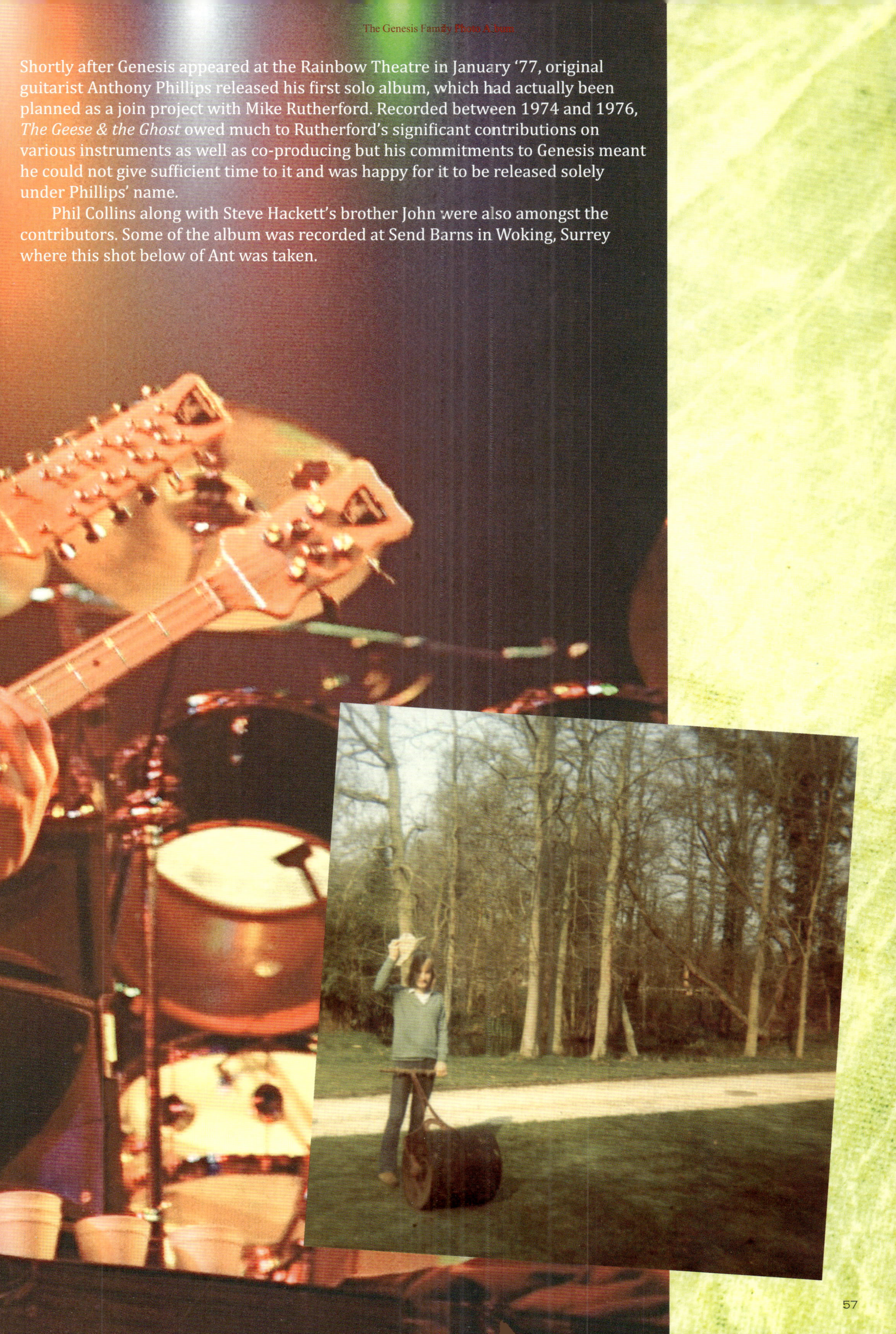

Shortly after Genesis appeared at the Rainbow Theatre in January '77, original guitarist Anthony Phillips released his first solo album, which had actually been planned as a join project with Mike Rutherford. Recorded between 1974 and 1976, *The Geese & the Ghost* owed much to Rutherford's significant contributions on various instruments as well as co-producing but his commitments to Genesis meant he could not give sufficient time to it and was happy for it to be released solely under Phillips' name.

Phil Collins along with Steve Hackett's brother John were also amongst the contributors. Some of the album was recorded at Send Barns in Woking, Surrey where this shot below of Ant was taken.

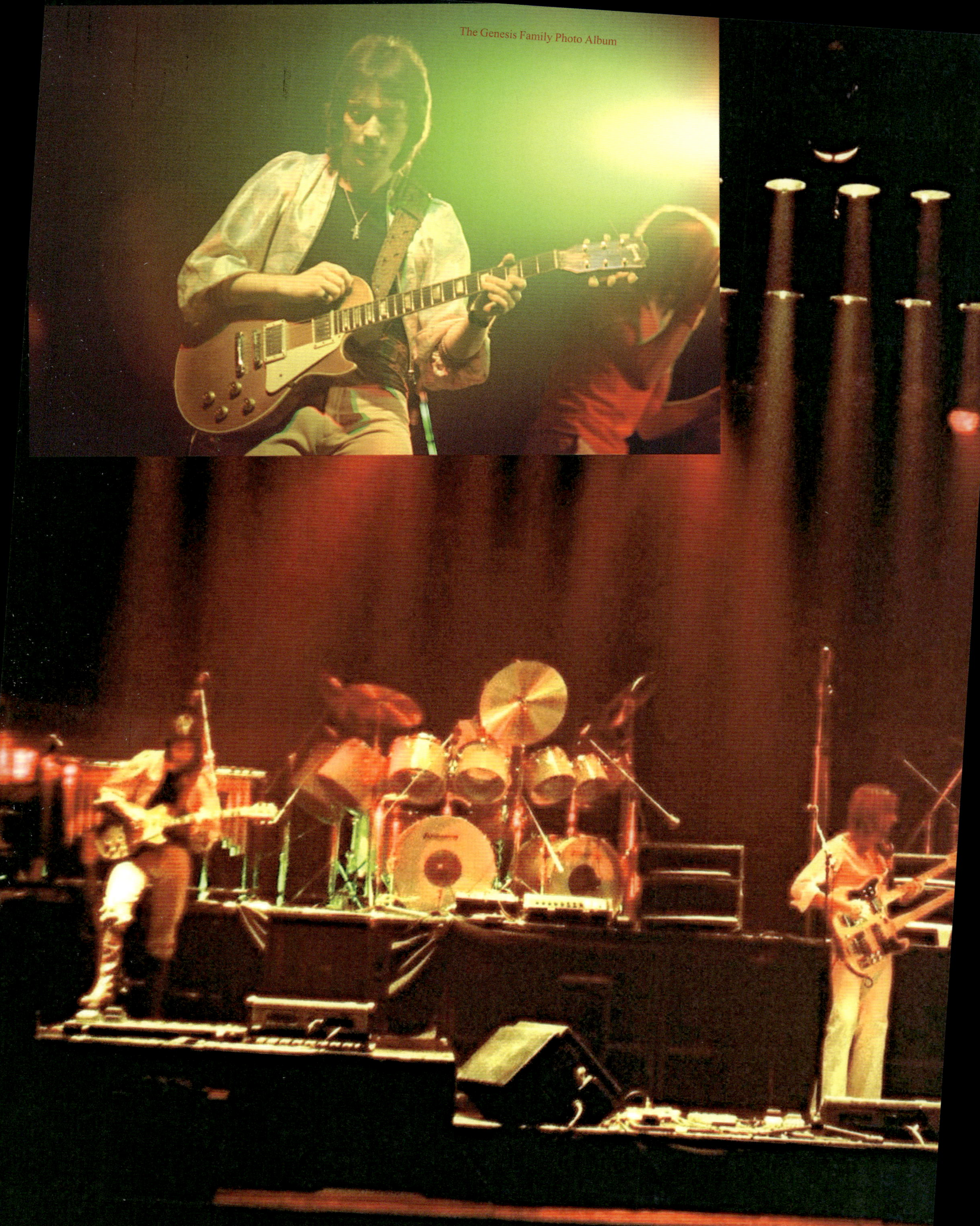

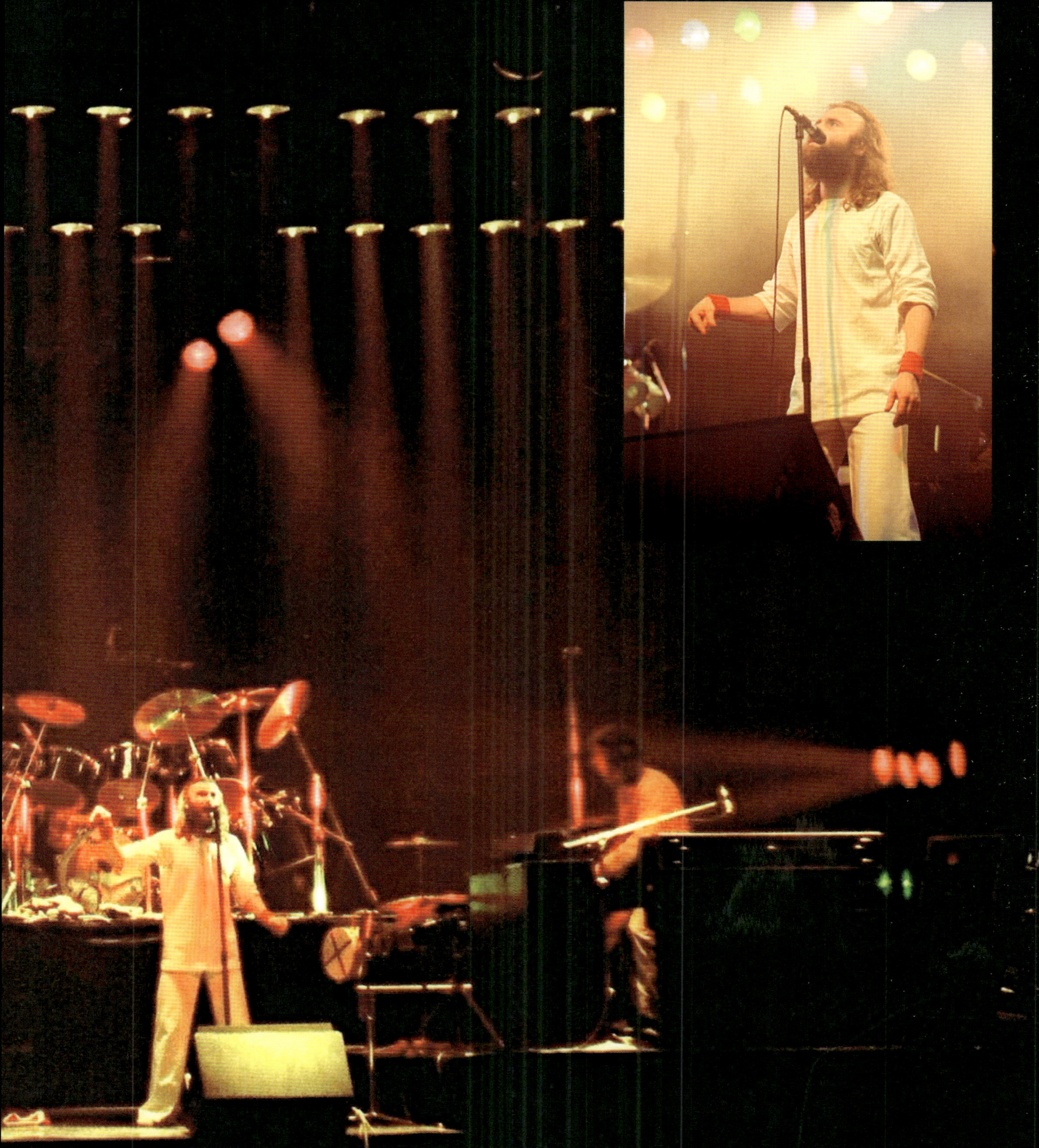

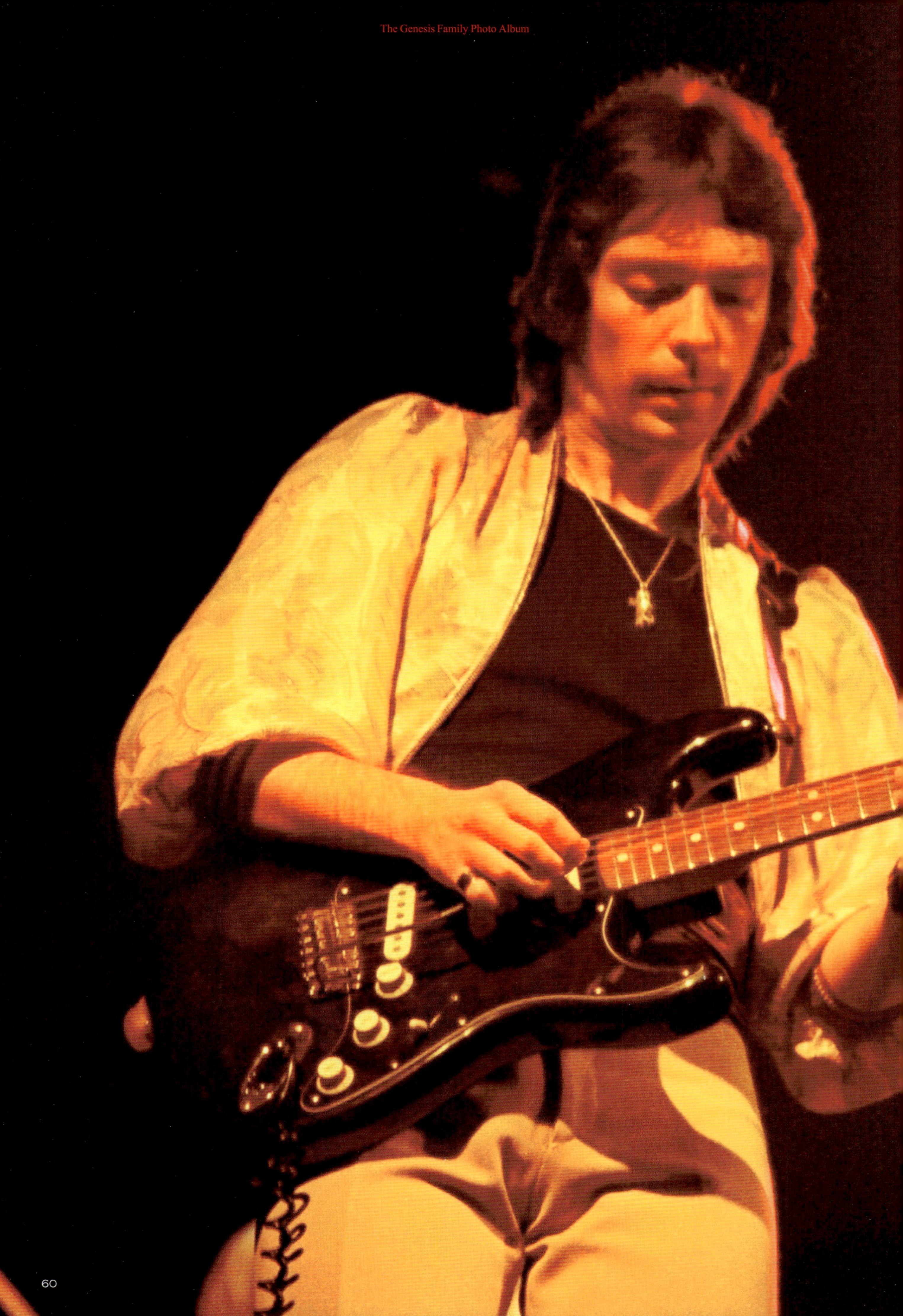

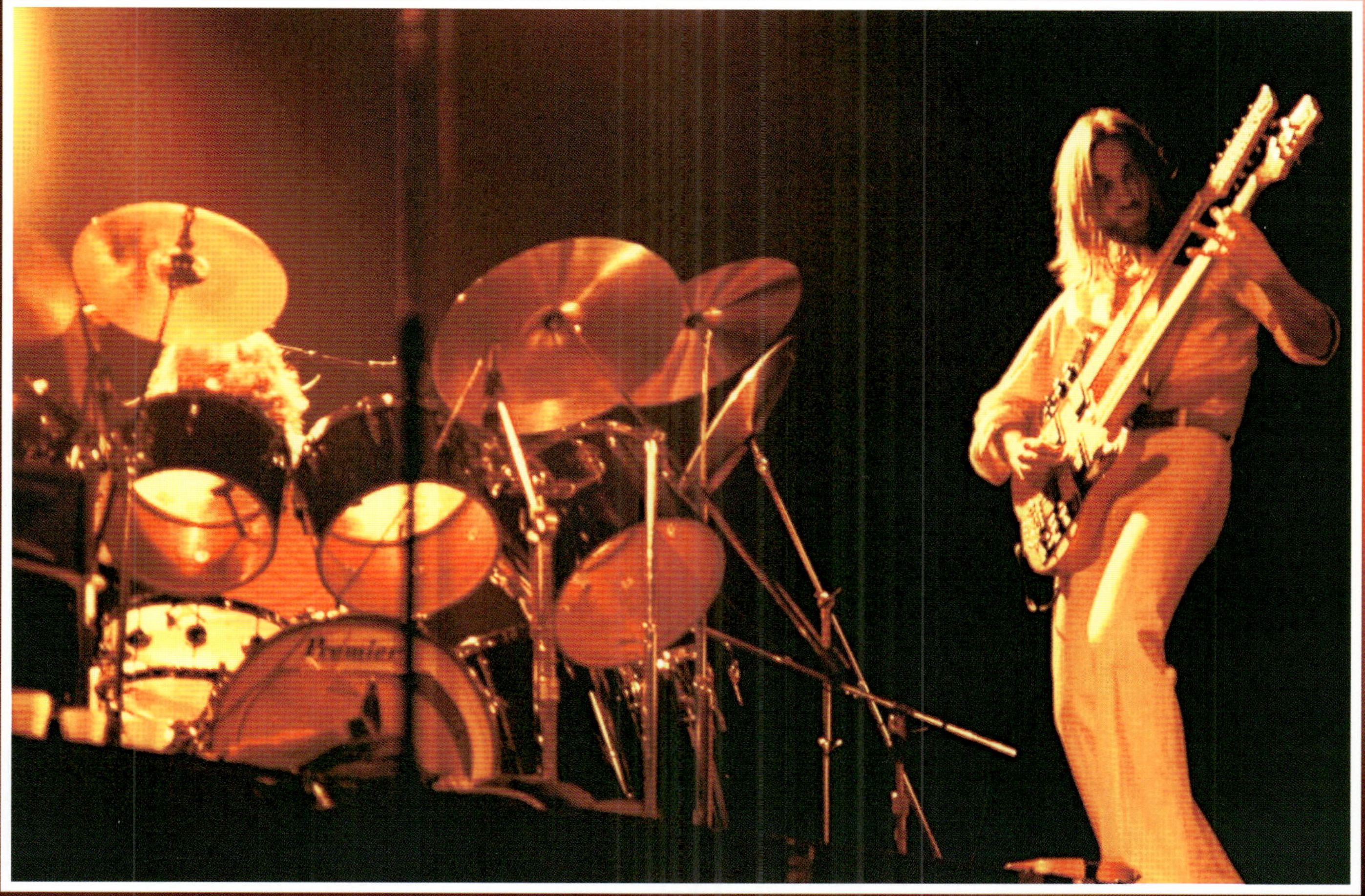

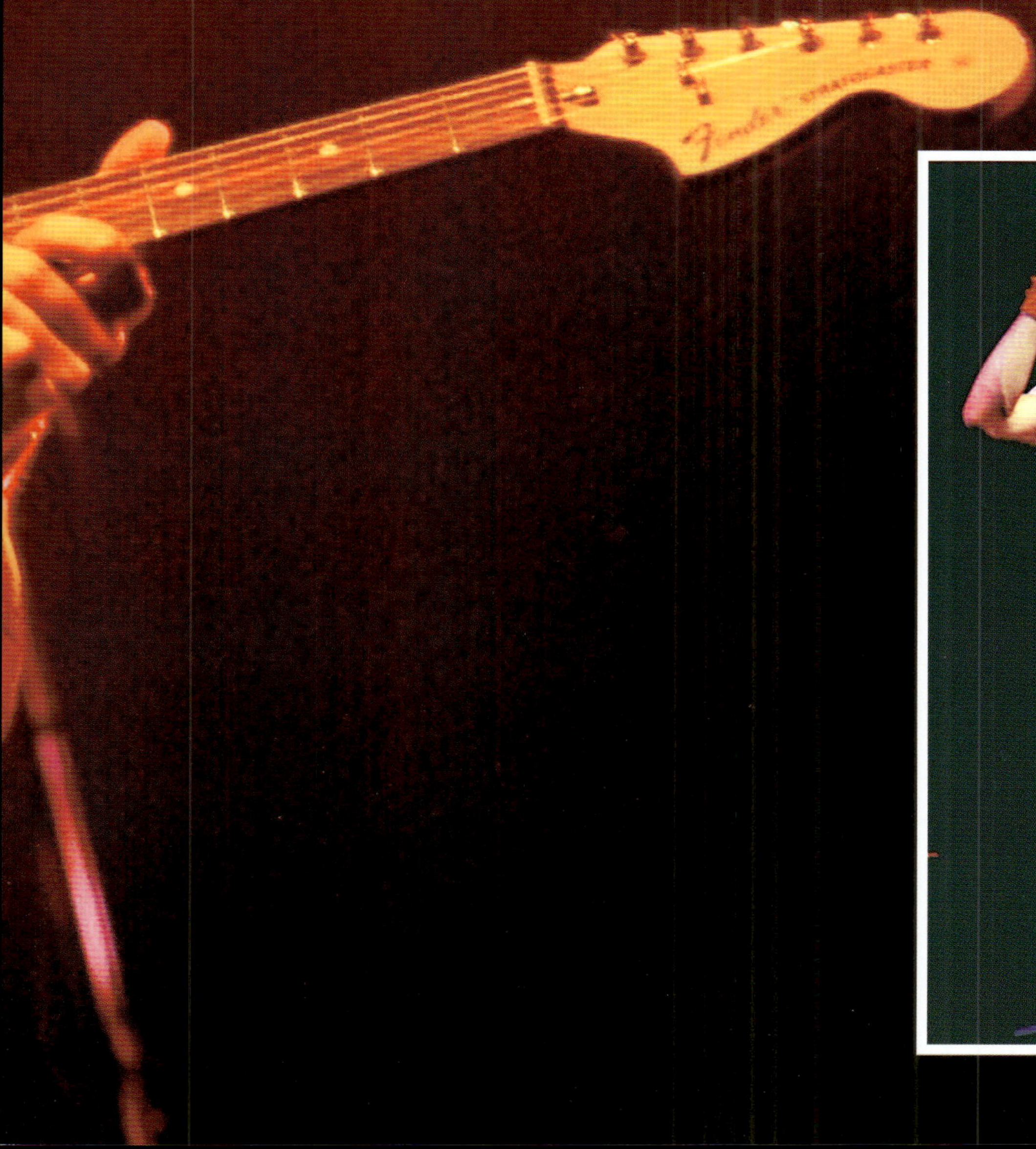

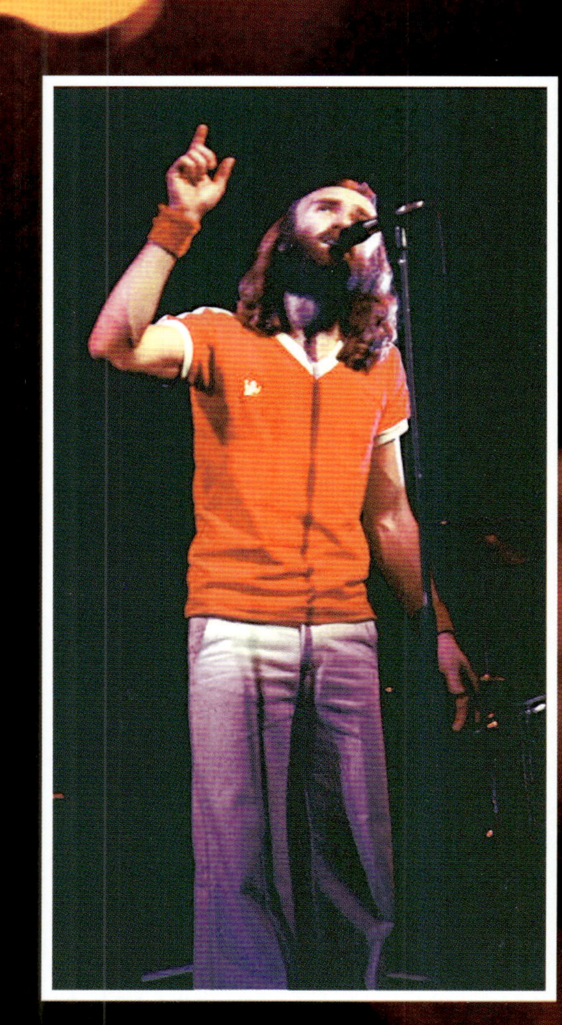

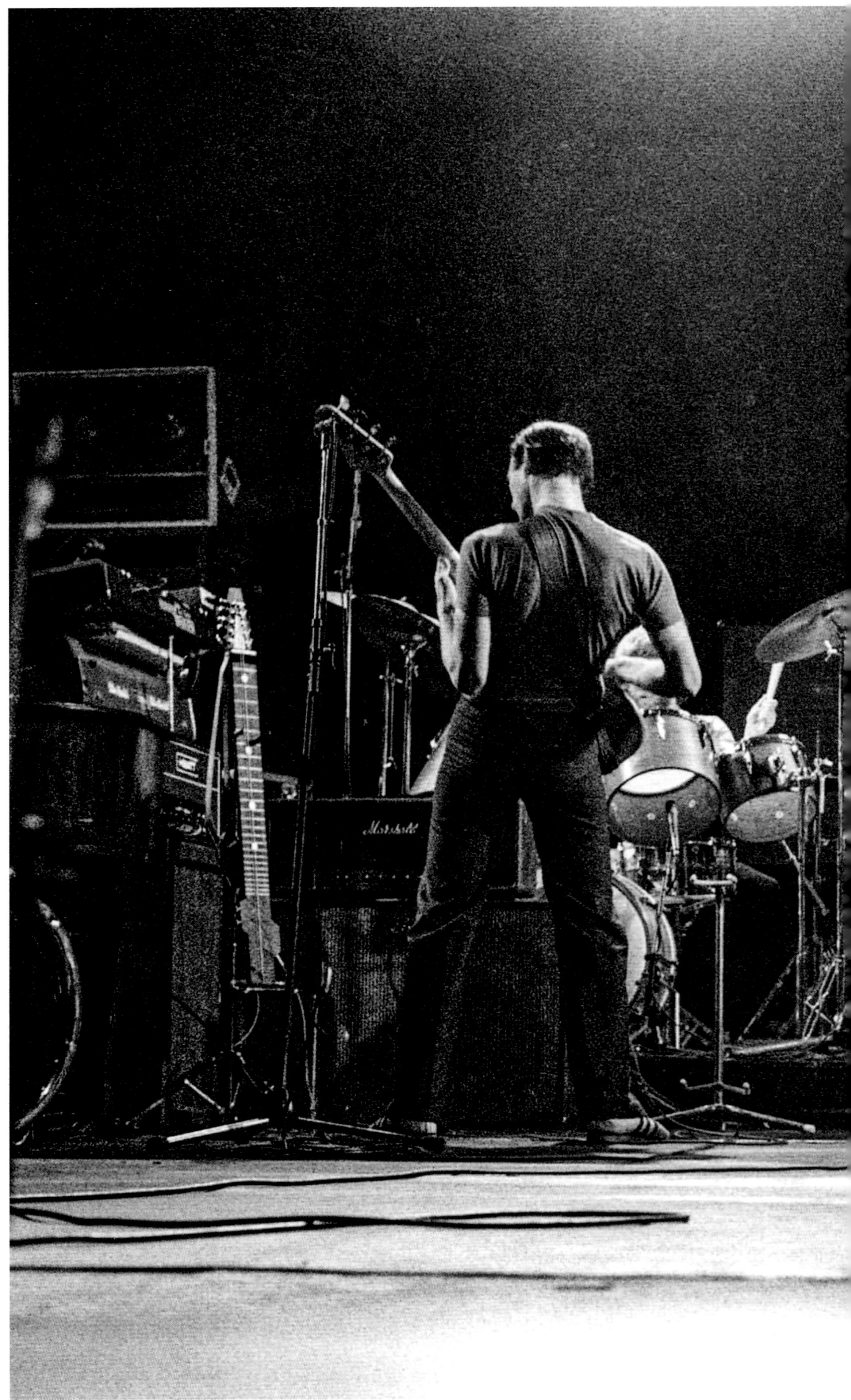

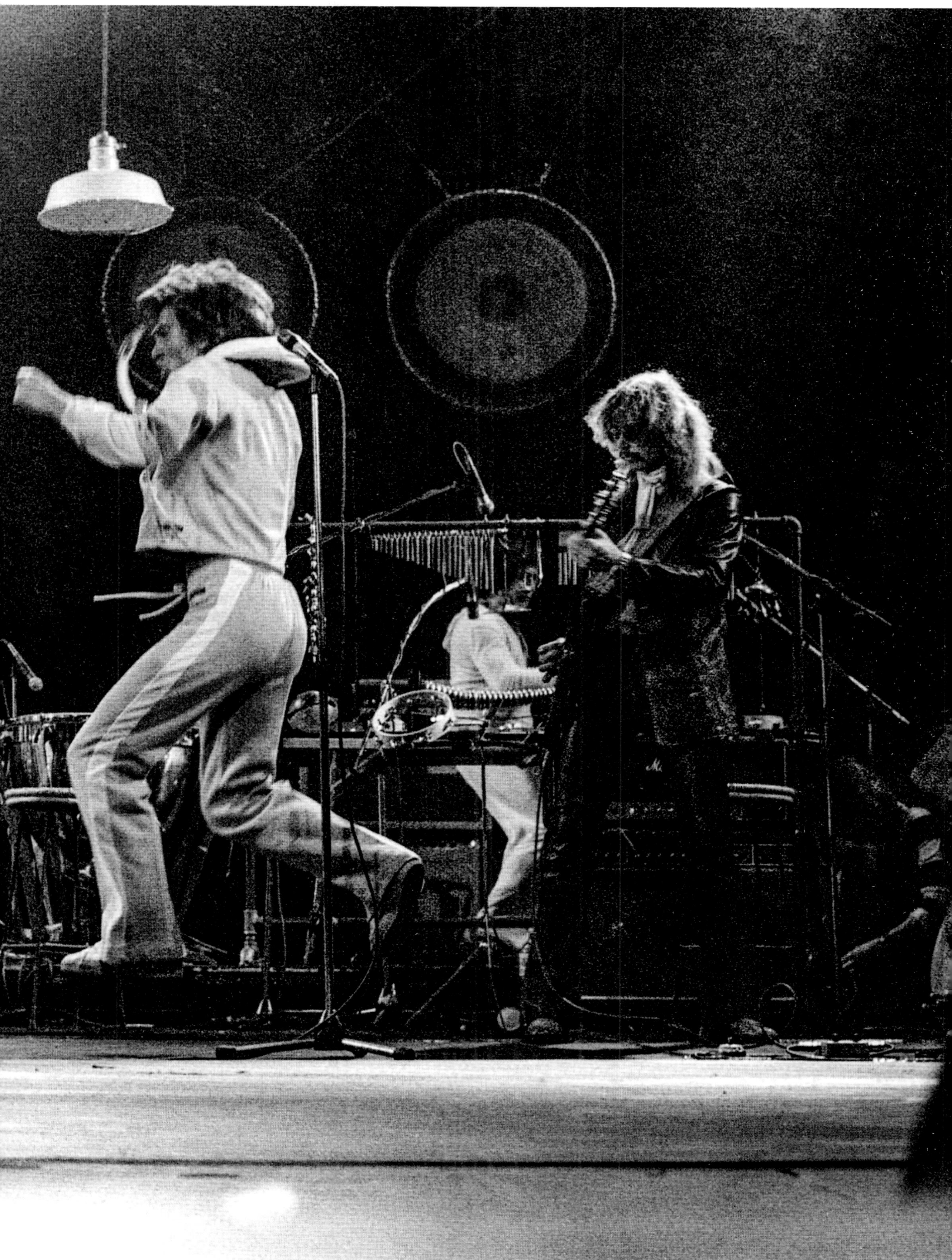

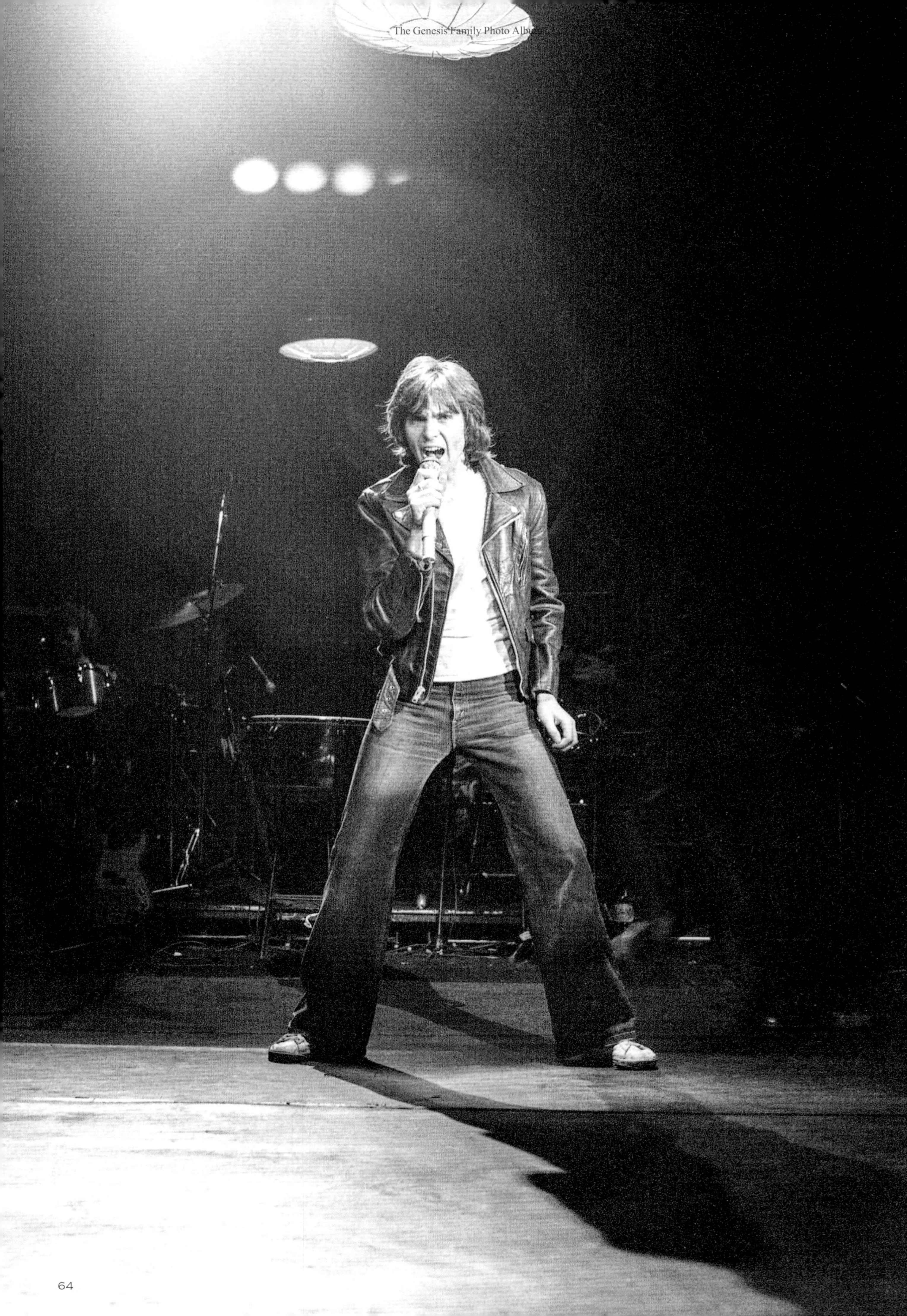

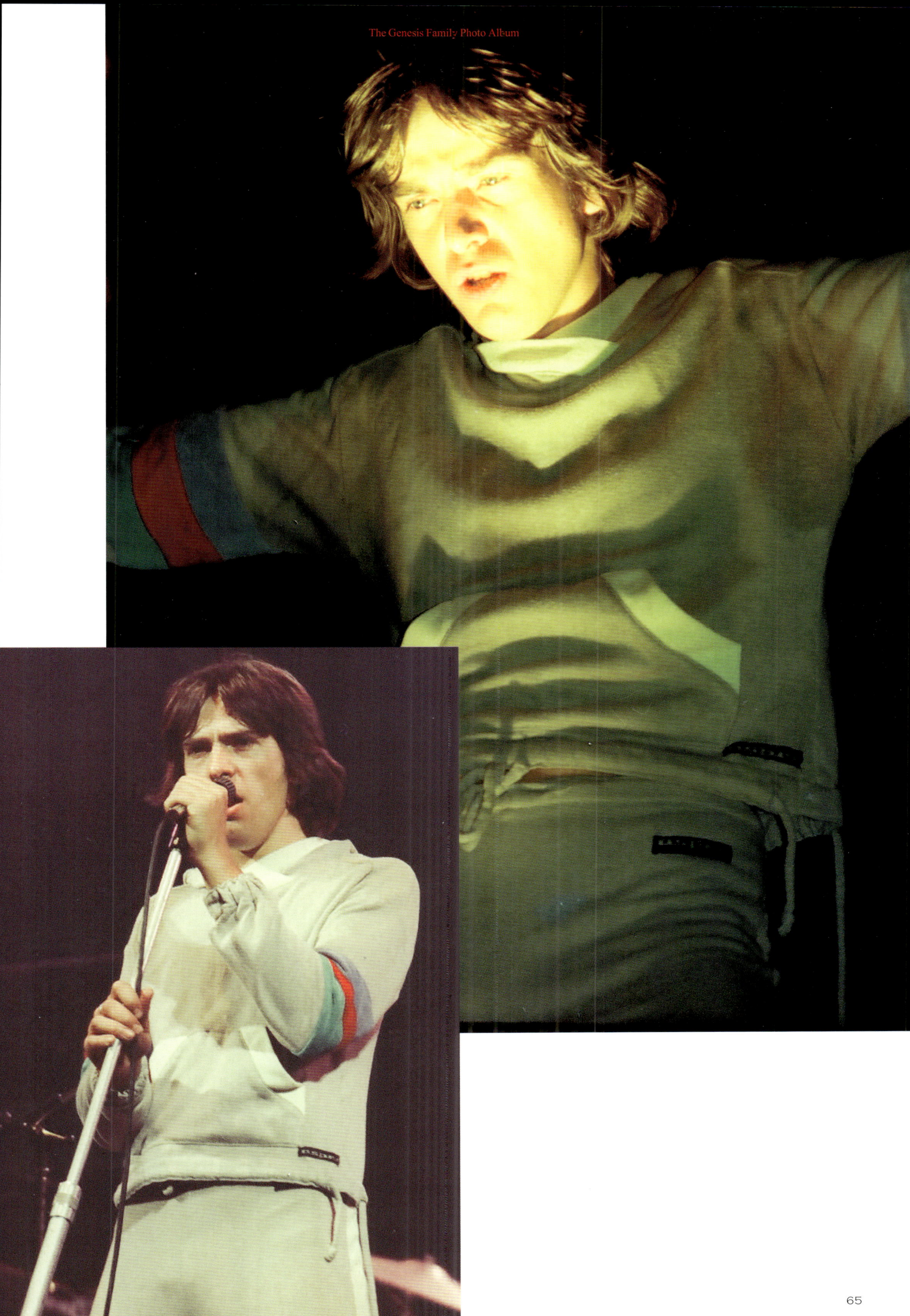

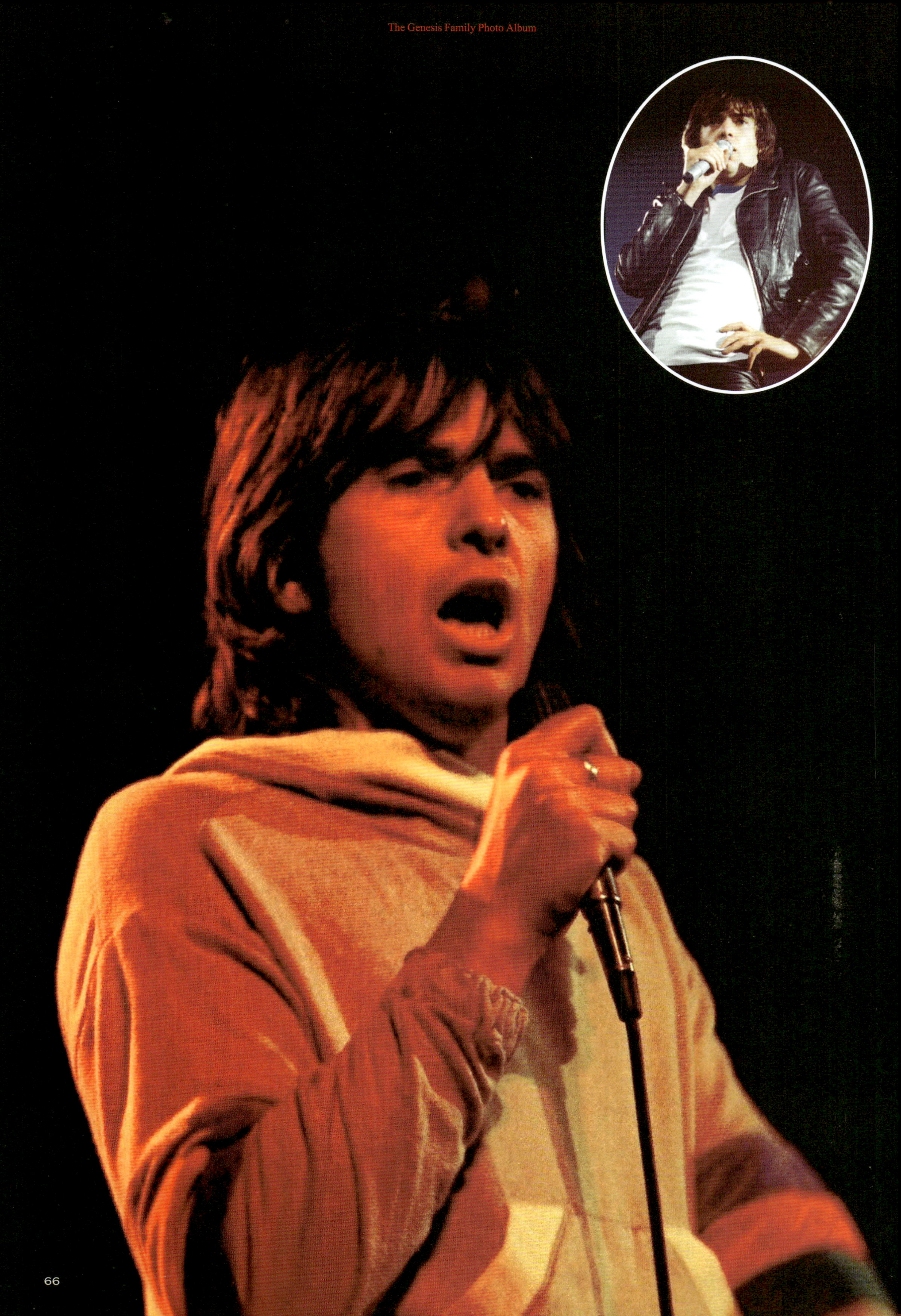

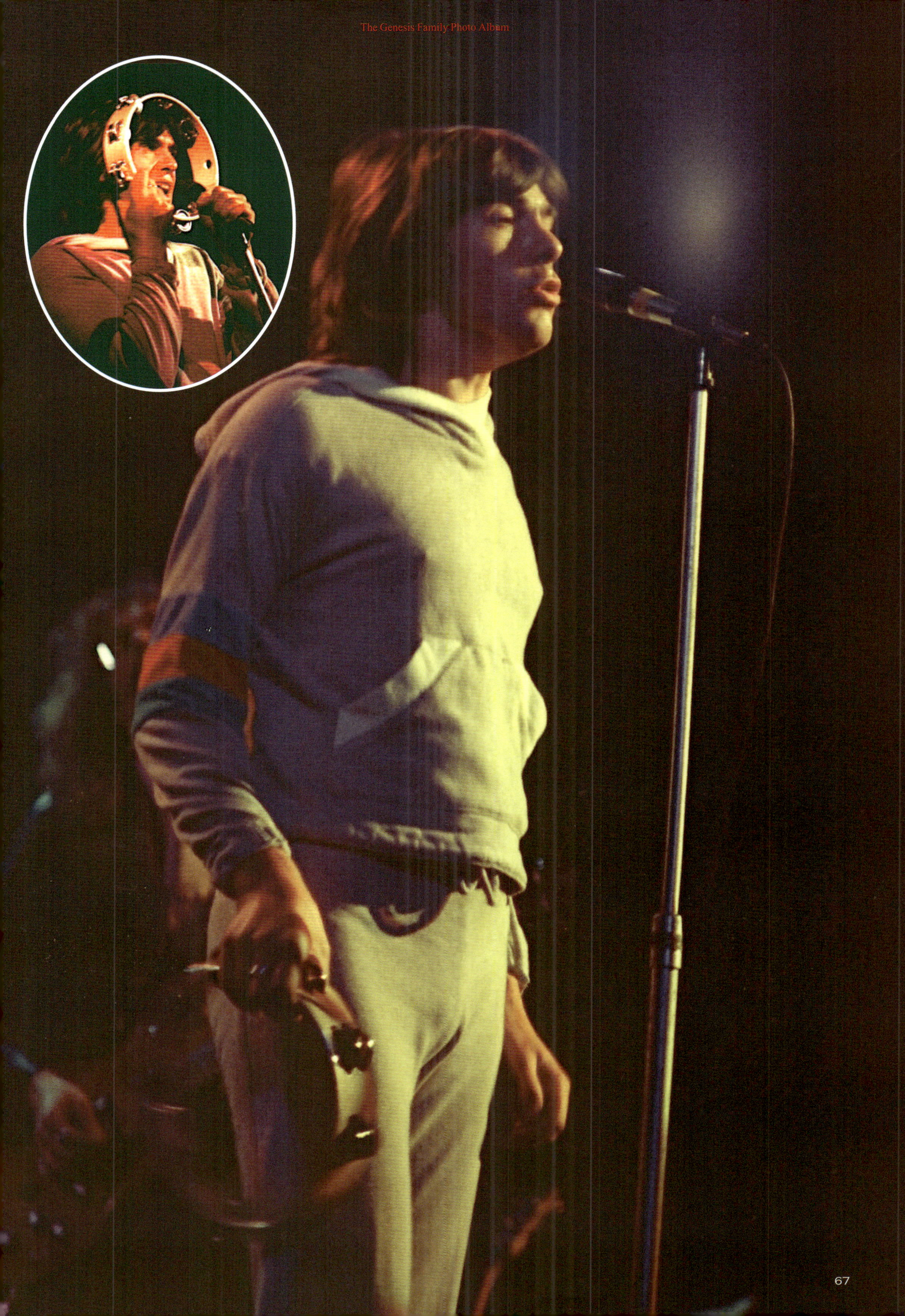

...And Three...

It seems like a life time ago now that Genesis became three with the departure of Steve Hackett. The aptly named first album as a trio, 1978's *...Then There Were Three...* gave Genesis its biggest hit single with 'Follow You Follow Me' but equally as appealing it gave fans yet another solo career to follow as well.

With Anthony Phillips also having returned to releasing albums, the Genesis Family continued to expand. Genesis, Peter Gabriel and Steve Hackett all toured in 1978. Genesis, more popular than ever performed to a huge audience at the Knebworth Festival; Gabriel played at New York's vast Madison Square Garden (and at a second Knebworth Festival), and Steve Hackett concluded a debut tour at the Hammersmith Odeon.

Their careers continued to flourish. By 1982 Phil Collins embarked on his first solo tour following his massive solo success with 'In The Air Tonight' and the album *Hello, I Must Be Going*.

The same year a one-off reunion with Peter Gabriel took everyone by surprise. Not on a muddy pitch in Newcastle, as the song went, but a muddy field in Milton Keynes!

Four years later and Mike Rutherford gets in on the act with his offshoot band Mike & The Mechanics, and as they say the rest is history. The Genesis Family hasn't looked back since.

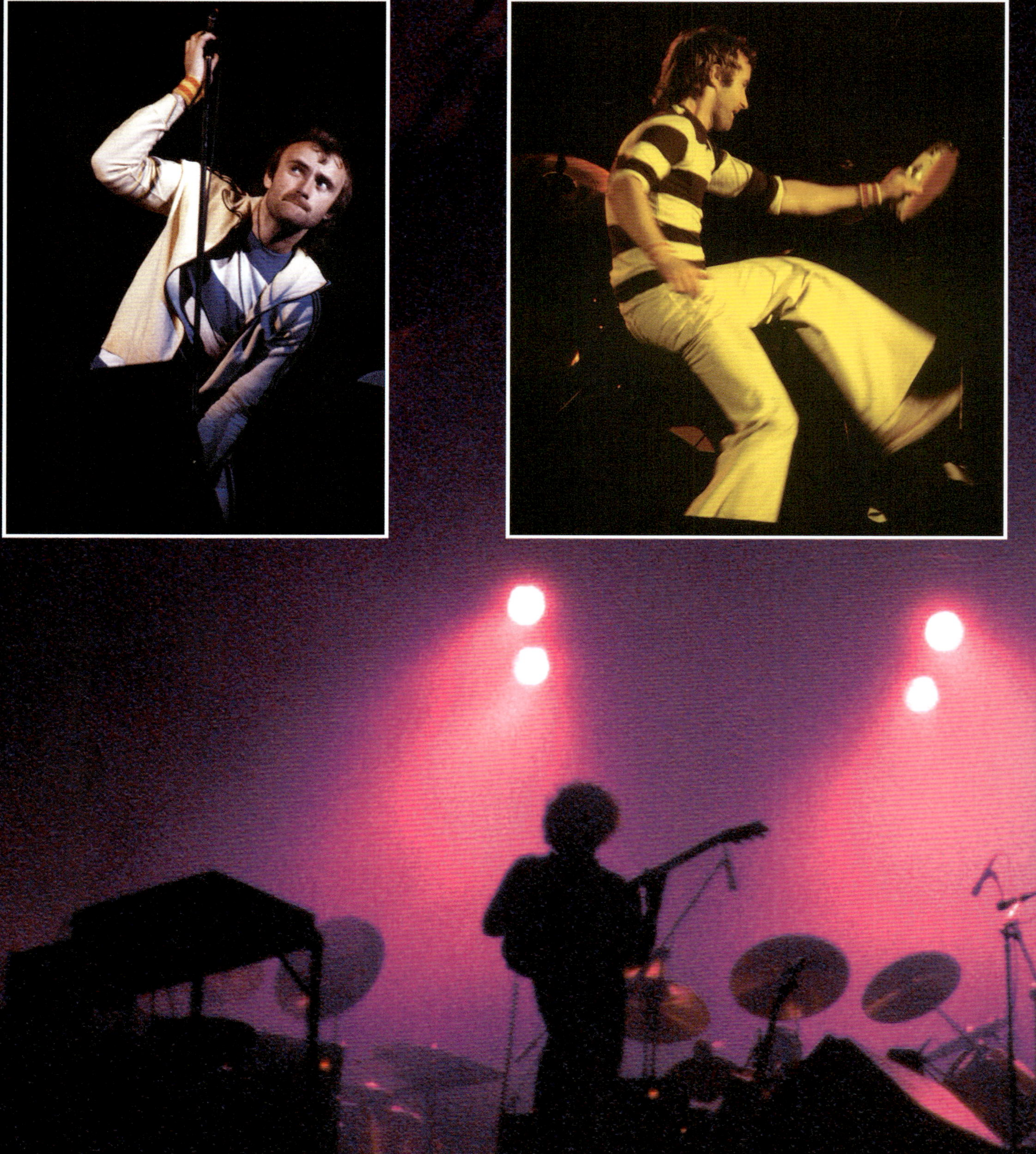

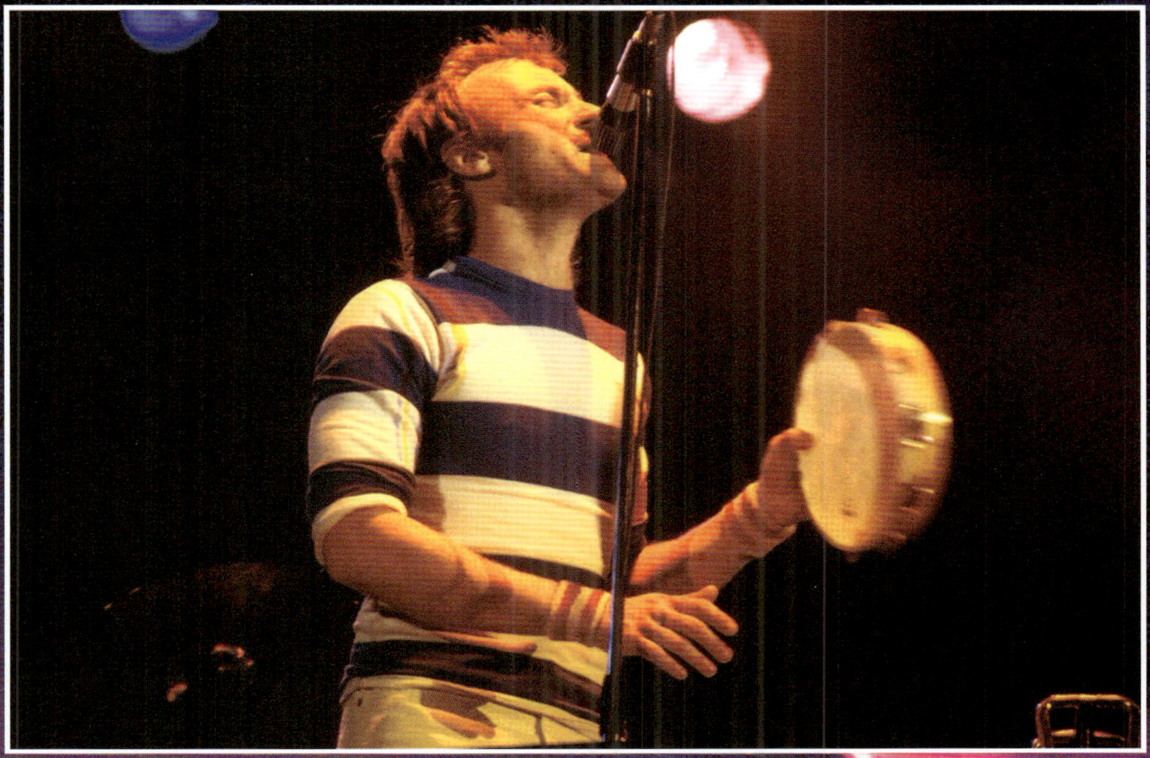

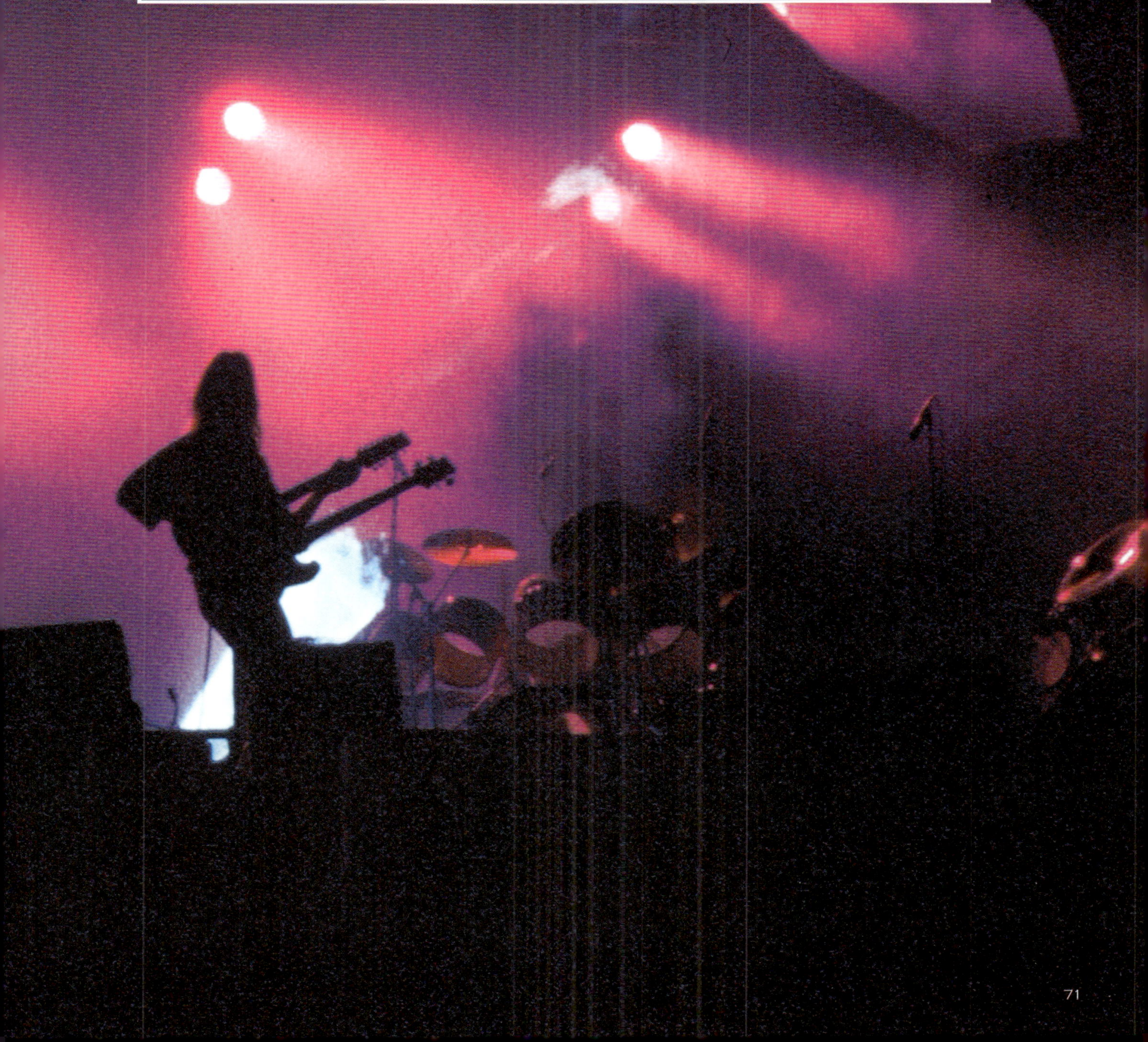

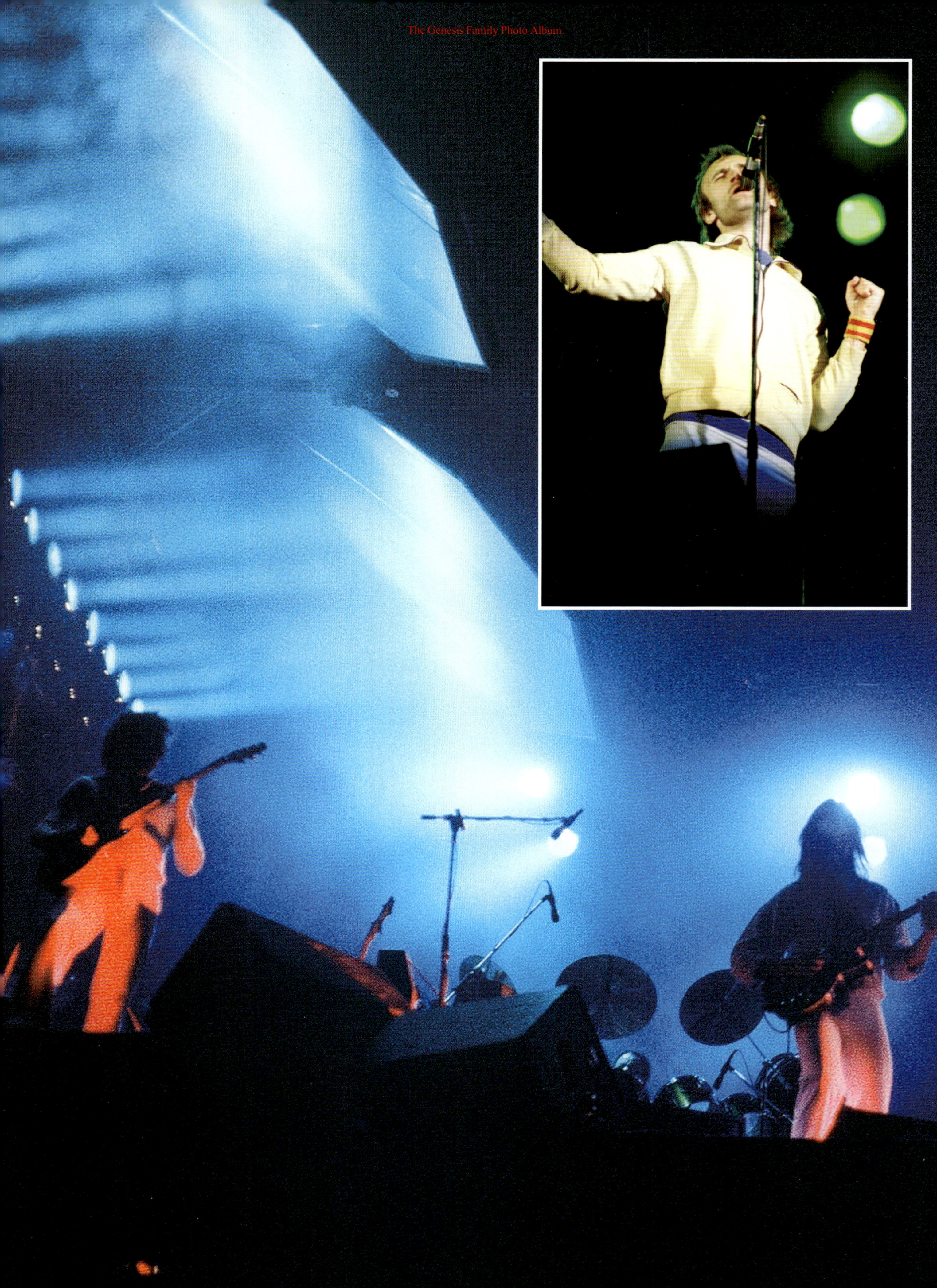

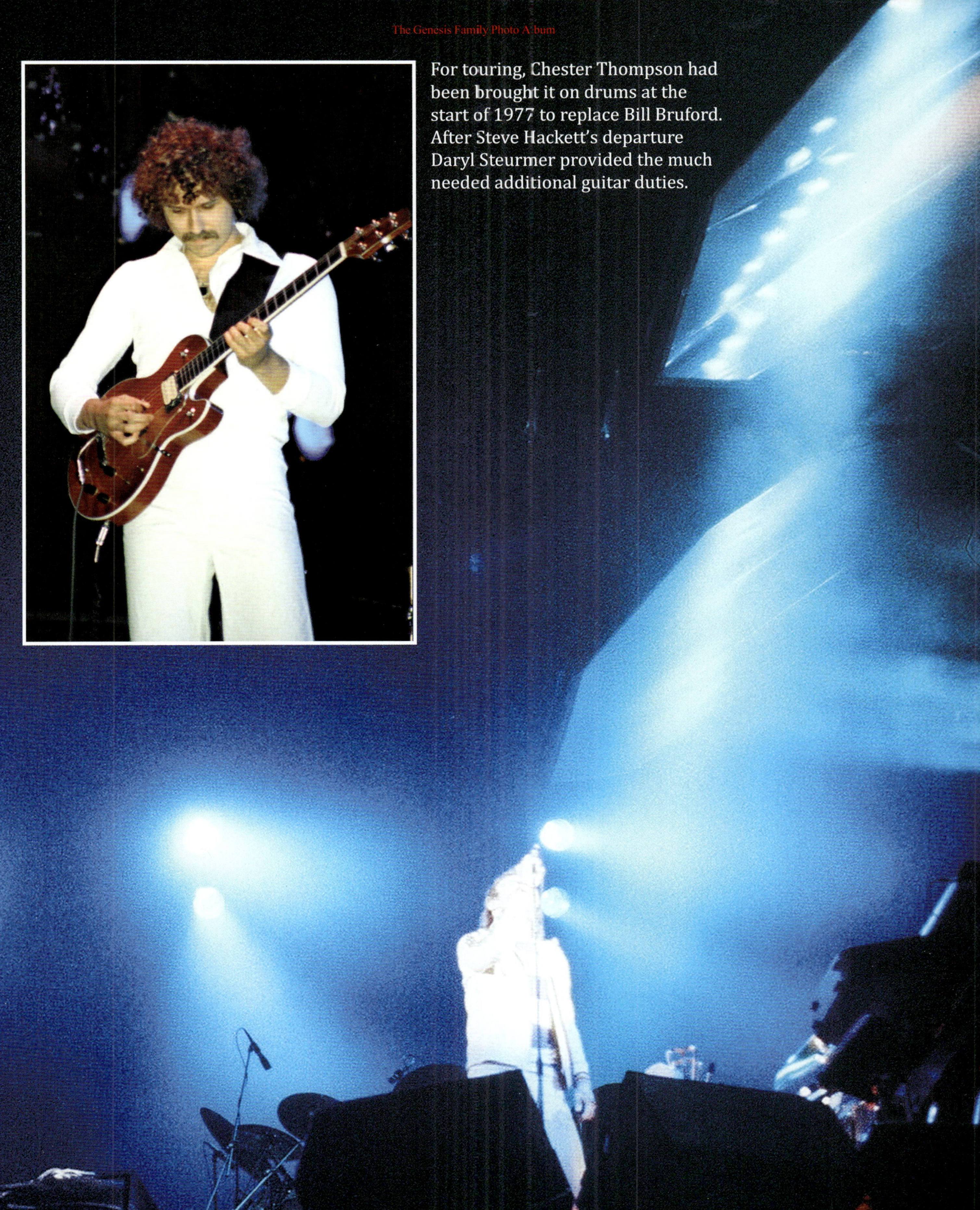

For touring, Chester Thompson had been brought it on drums at the start of 1977 to replace Bill Bruford. After Steve Hackett's departure Daryl Steurmer provided the much needed additional guitar duties.

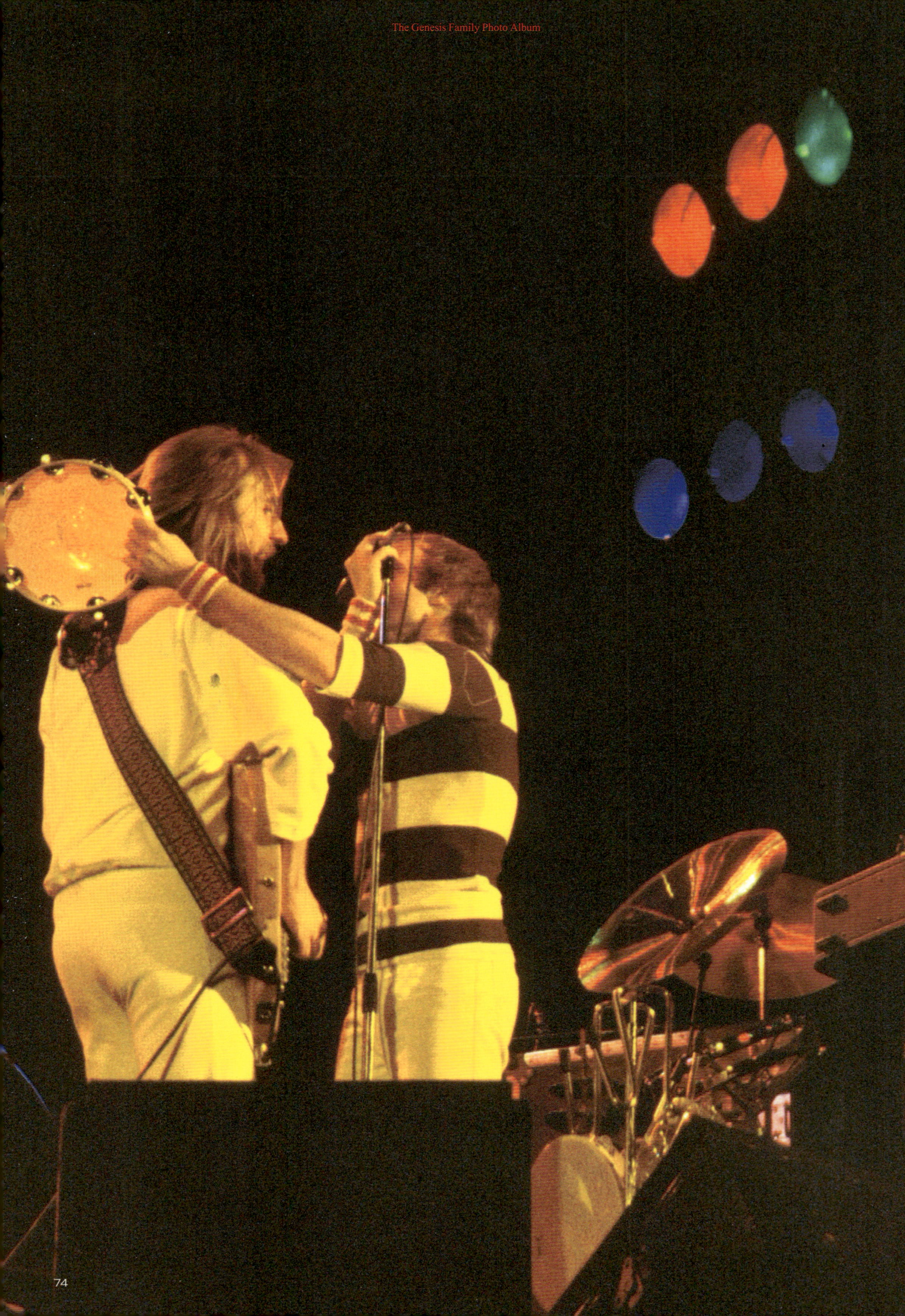

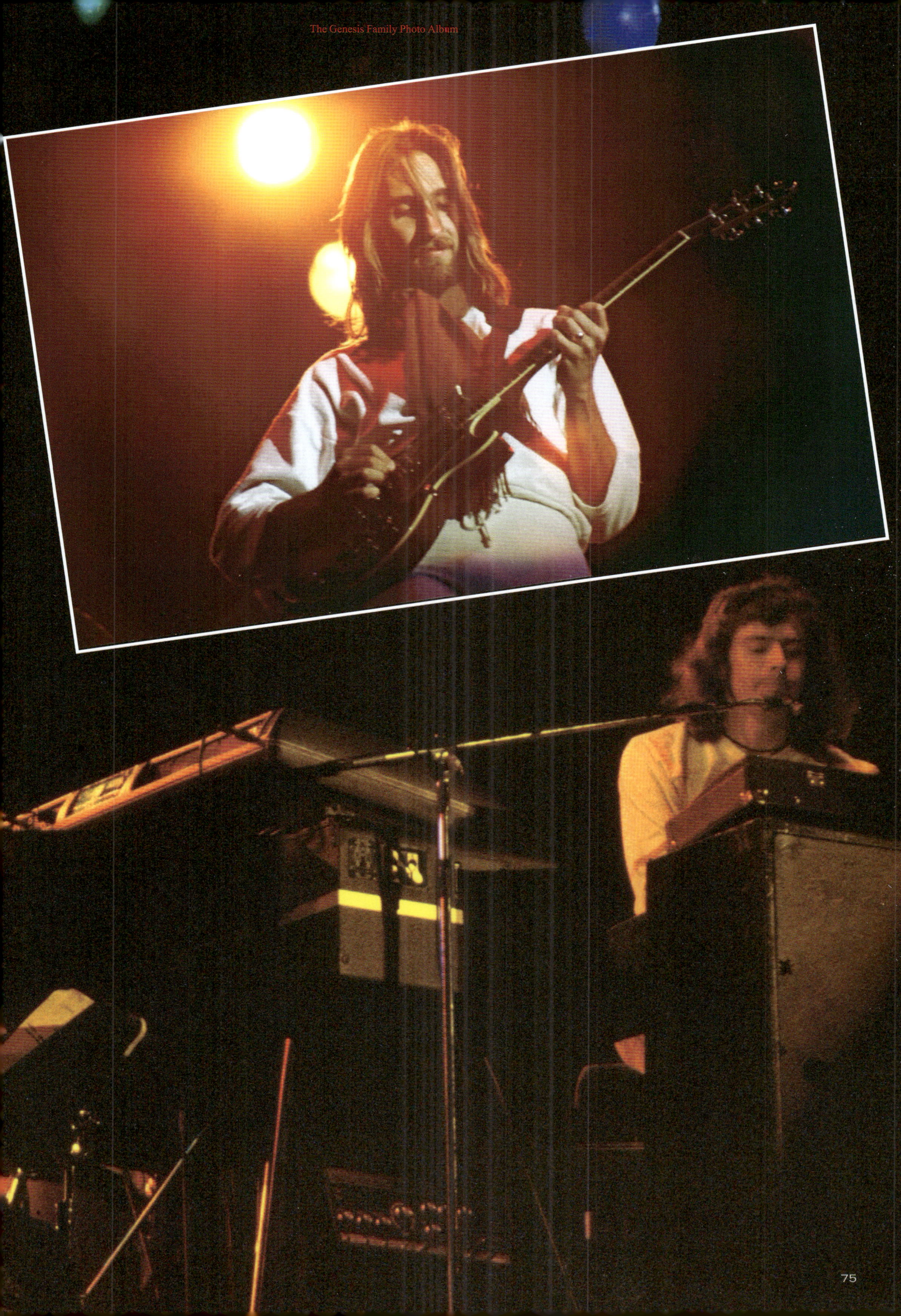

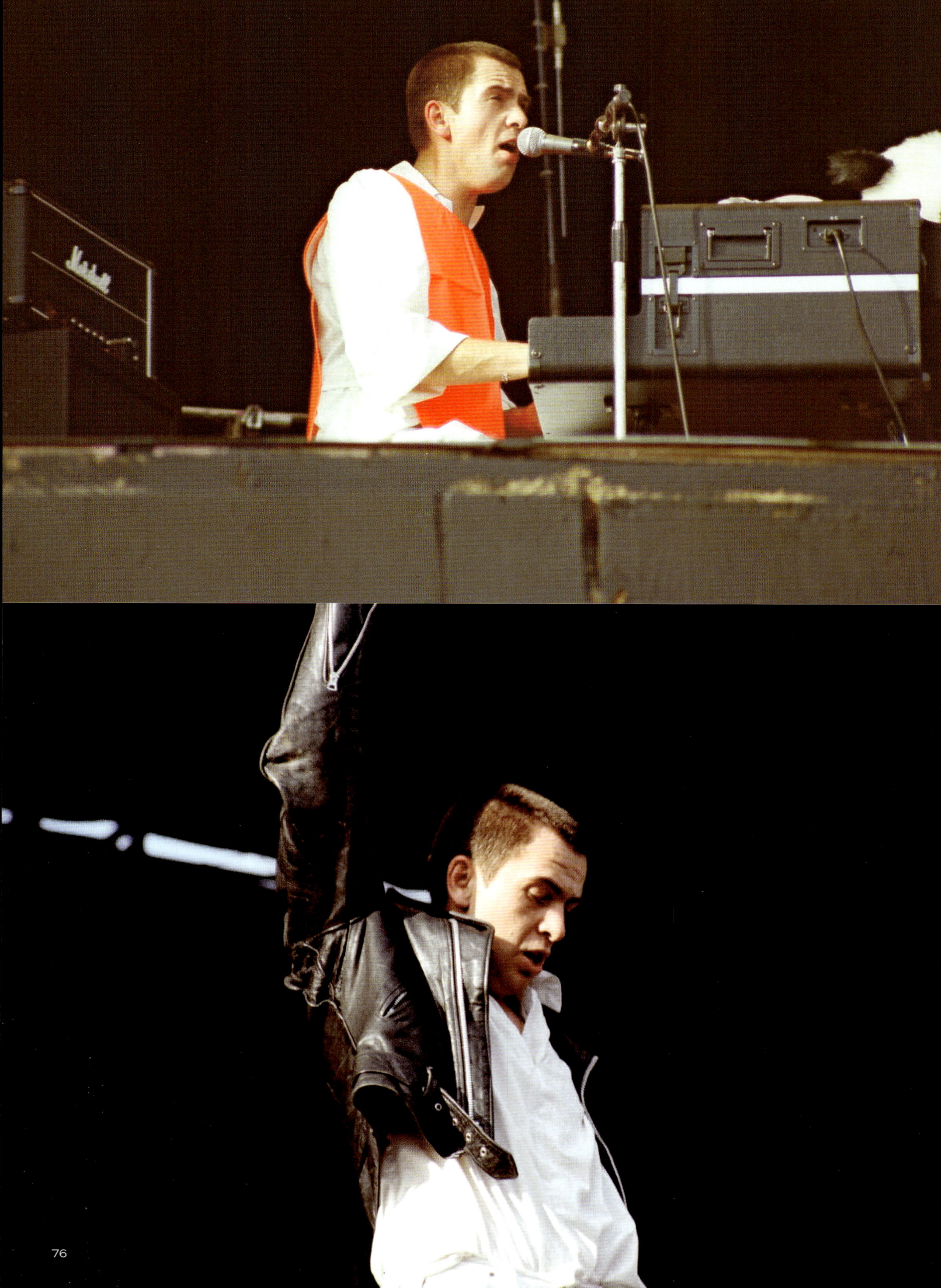

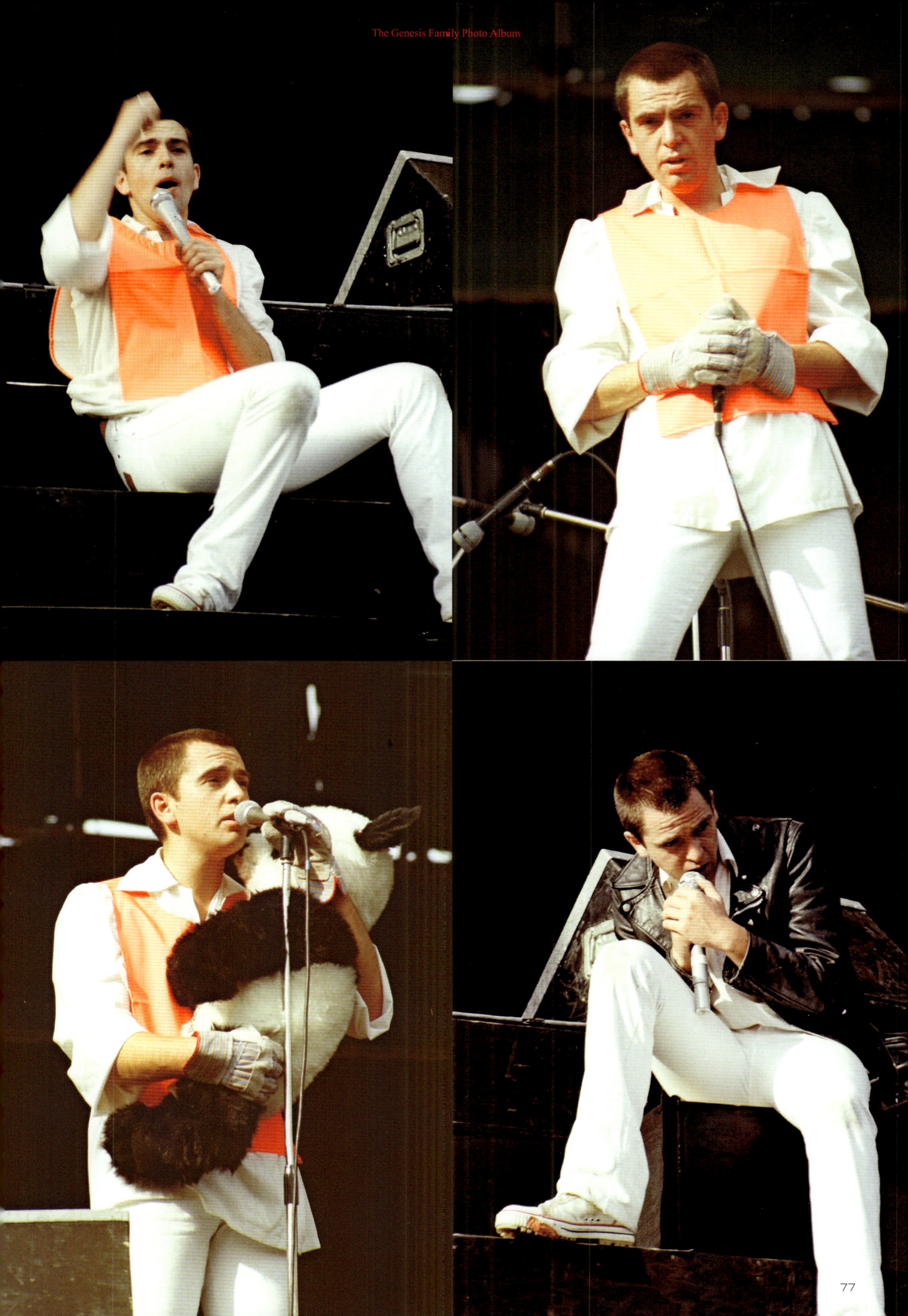

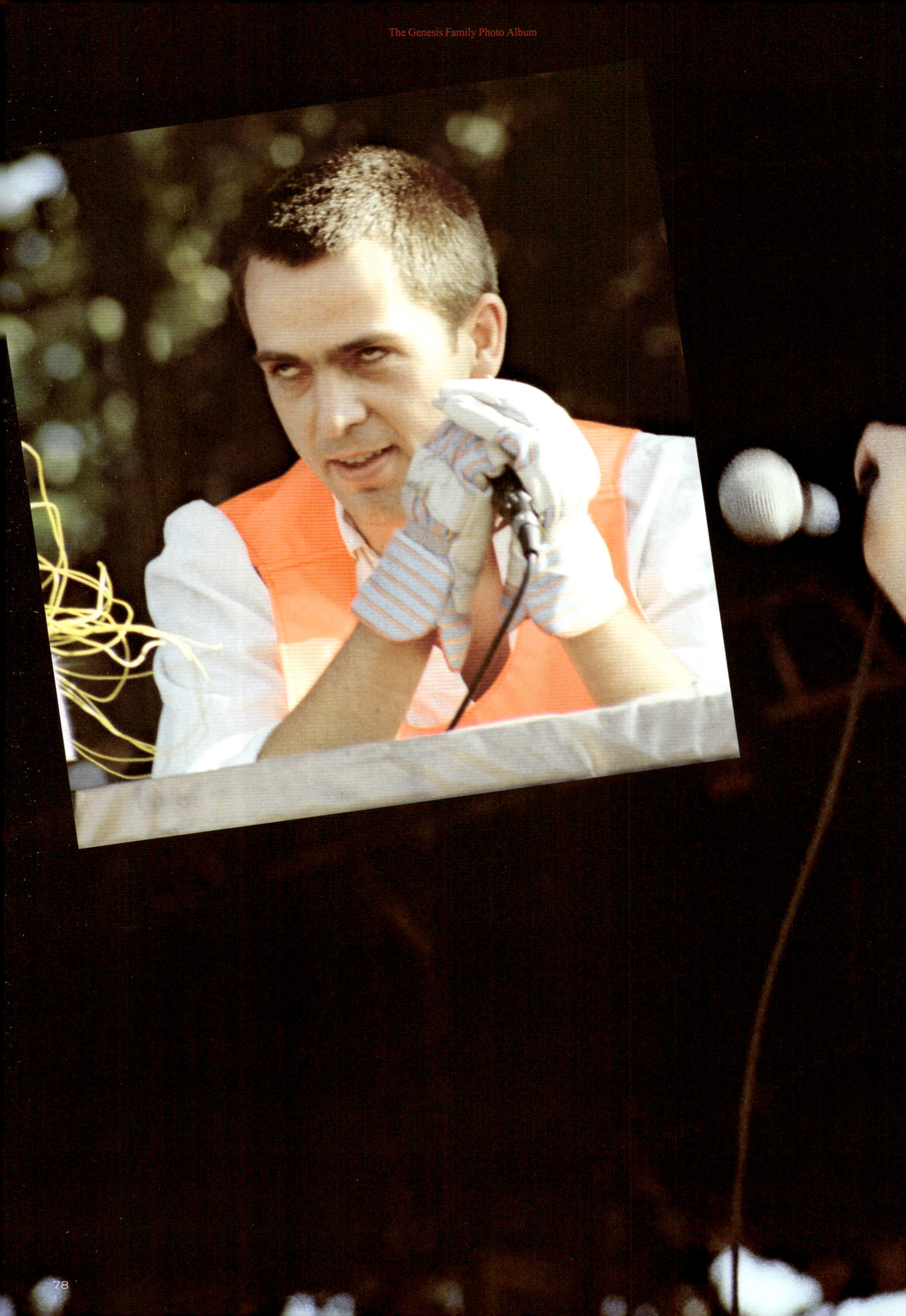

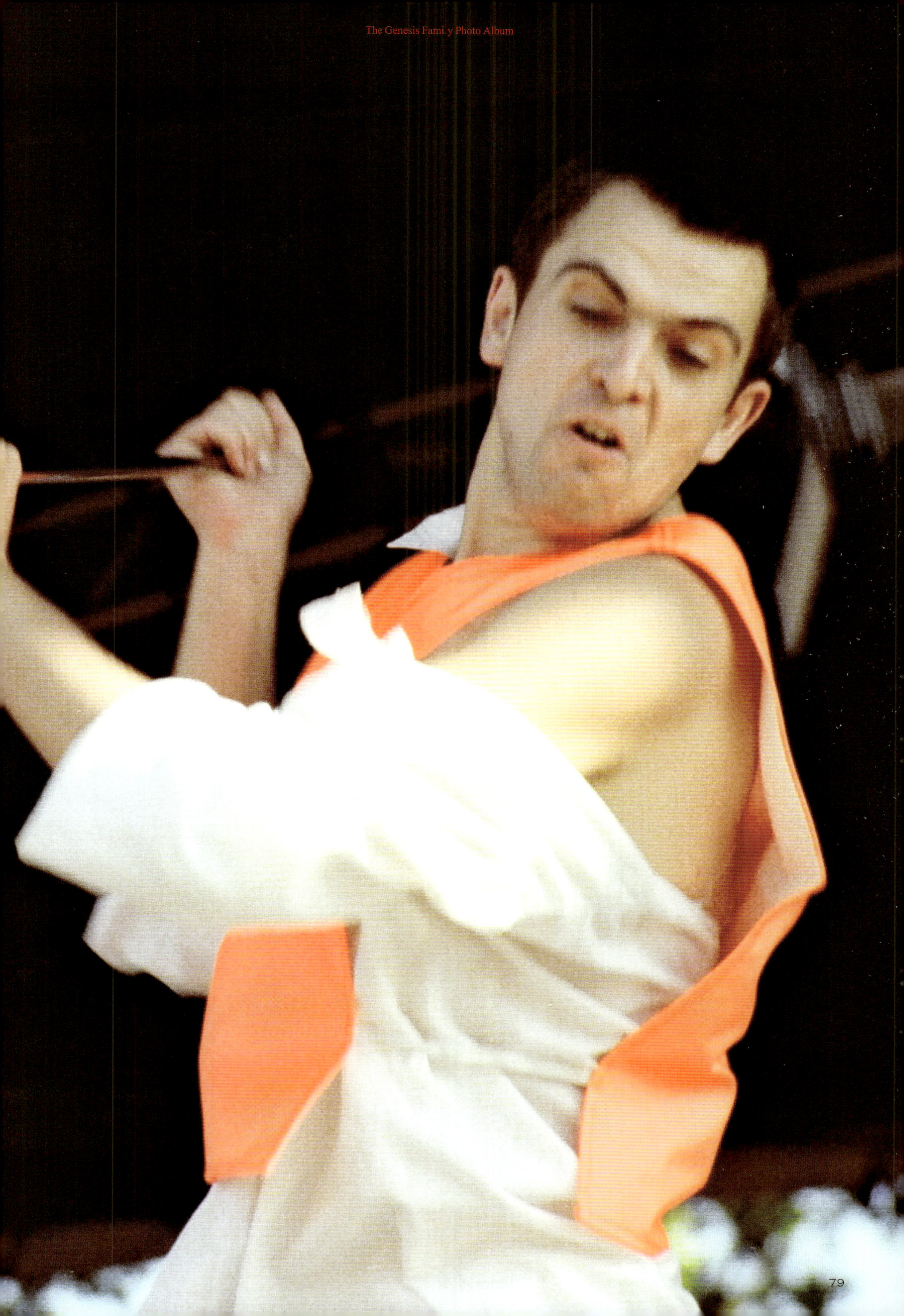

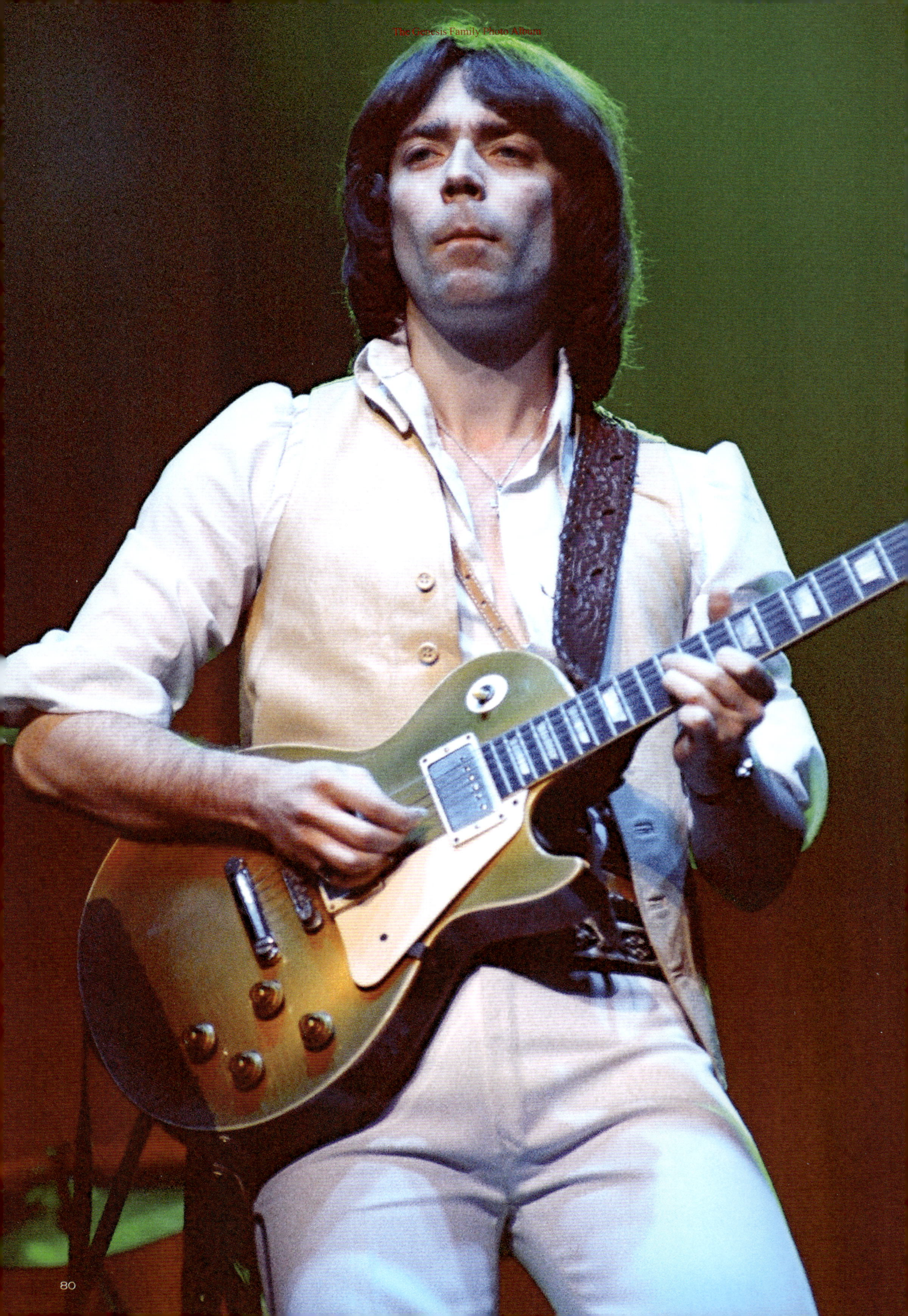

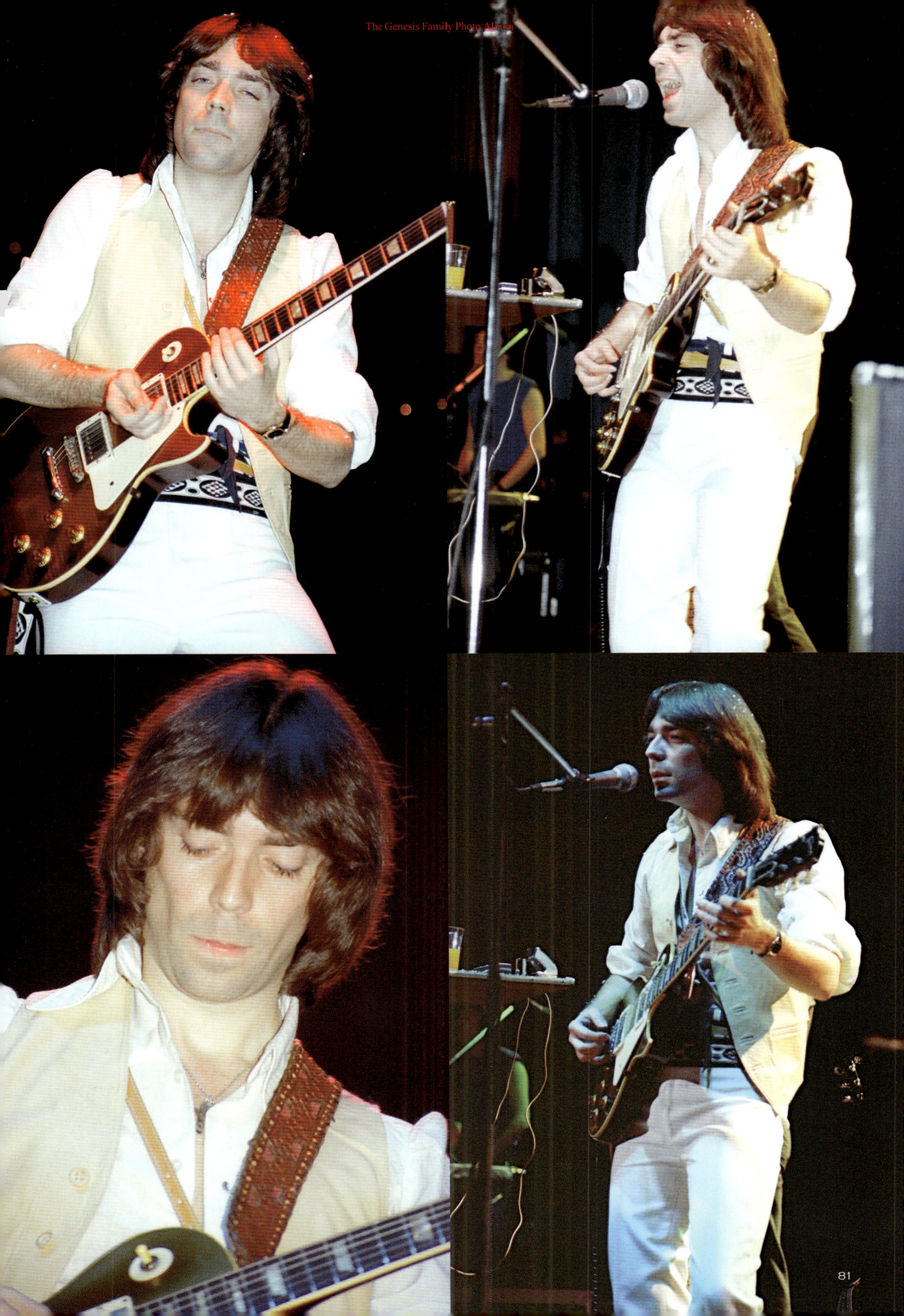

"All change!" Another year and another new look for Peter Gabriel.
For this performance at the Reading Festival 26th August 1979 Peter was joined by
Phil Collins who entered the stage beating out the rhythm of 'Biko'.
The previous day Steve Hackett also performed.

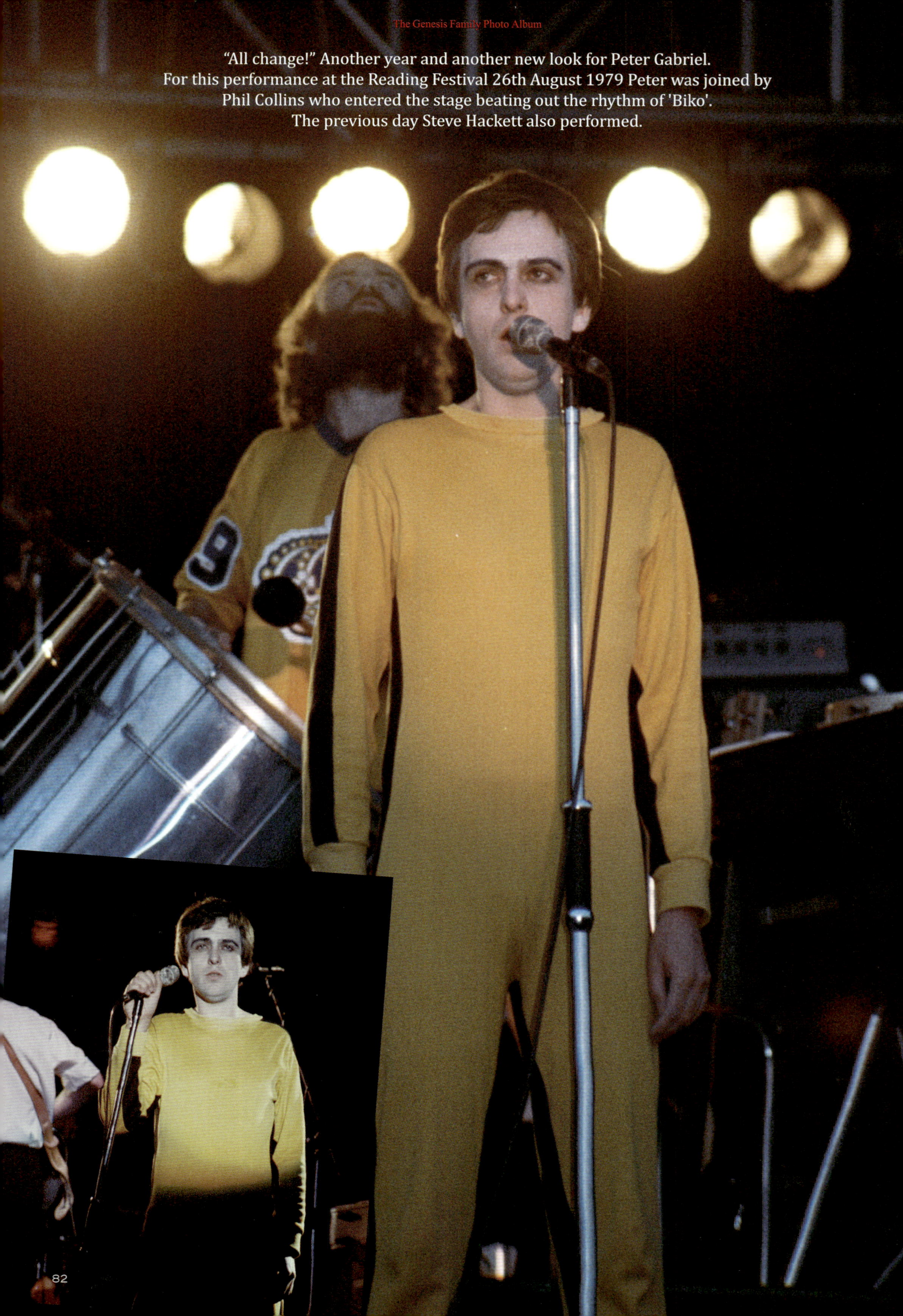

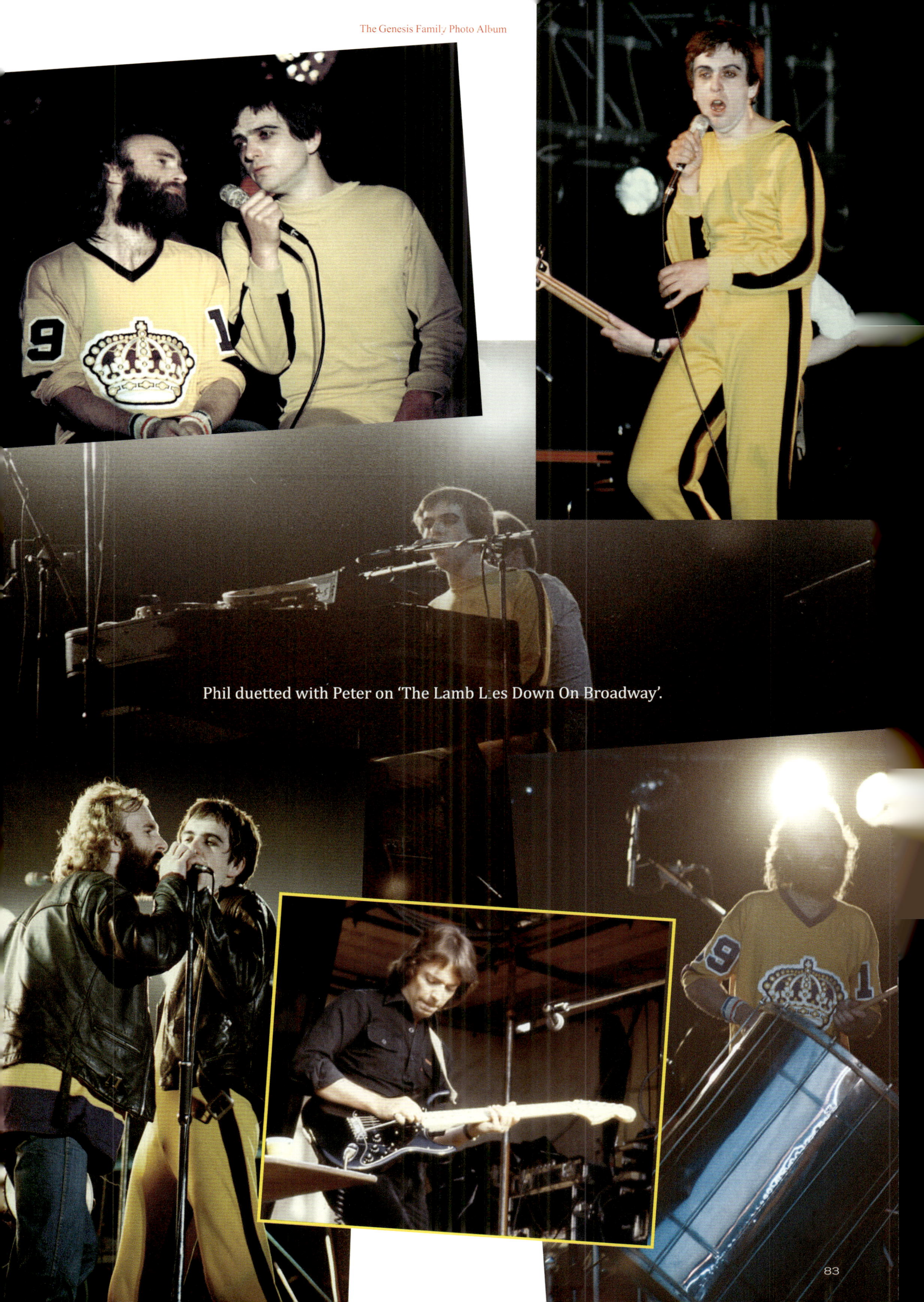

Phil duetted with Peter on 'The Lamb Lies Down On Broadway'.

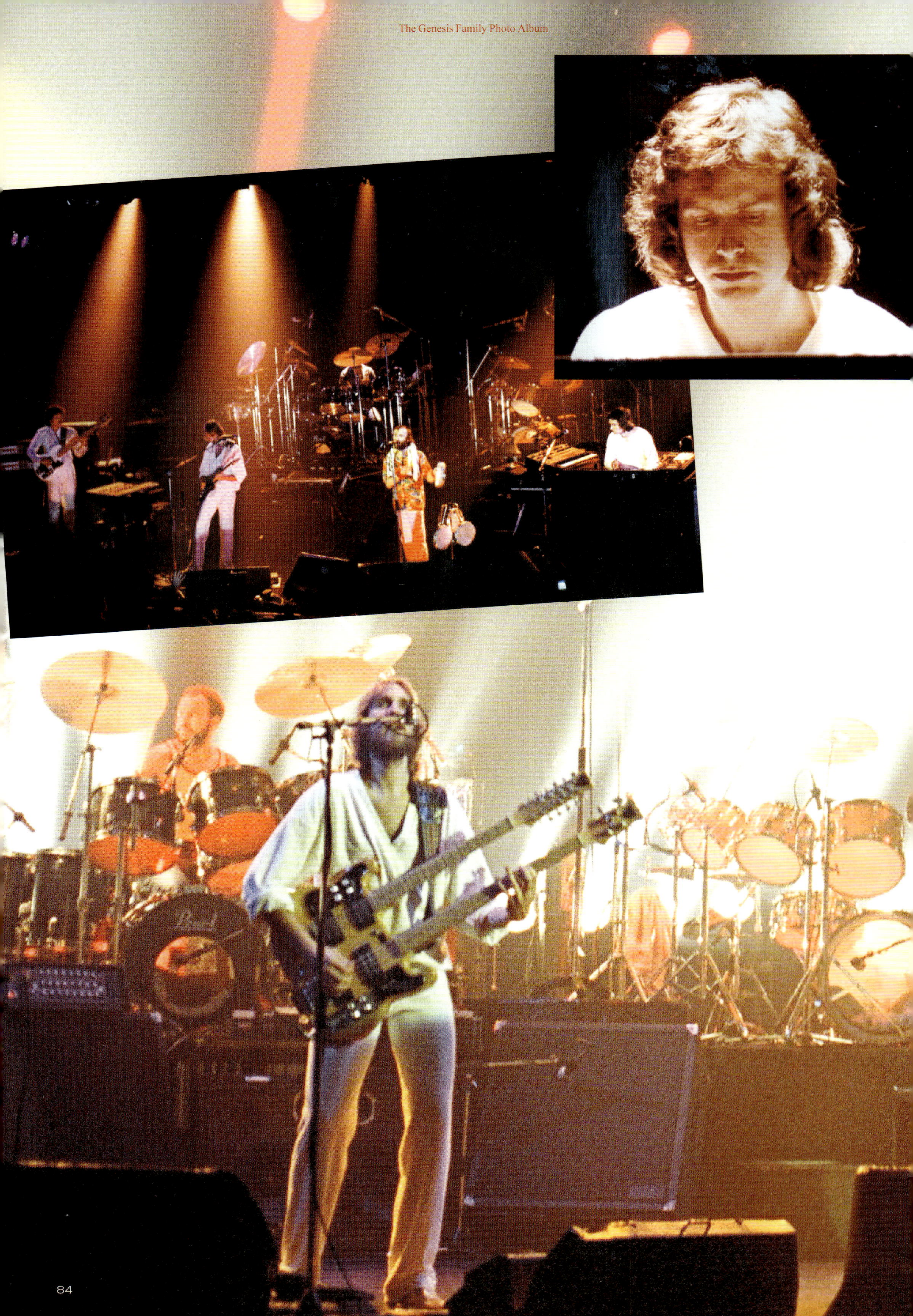

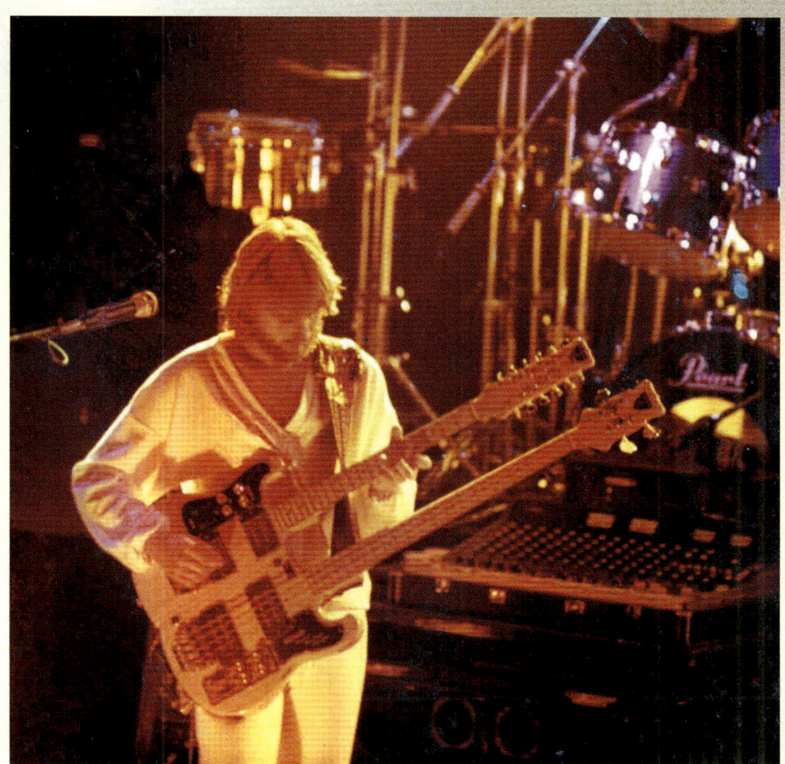

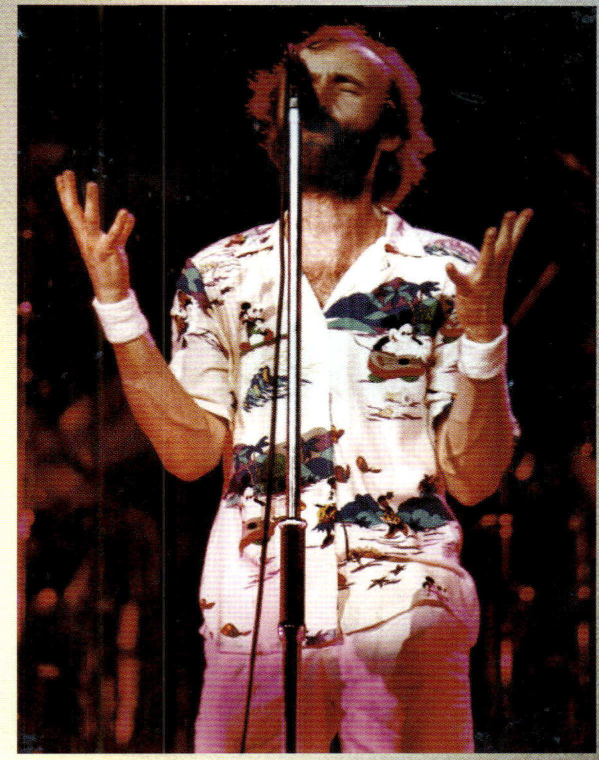

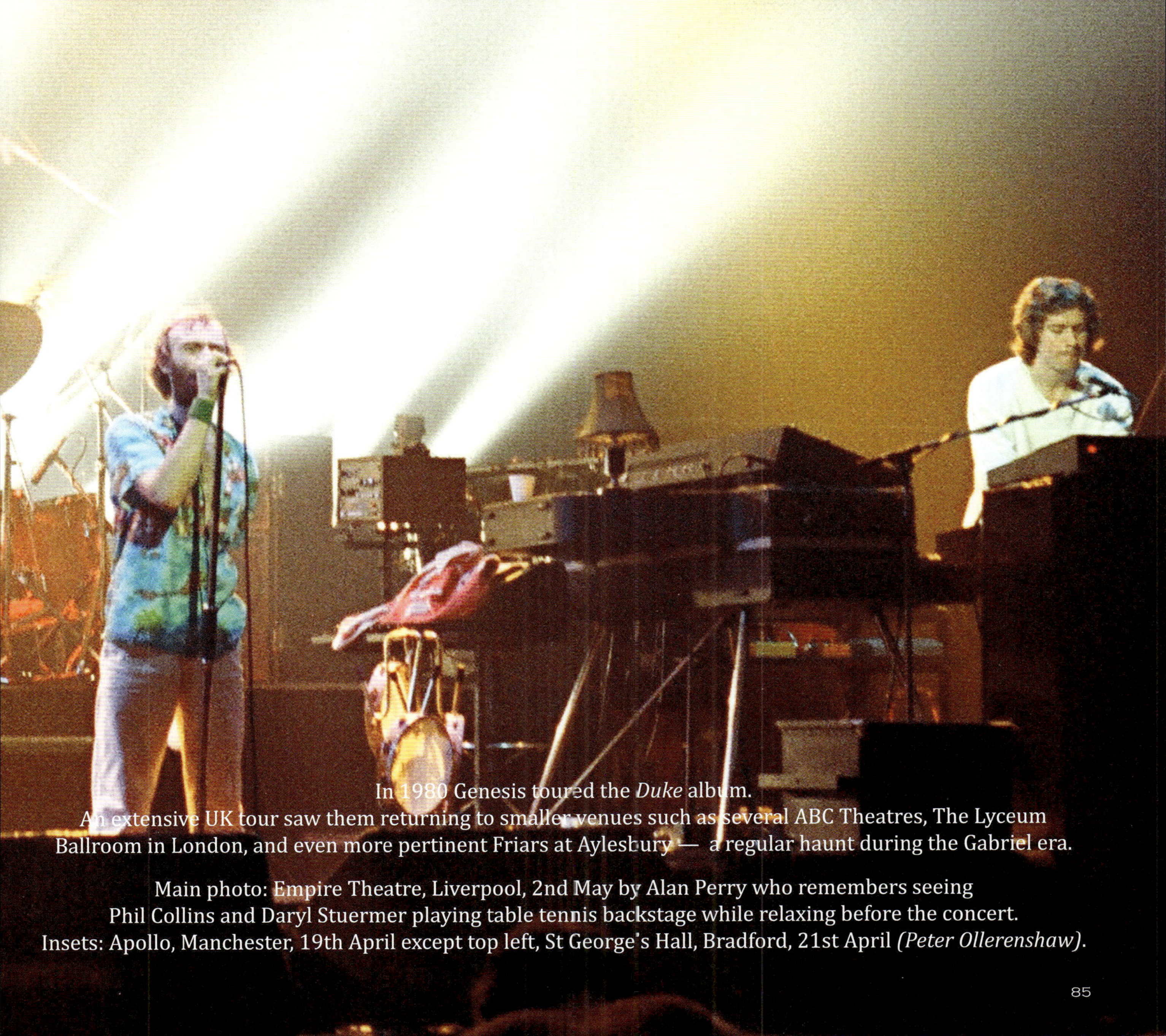

In 1980 Genesis toured the *Duke* album.
An extensive UK tour saw them returning to smaller venues such as several ABC Theatres, The Lyceum
Ballroom in London, and even more pertinent Friars at Aylesbury — a regular haunt during the Gabriel era.

Main photo: Empire Theatre, Liverpool, 2nd May by Alan Perry who remembers seeing
Phil Collins and Daryl Stuermer playing table tennis backstage while relaxing before the concert.
Insets: Apollo, Manchester, 19th April except top left, St George's Hall, Bradford, 21st April *(Peter Ollerenshaw)*.

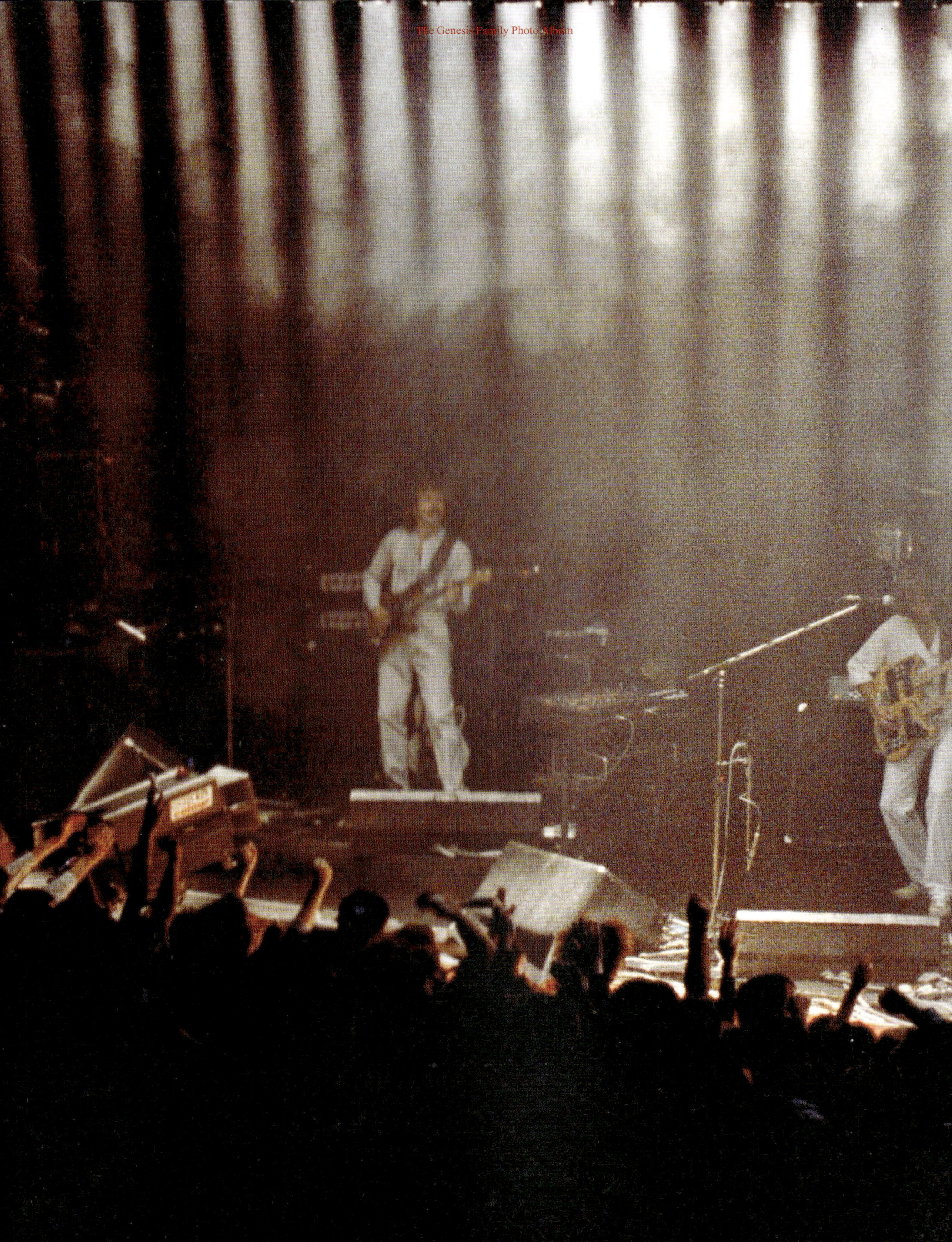

The Lyceum Ballroom, London, 7th May 1980. As you can see from this photo this concert was filmed. Forty minutes of the show were broadcasted soon after by the BBC on *The Whistle Test*. Audio of virtually the full show was also broadcasted by the BBC on *The Friday Rock Show* on Radio One.

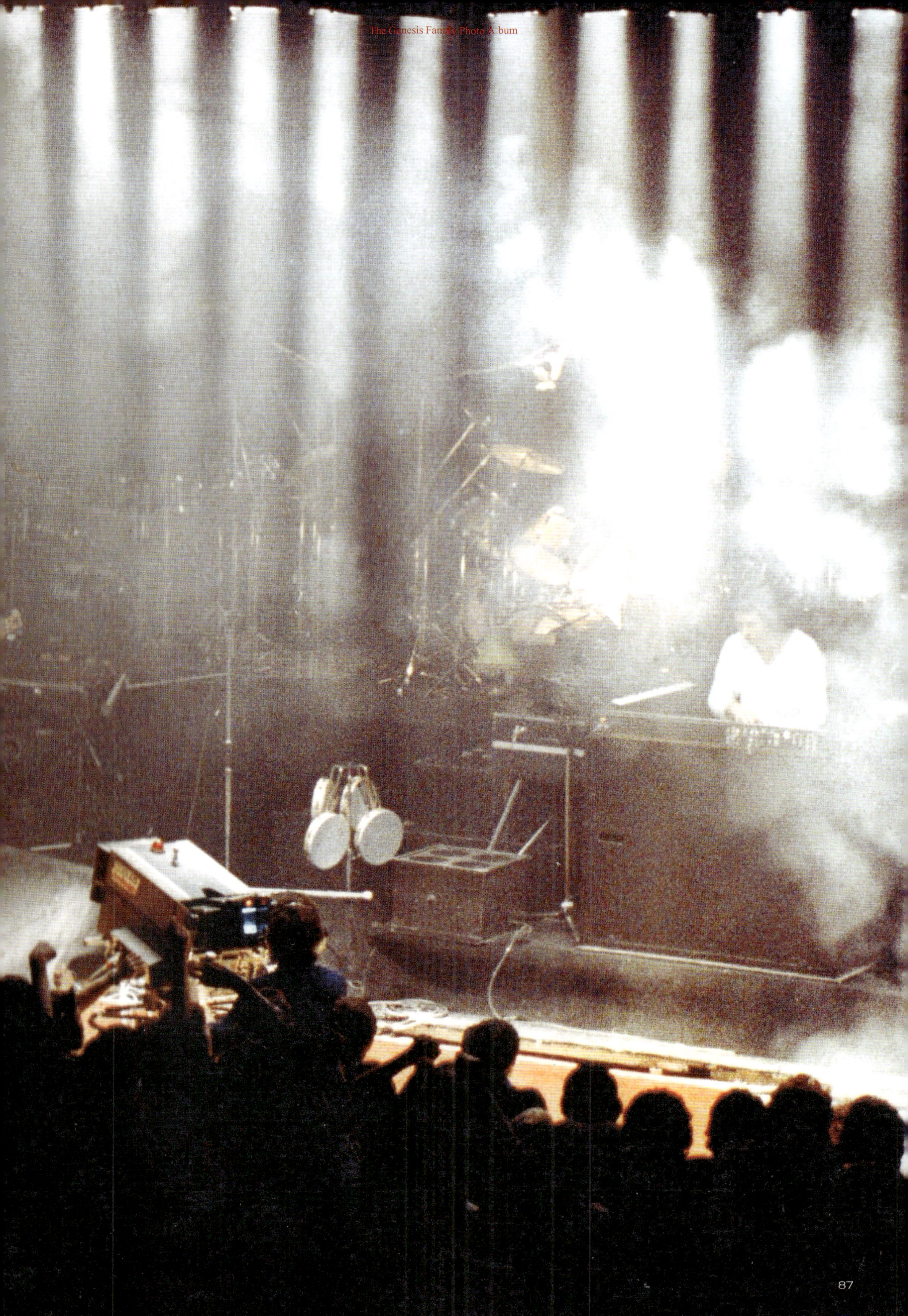

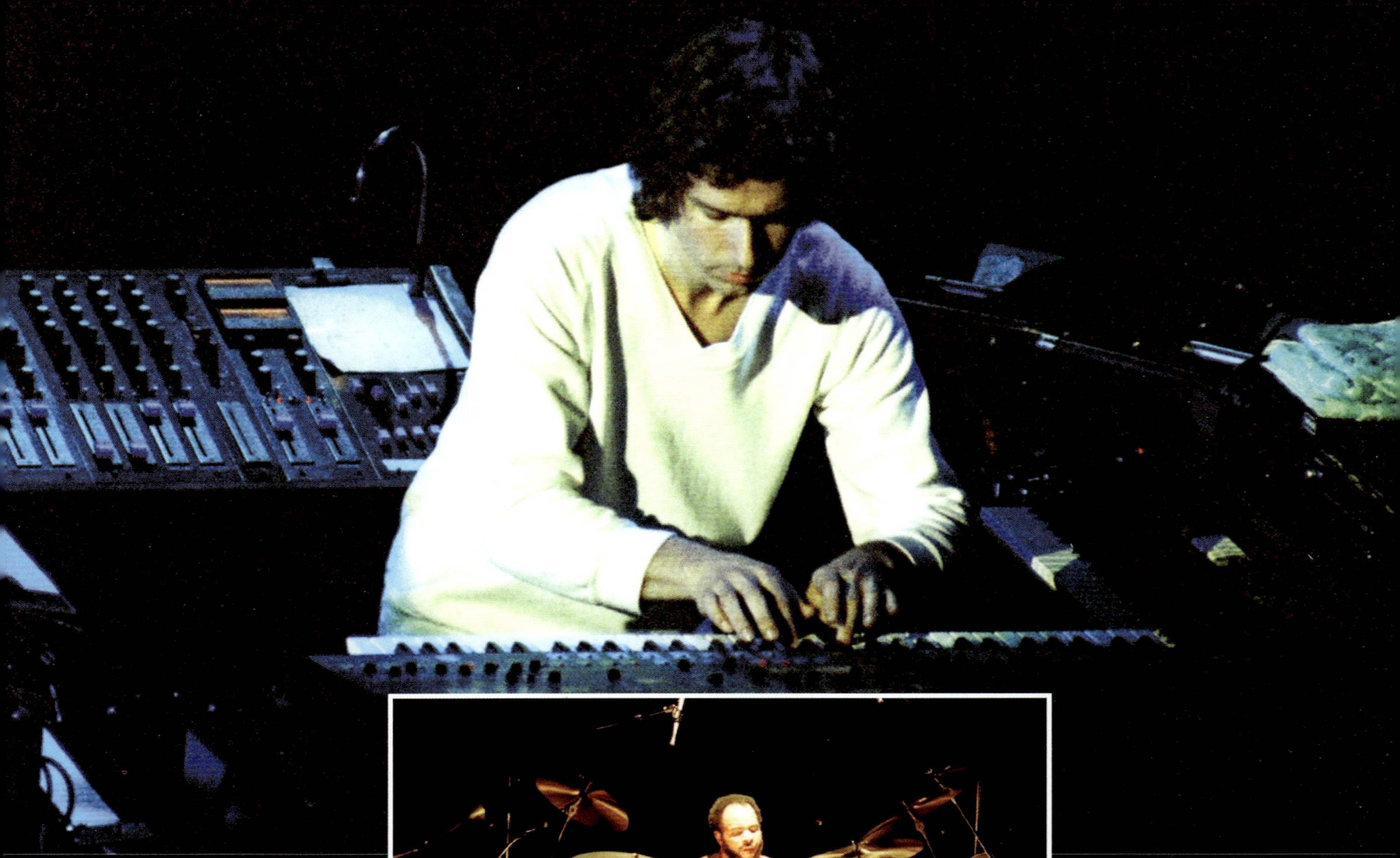

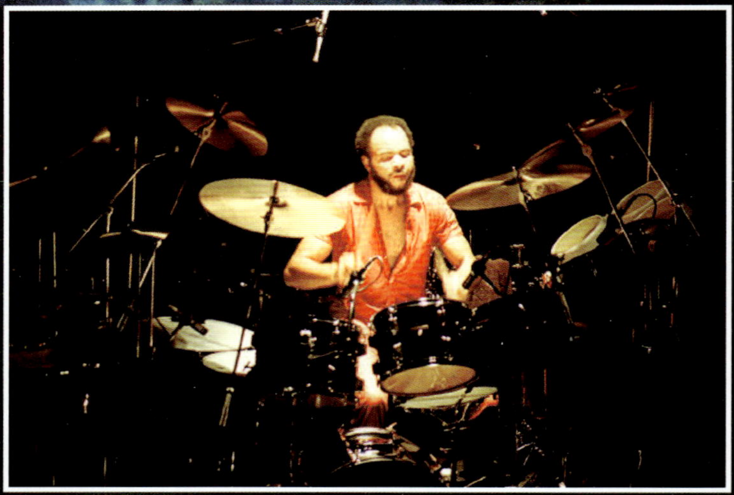

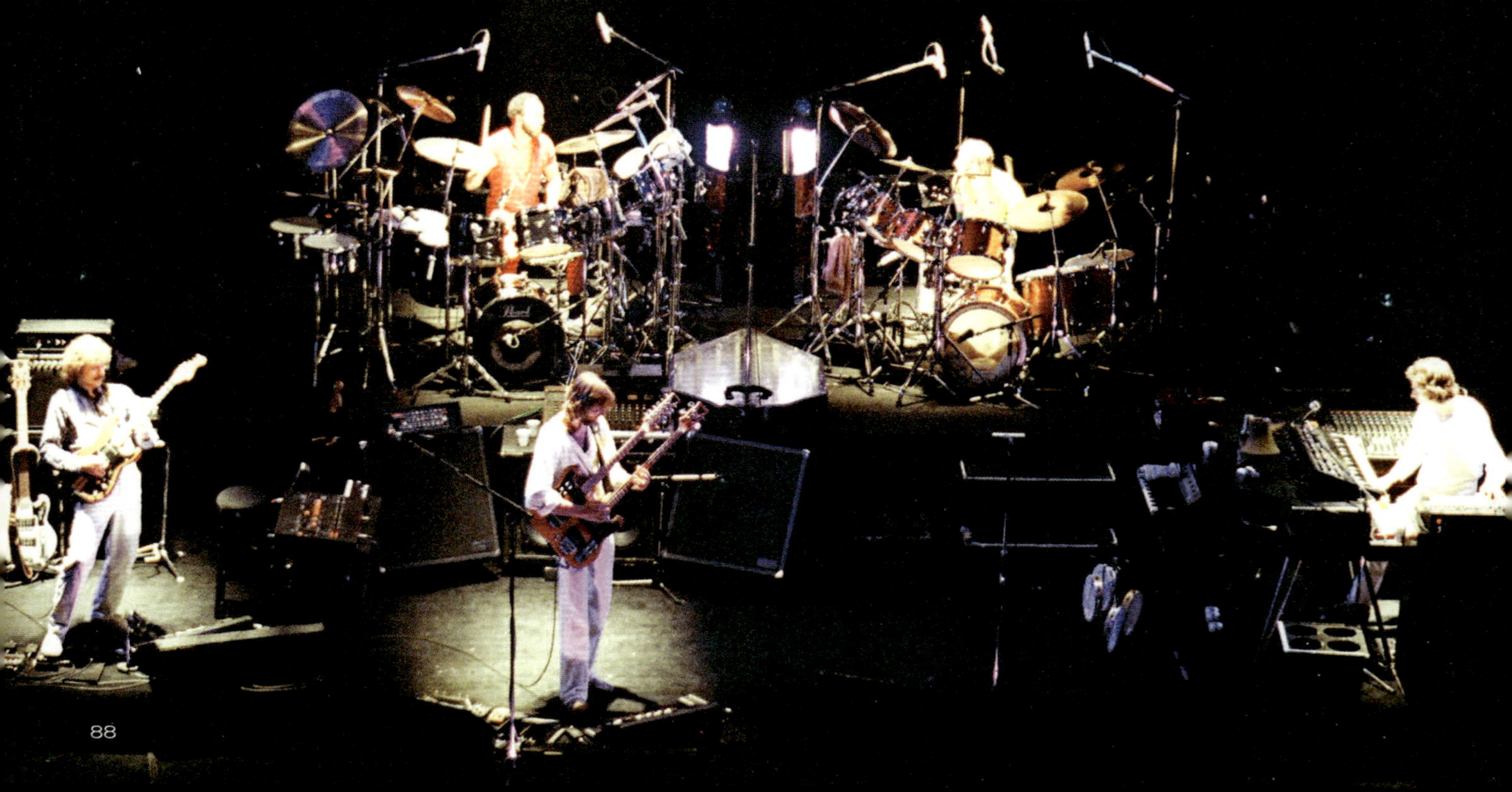

Having played at the Reading Festival in 1979, Steve returned two years later with his band in support of his fourth album, *Cured*. The first time he had played at Reading was with Genesis in 1973. Just over a year on from this gig they were all back together again at another outdoor show that no one could possibly have foreseen.

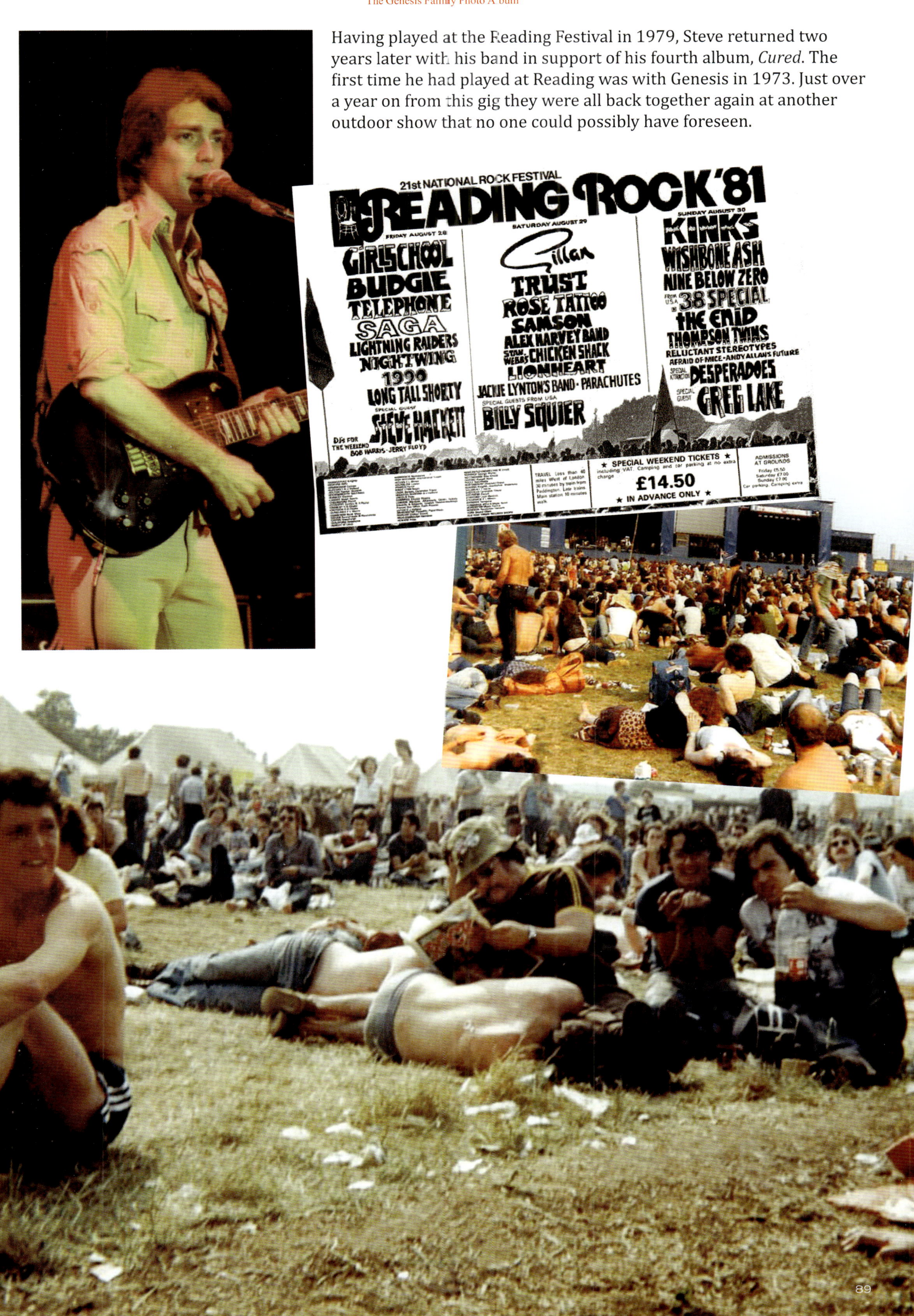

Back in New York City. Well, Milton Keynes actually. Billed as Six Of The Best, a one-off reunion with Peter Gabriel that allowed him to don the old costumes again as they performed old favourites such as 'Musical Box' and 'Supper's Ready'. Steve Hackett joined for the encore to make a truly memorable occasion in Genesis' history.

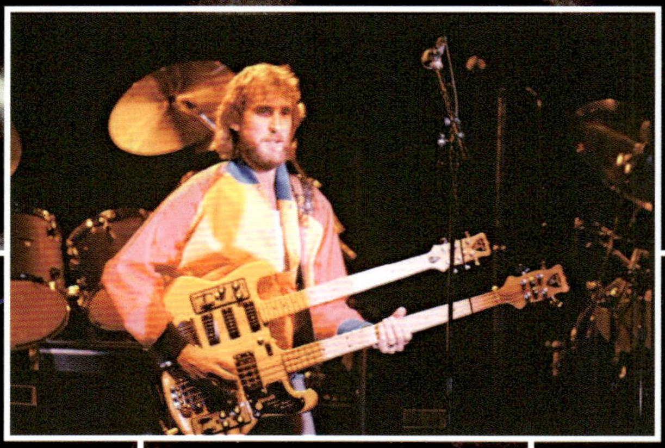

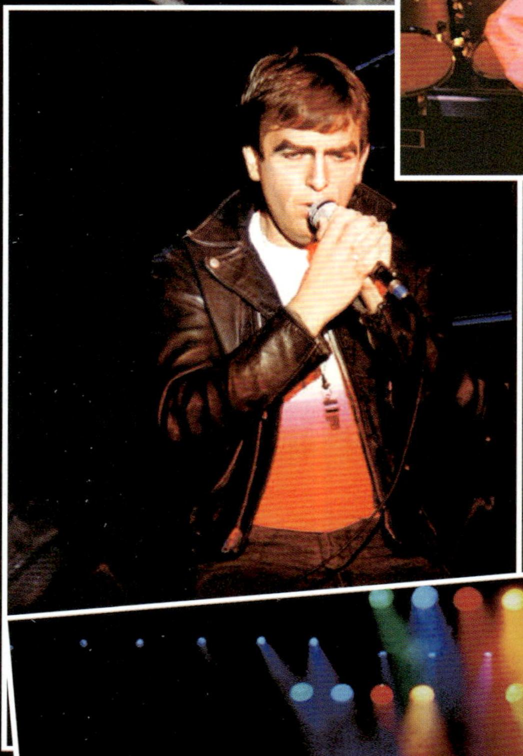

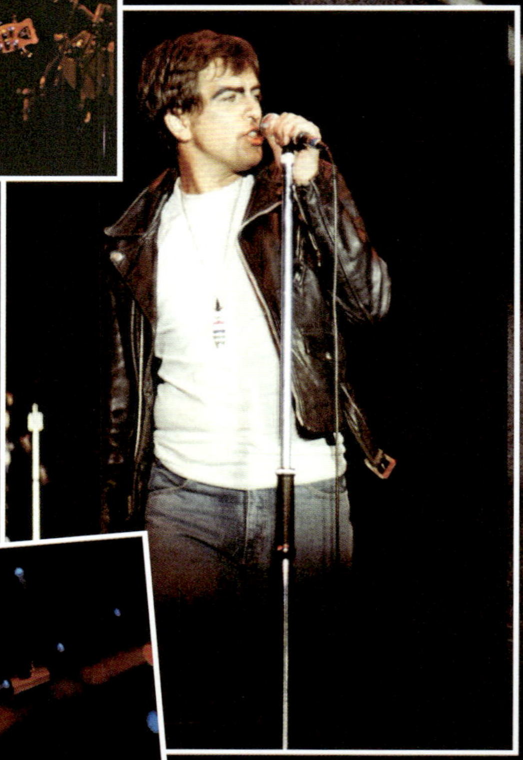

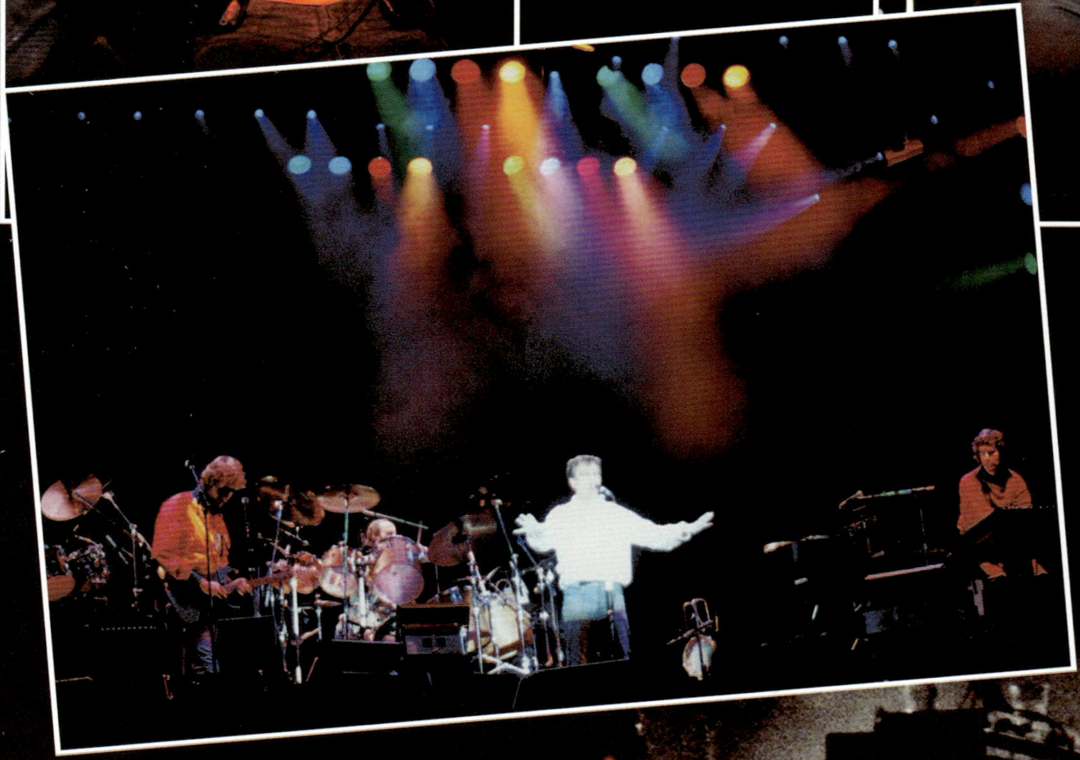

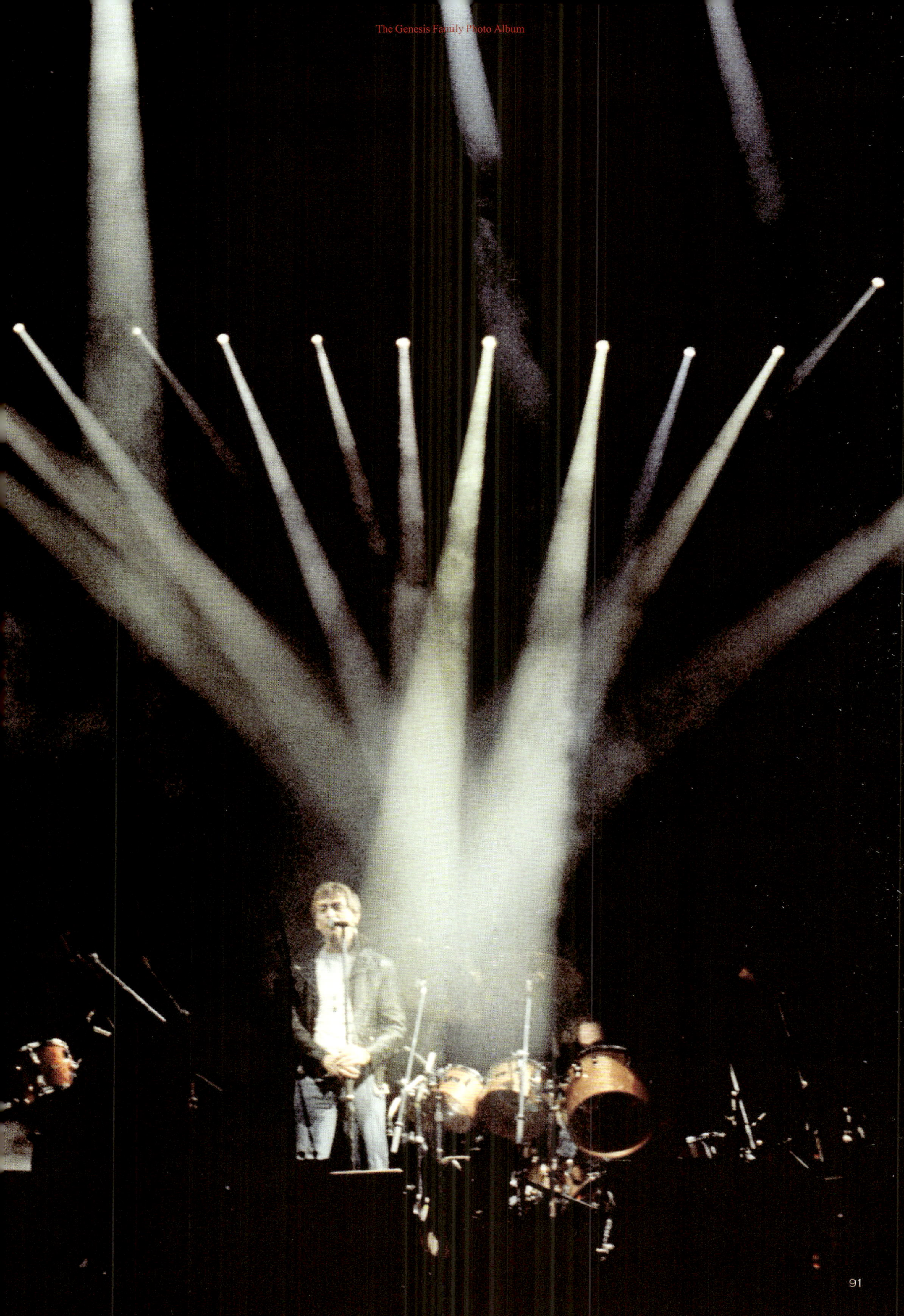

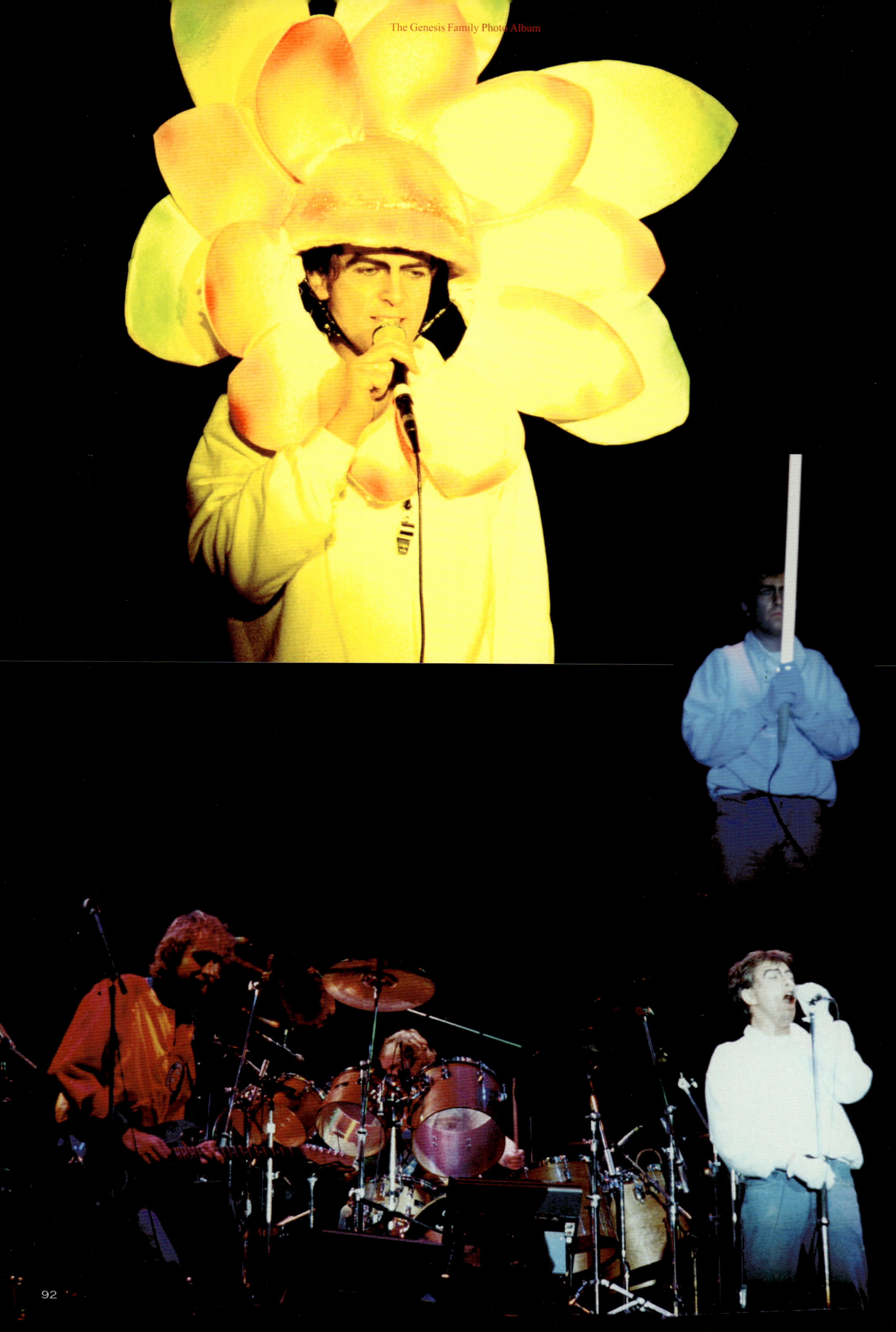

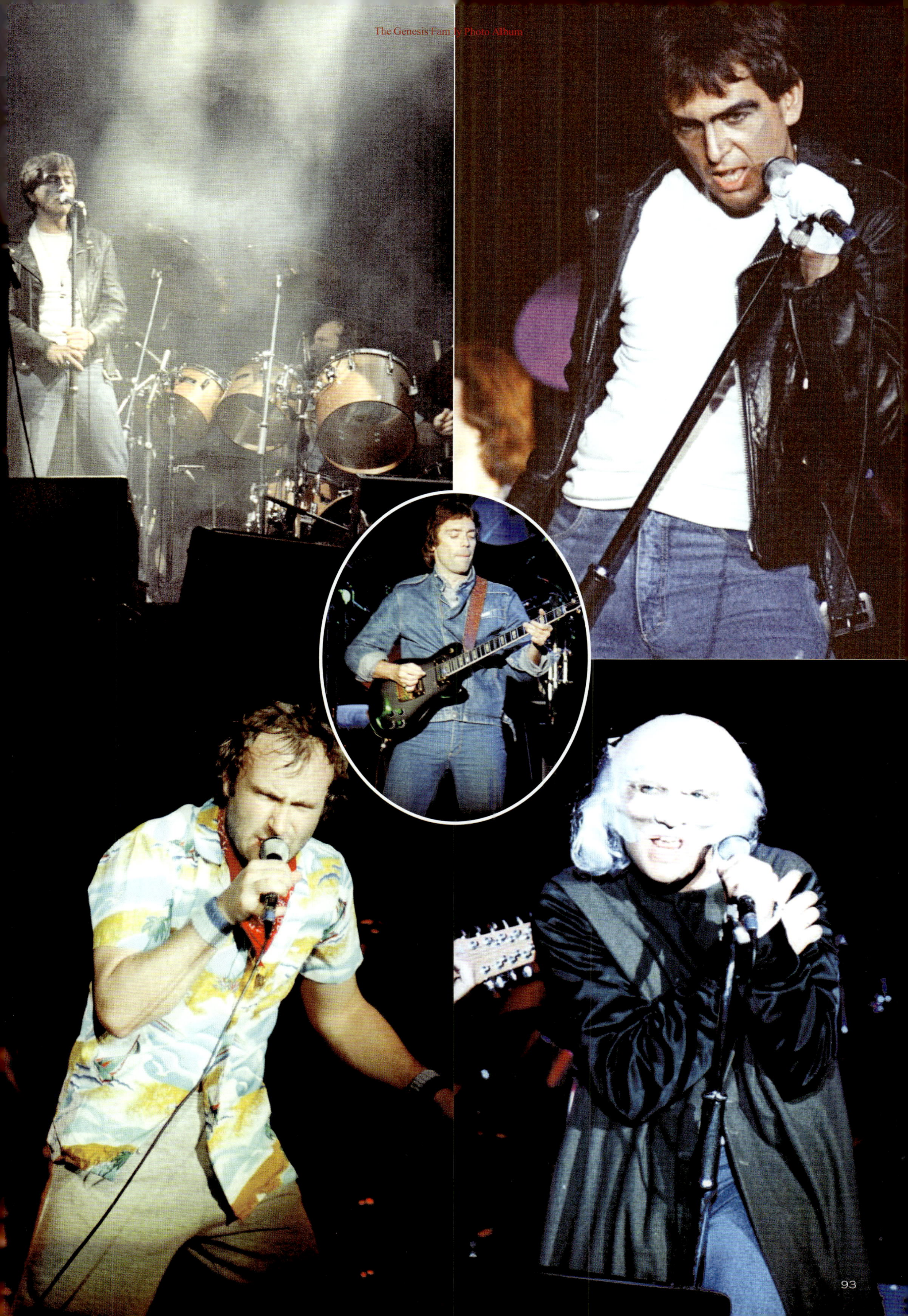

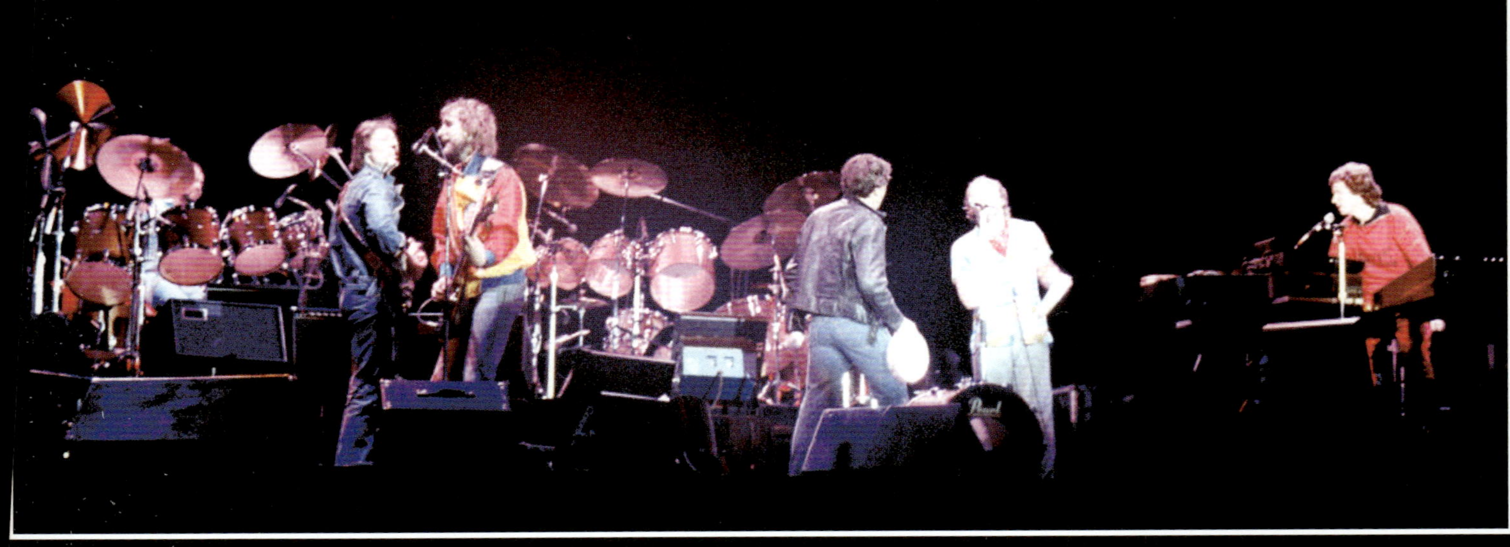

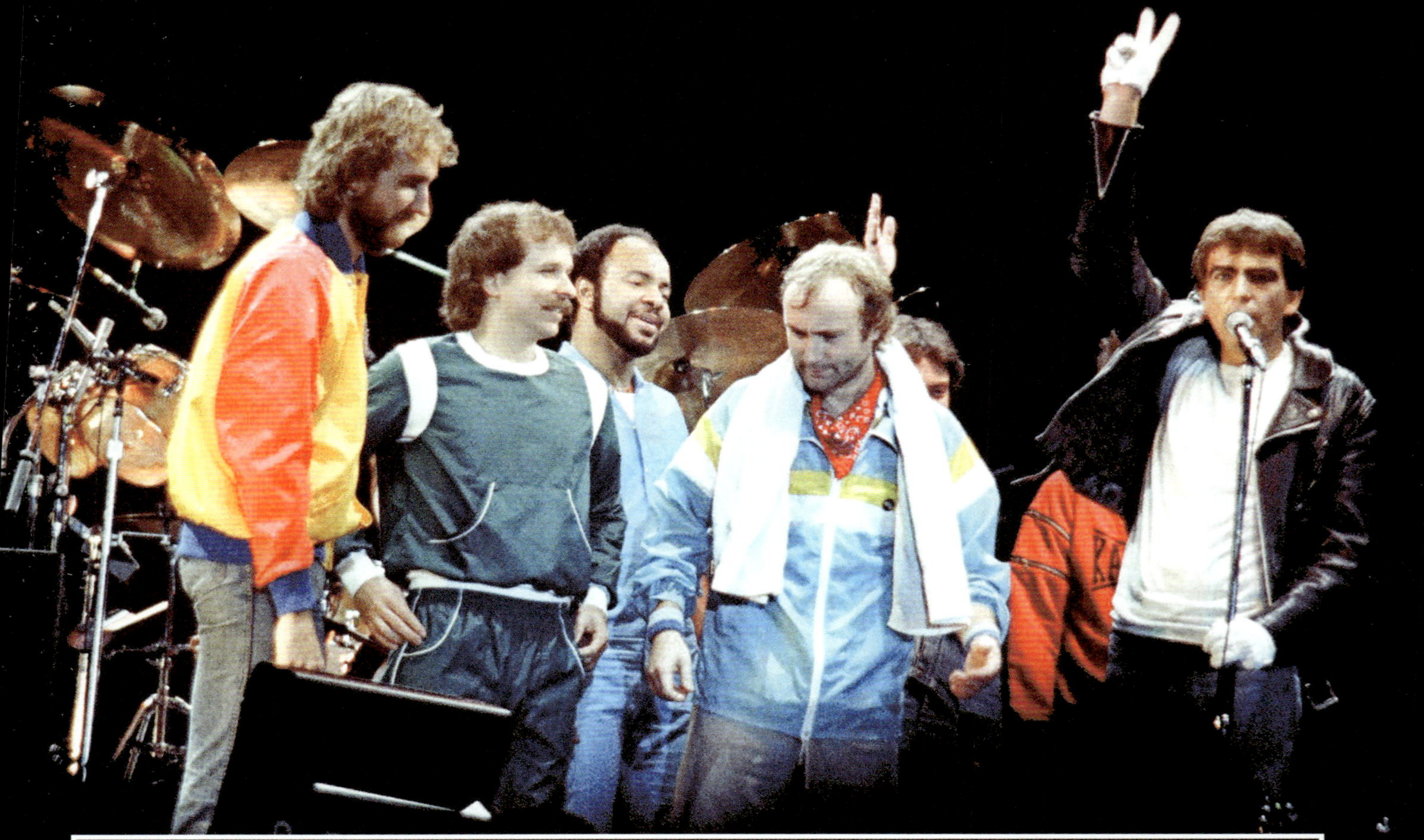

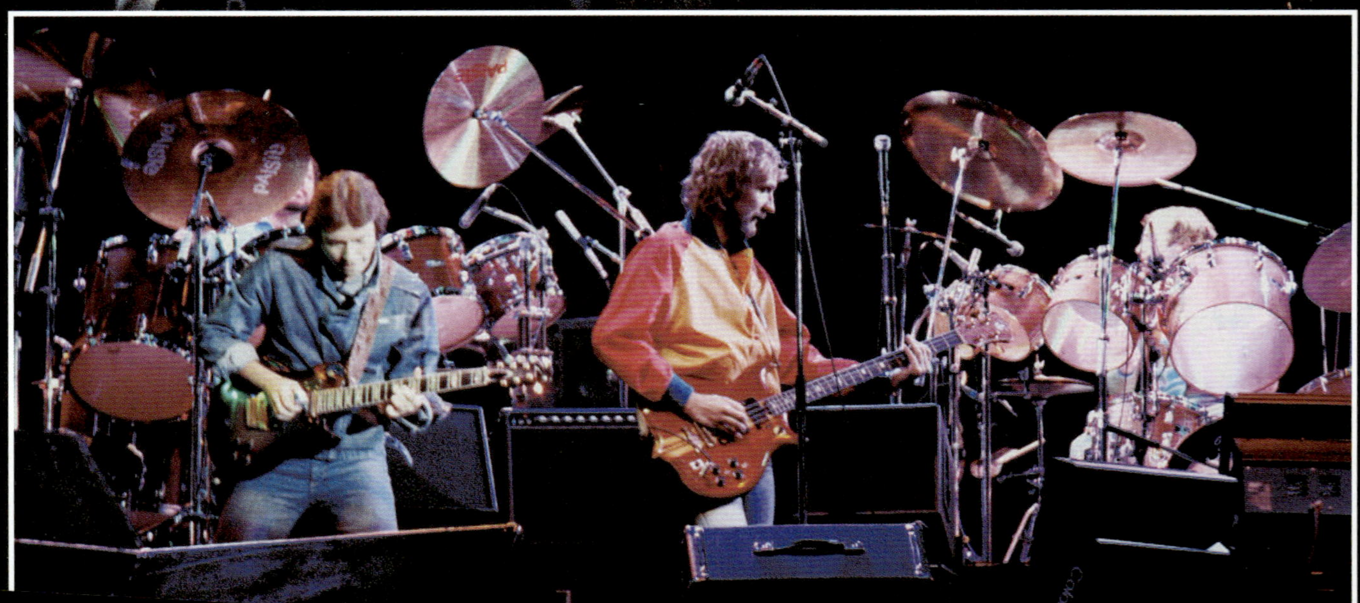

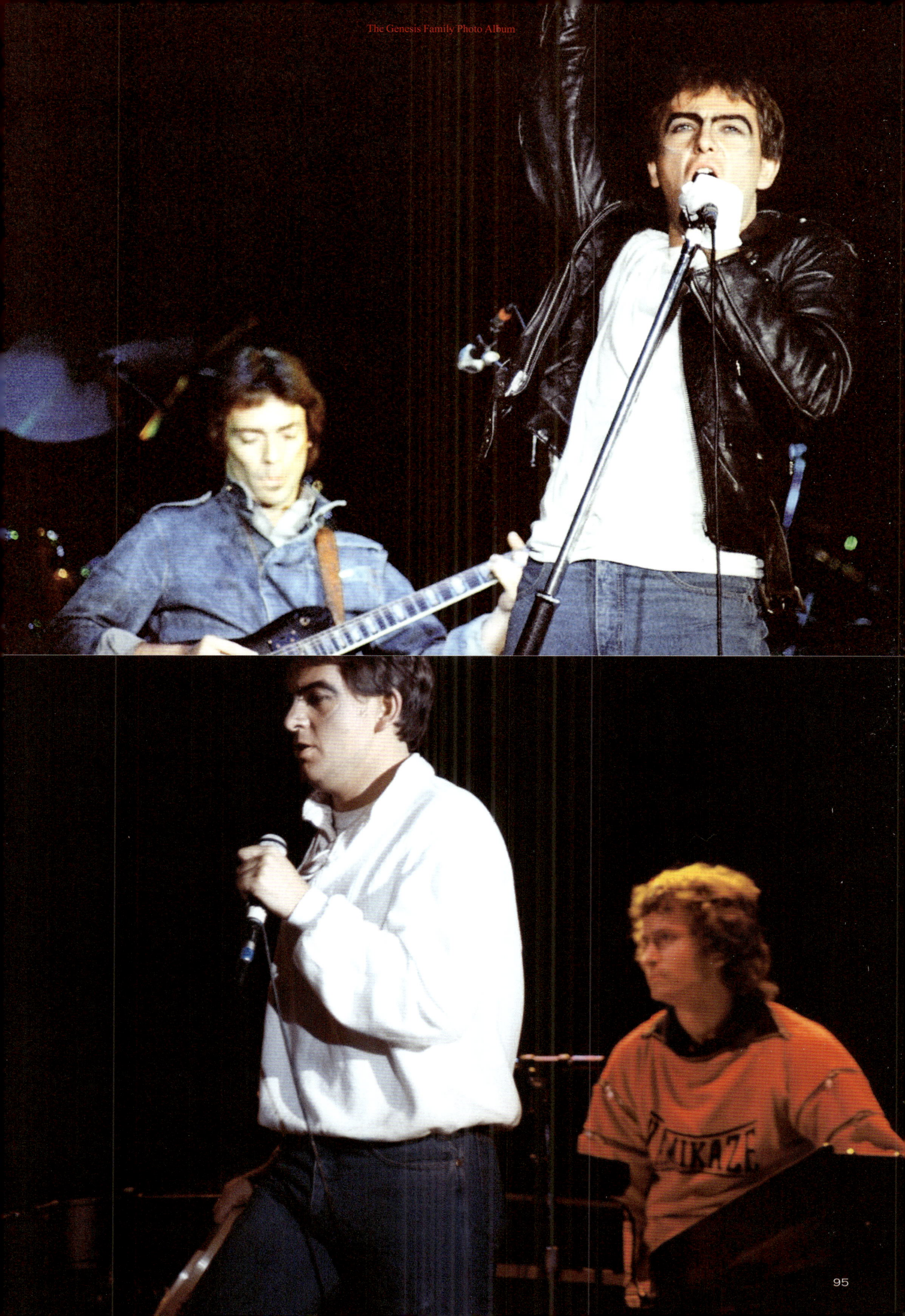

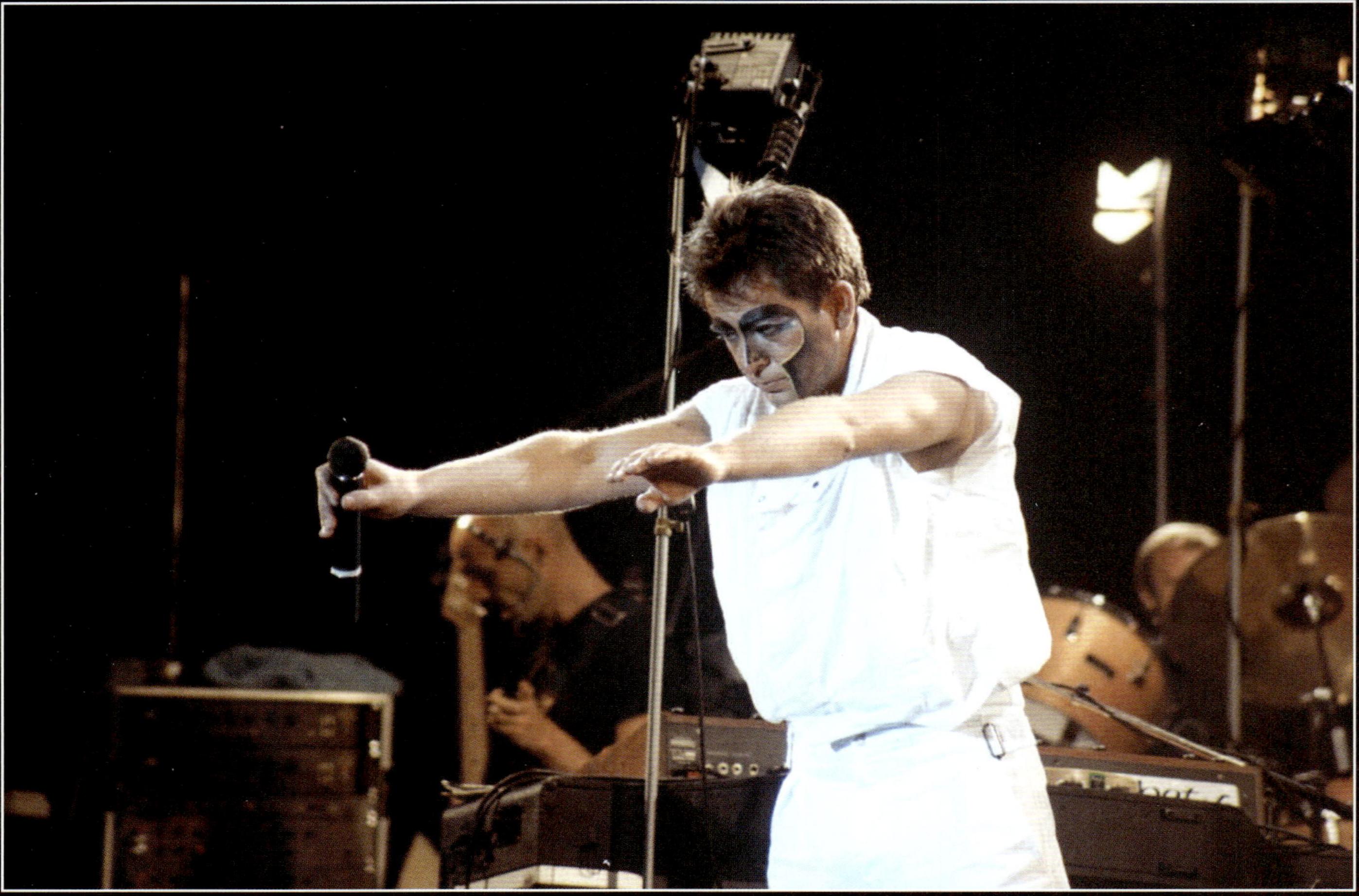

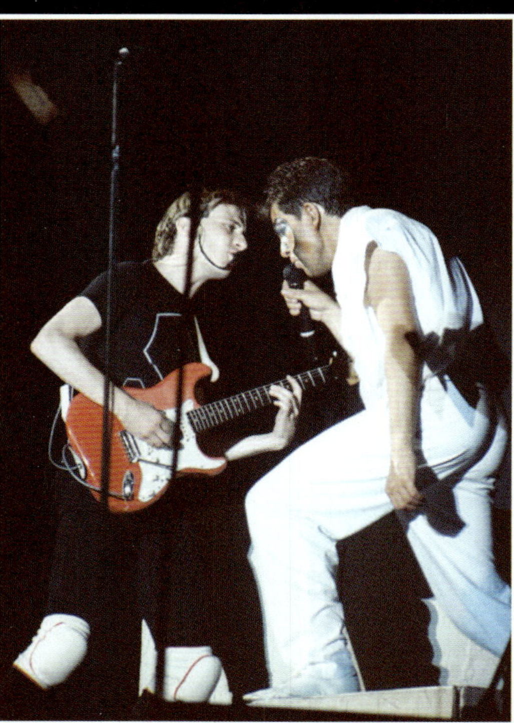

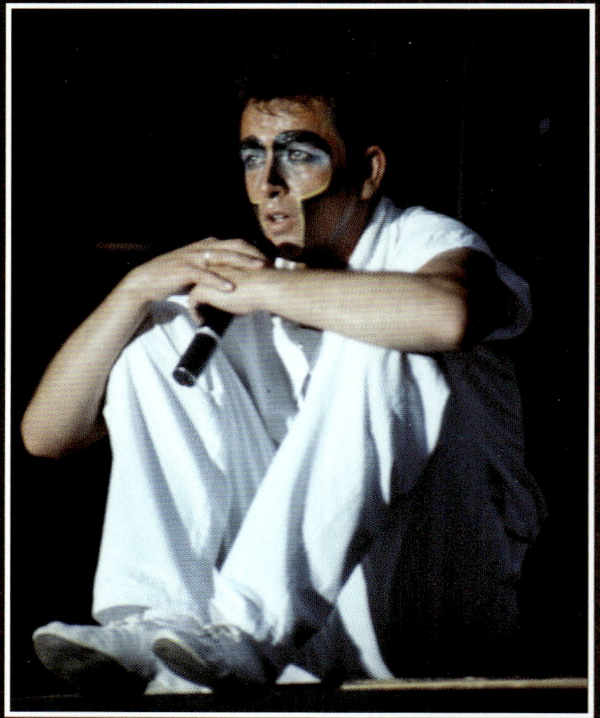

It was business as normal after the Milton Keynes spectacle. Gabriel toured the States for the rest of the year and returned to Europe the following summer. The one UK show was at Selhurst Park, the home of Crystal Palace Football Club, teaming up once again with Phil for this show.

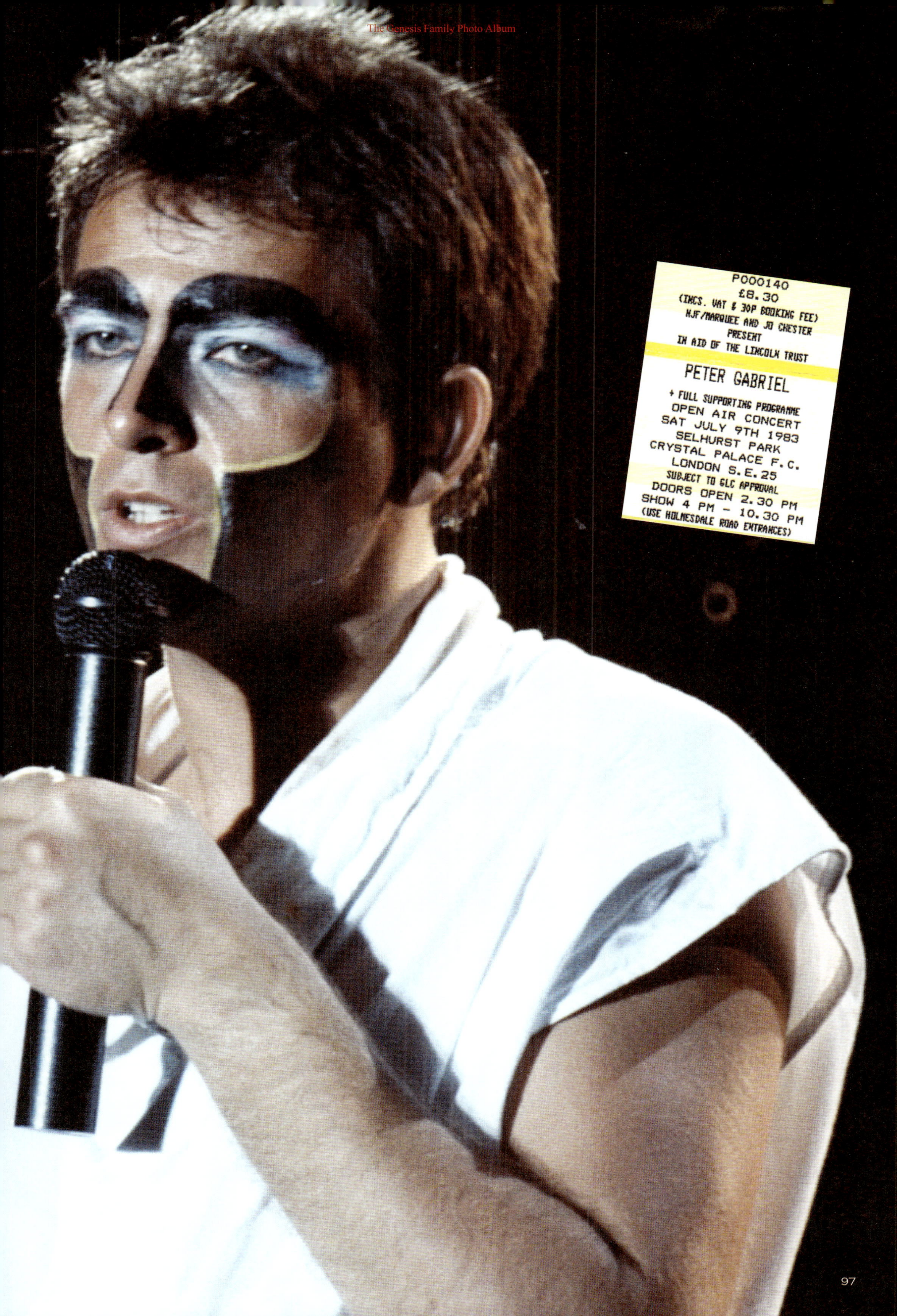
P000140
£8.30
(INCS. VAT & 30P BOOKING FEE)
NJF/MARQUEE AND JO CHESTER
PRESENT
IN AID OF THE LINCOLN TRUST
PETER GABRIEL
+ FULL SUPPORTING PROGRAMME
OPEN AIR CONCERT
SAT JULY 9TH 1983
SELHURST PARK
CRYSTAL PALACE F.C.
LONDON S.E.25
SUBJECT TO GLC APPROVAL
DOORS OPEN 2.30 PM
SHOW 4 PM - 10.30 PM
(USE HOLMESDALE ROAD ENTRANCES)

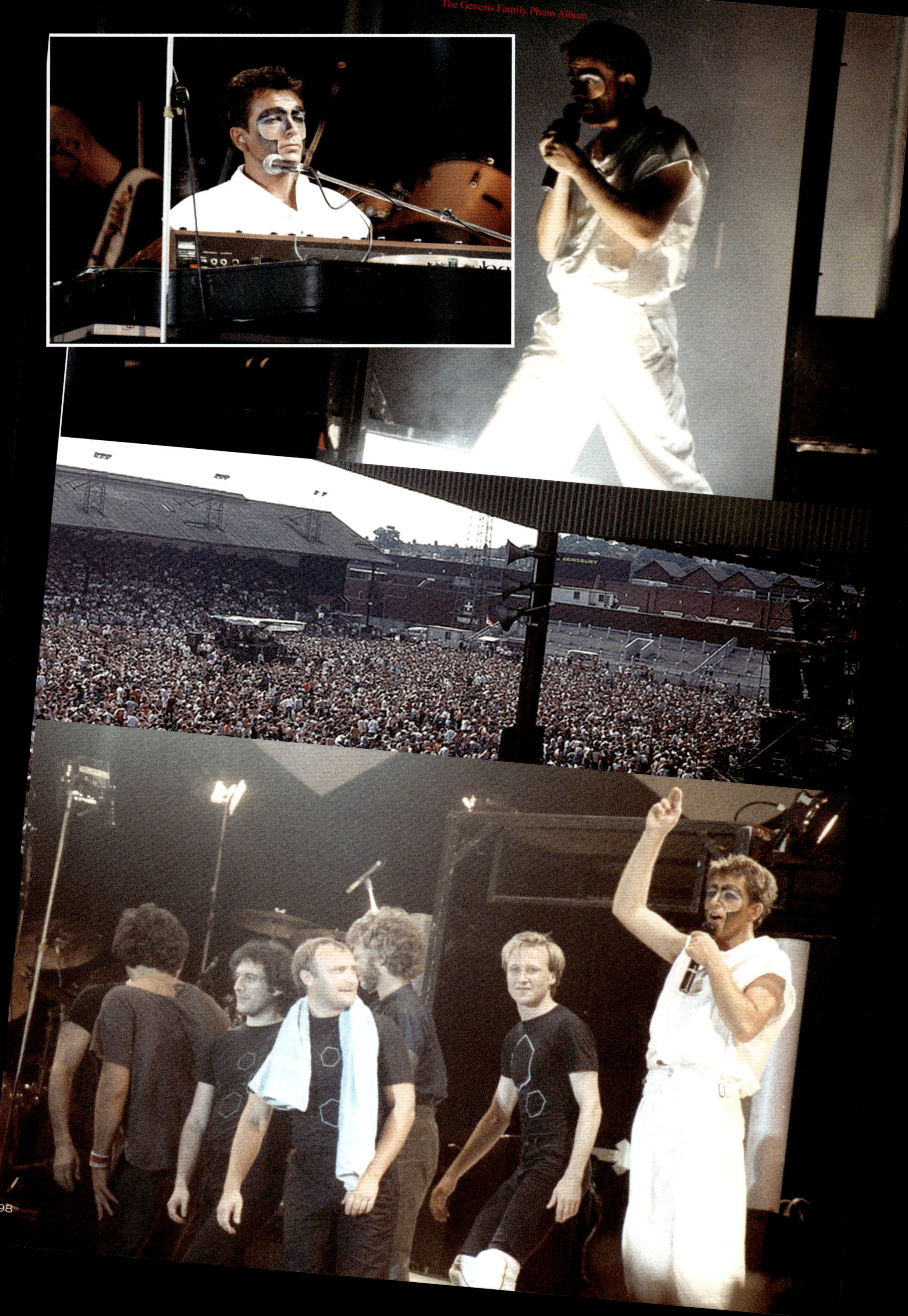

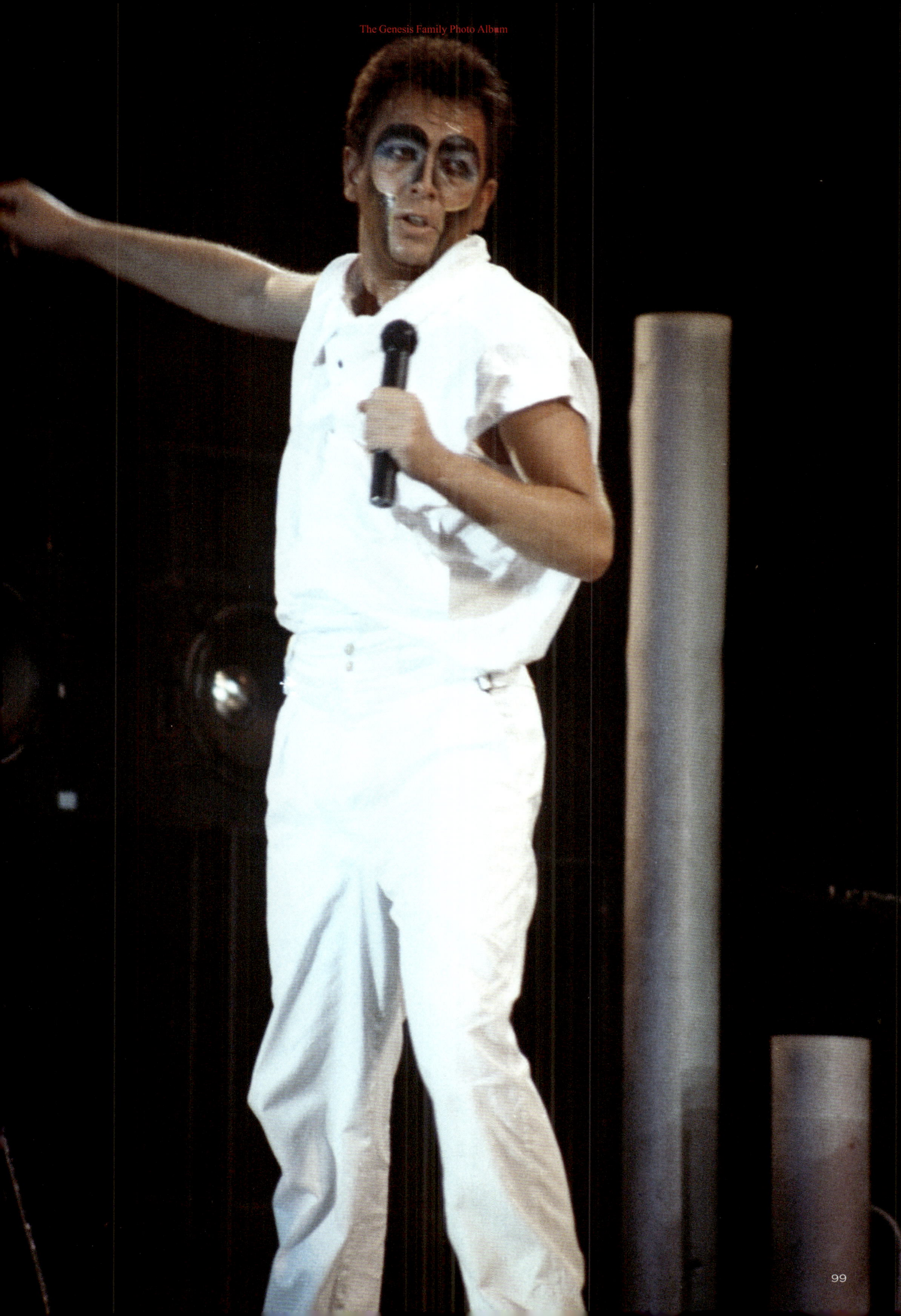

There could not be more striking contrasts. Peter, the consummate live performer and on the opposite page, Anthony Phillips who quit Genesis in 1970 because of stage fright. This photo of Ant was taken in 1986 during a period where he released several albums utilising the *Private Parts And Pieces* title of his 1978 release.

Also in contrast to Peter and his rock theatrics, in 1983 Steve did an acoustic tour with his brother John. By 1986 he had formed the GTR band with Yes Guitarist Steve Howe and toured the States and Europe before going back to his acoustic duo in '88.

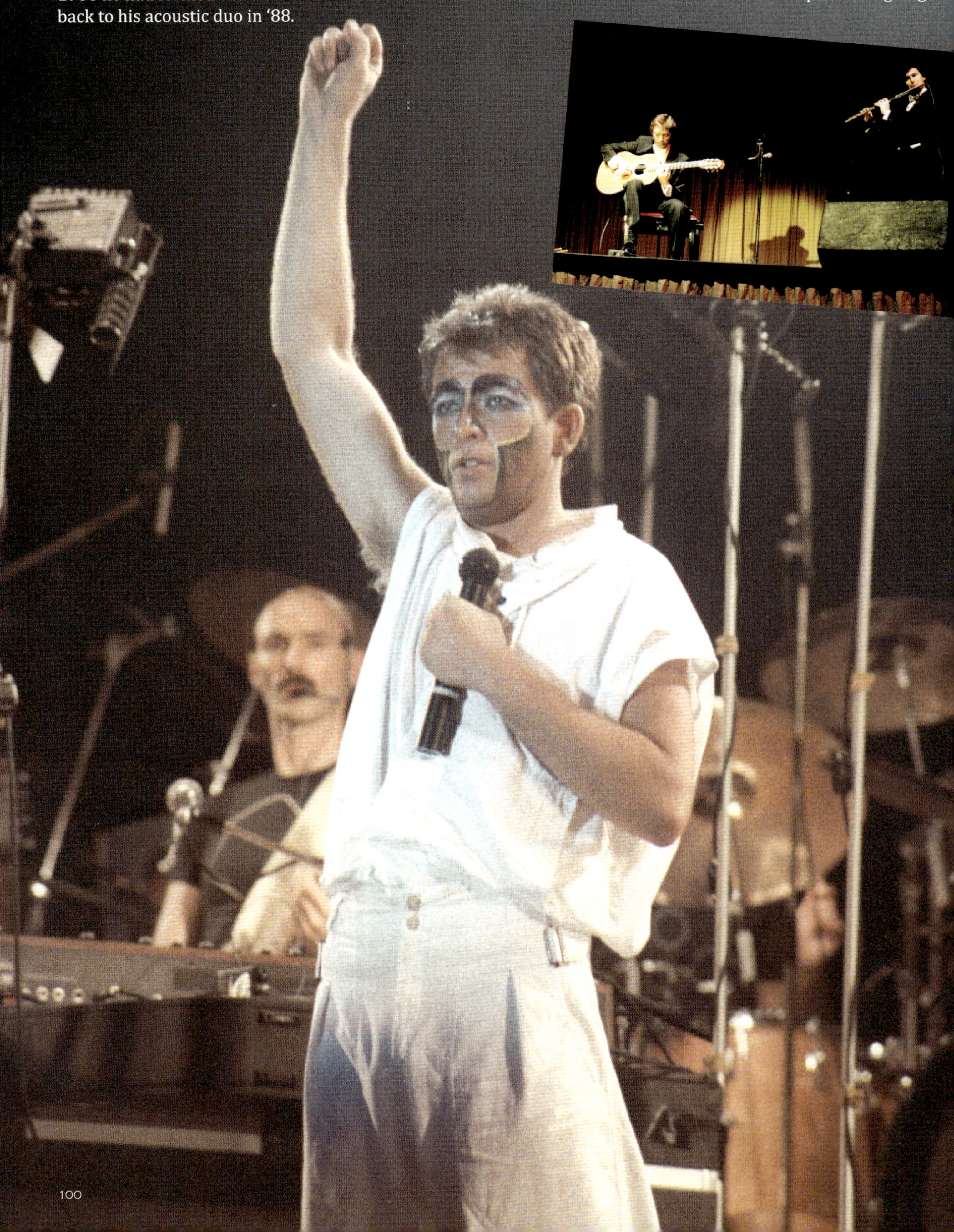

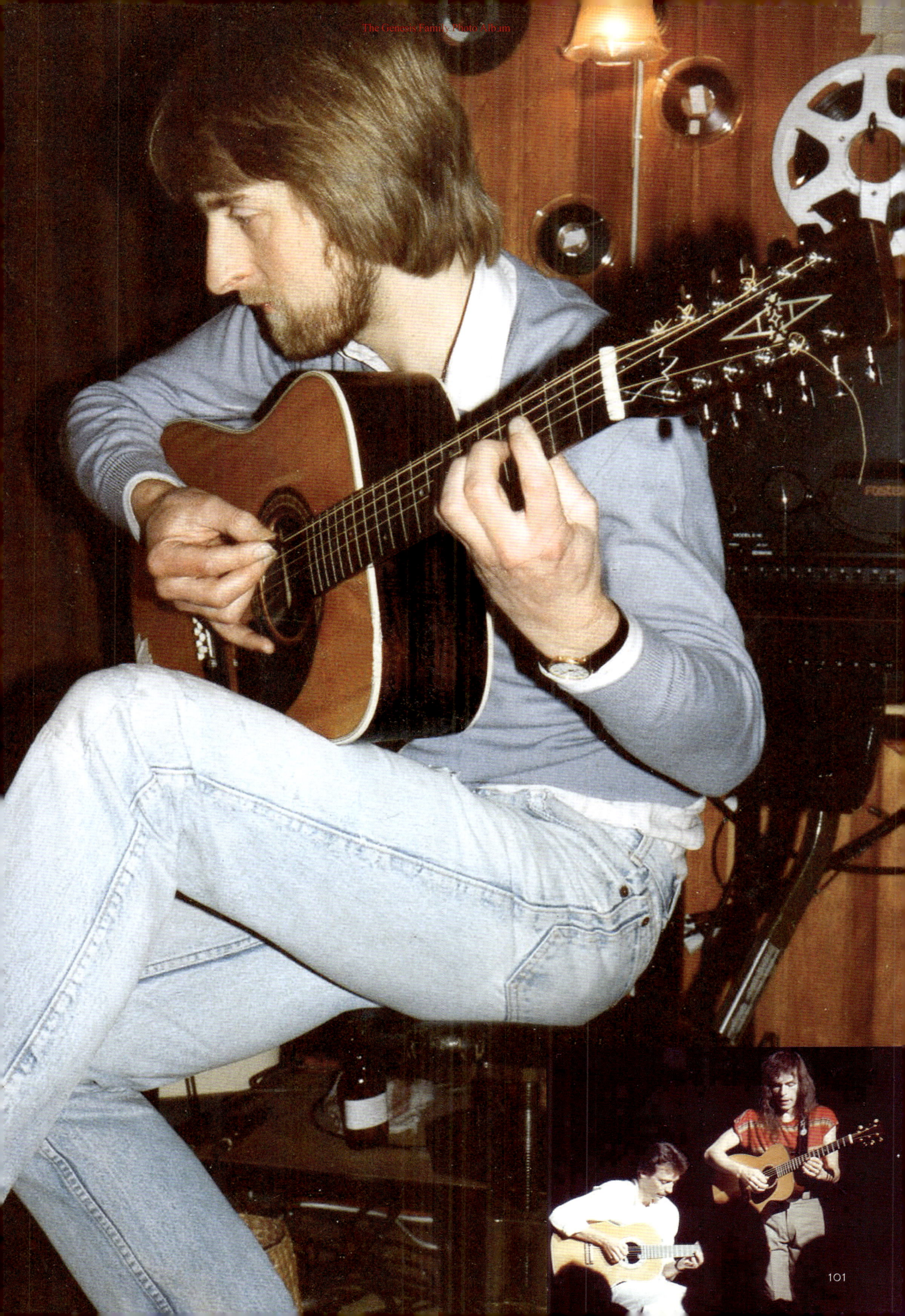

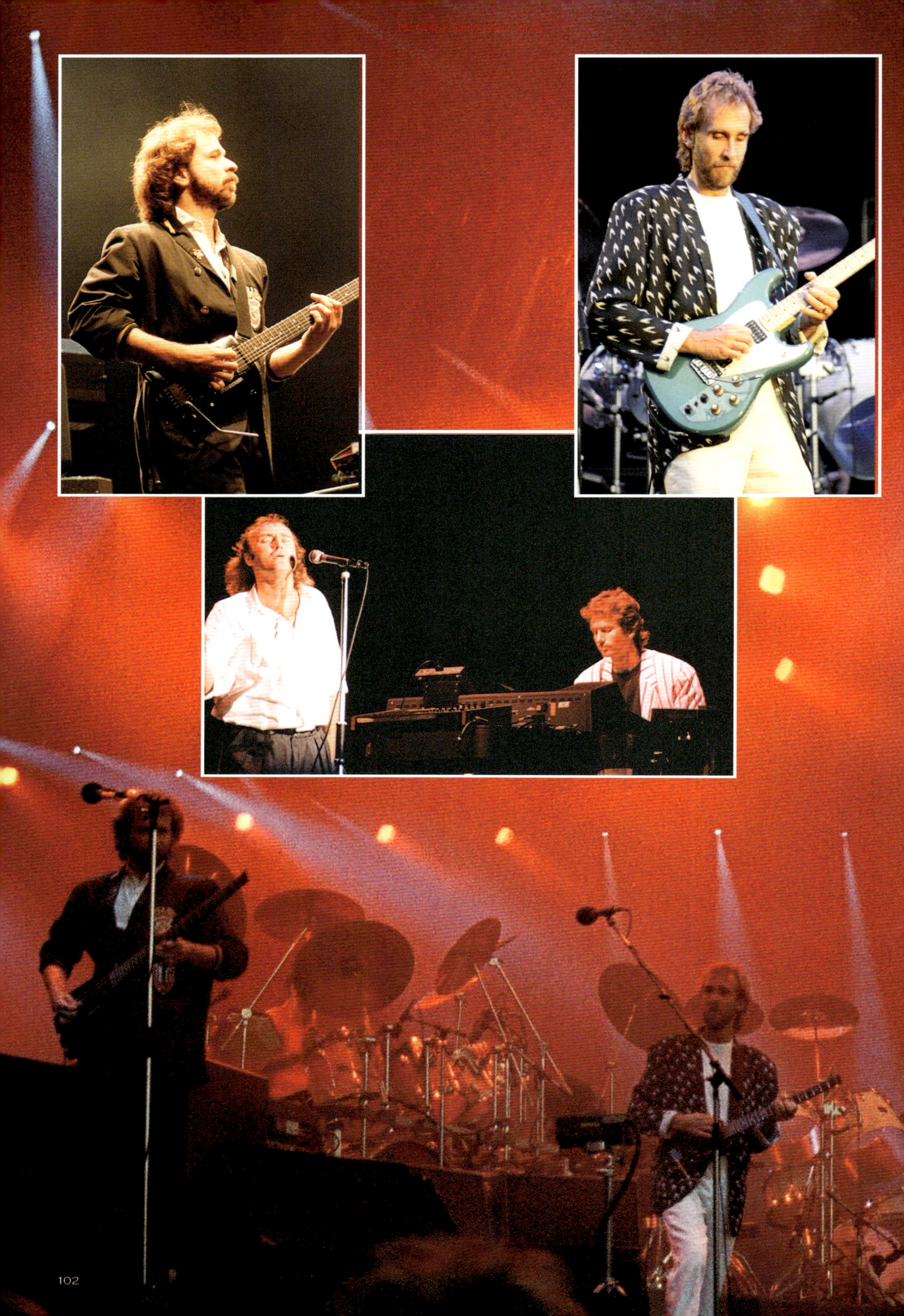

By 1986, Genesis was arguably at its commercial peak and toured the States playing five nights at the vast Madison Square Gardens in New York and four shows at the Forum in Los Angeles plus a 17-date tour of Australia. In 1987 they returned to the States before touring Japan including four nights at Tokyo's famous Budokan, followed by an array of stadium concerts across Europe that culminated with four nights at Wembley Stadium in London, where these photos were taken.

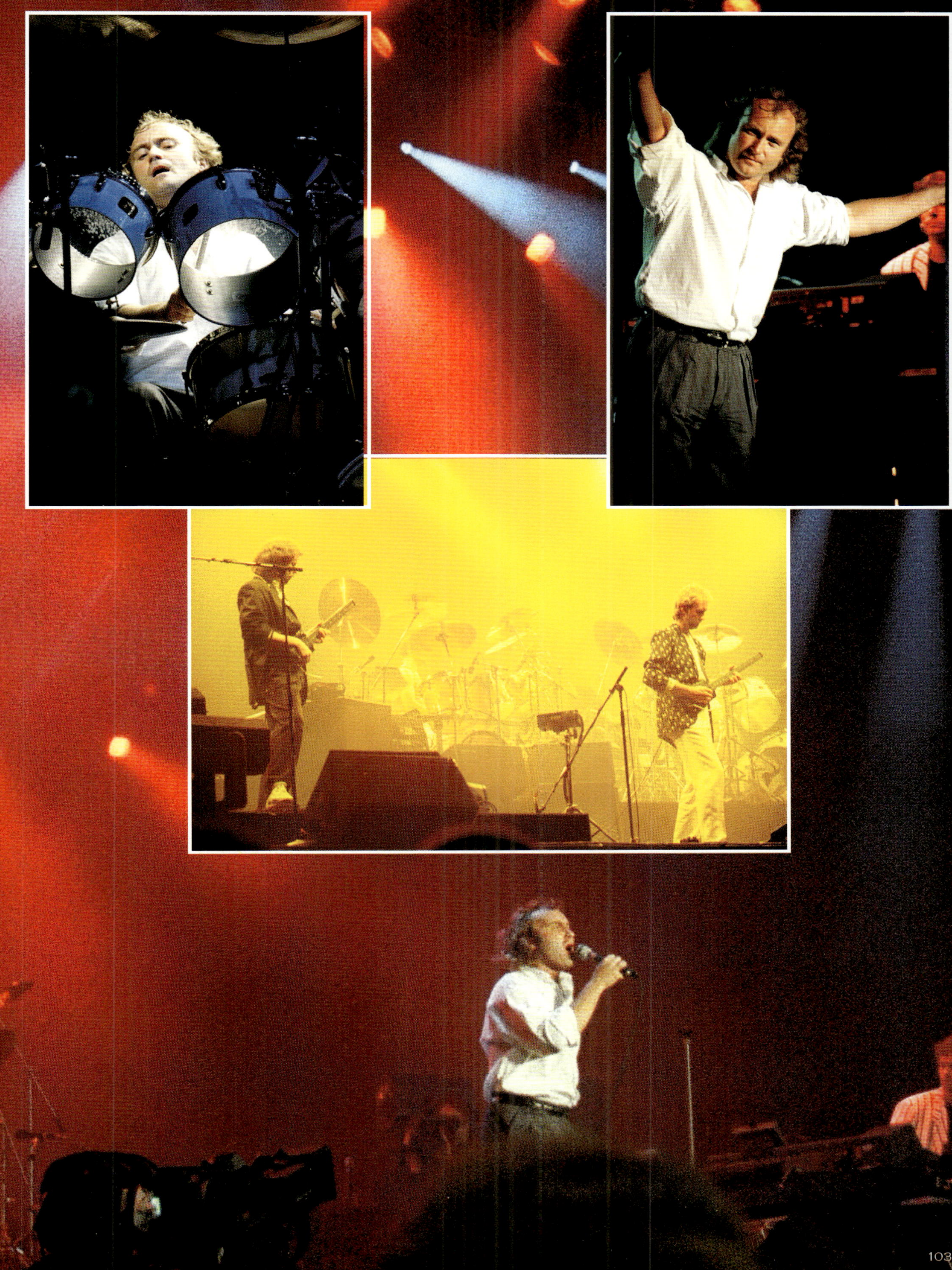

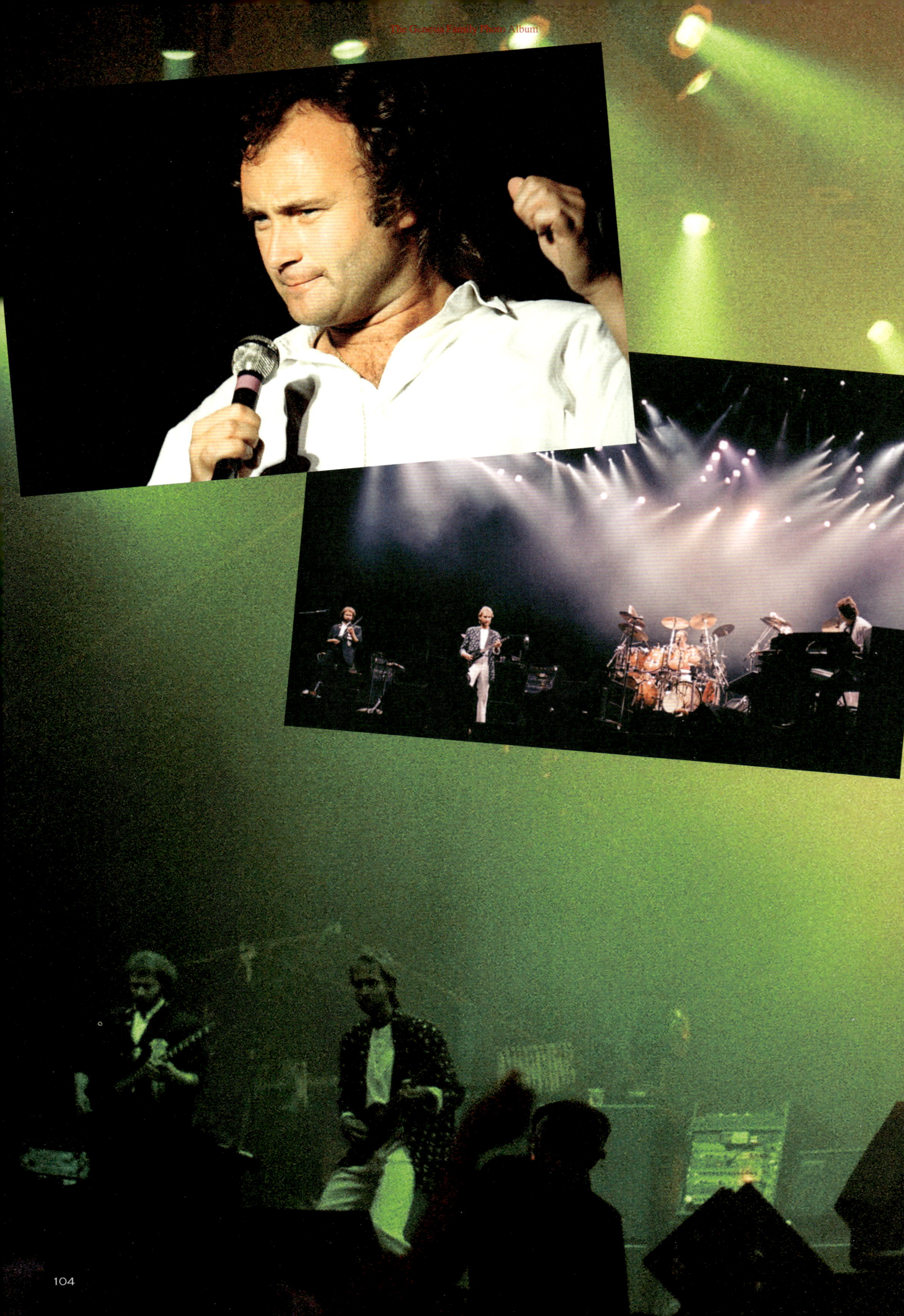

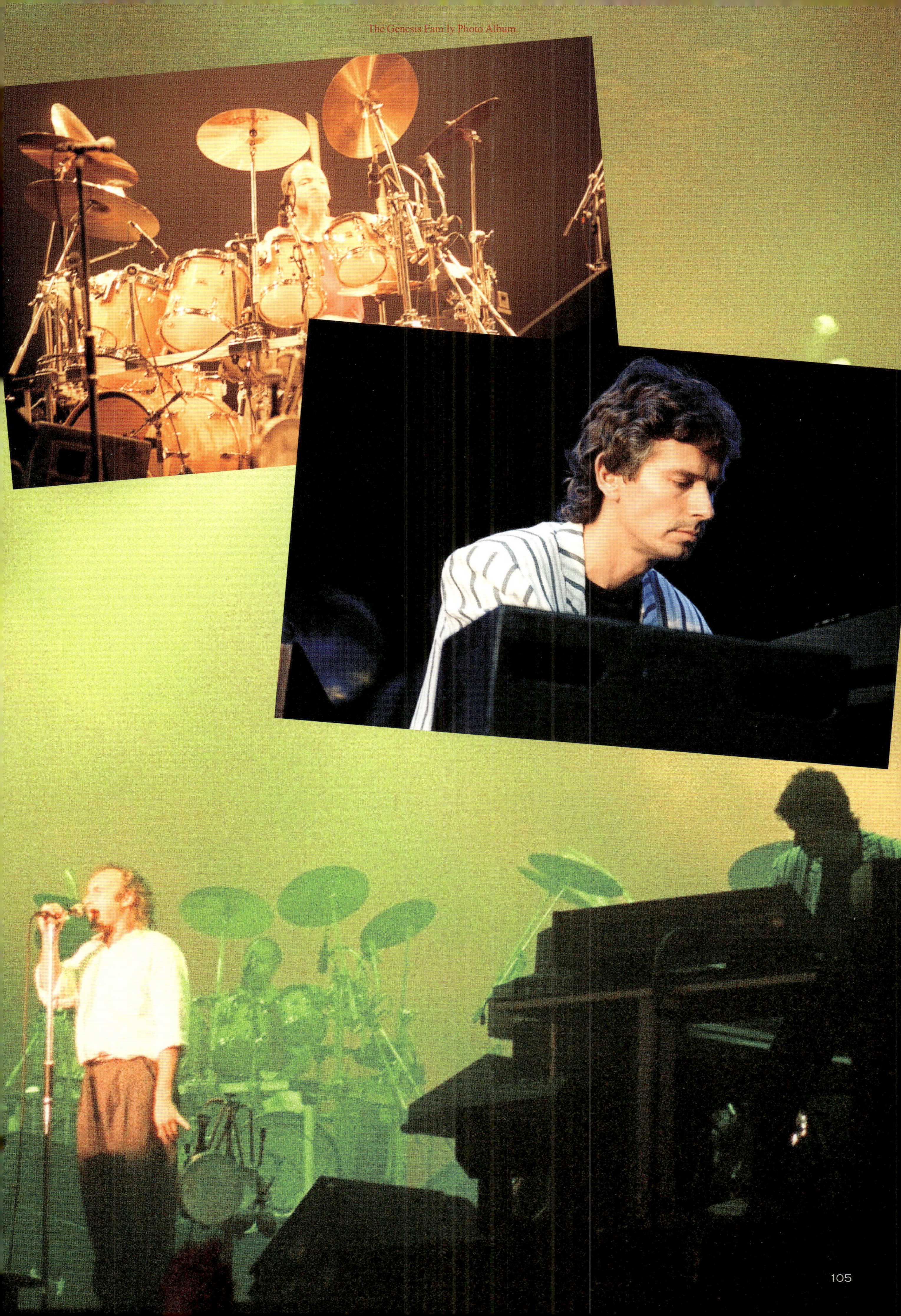

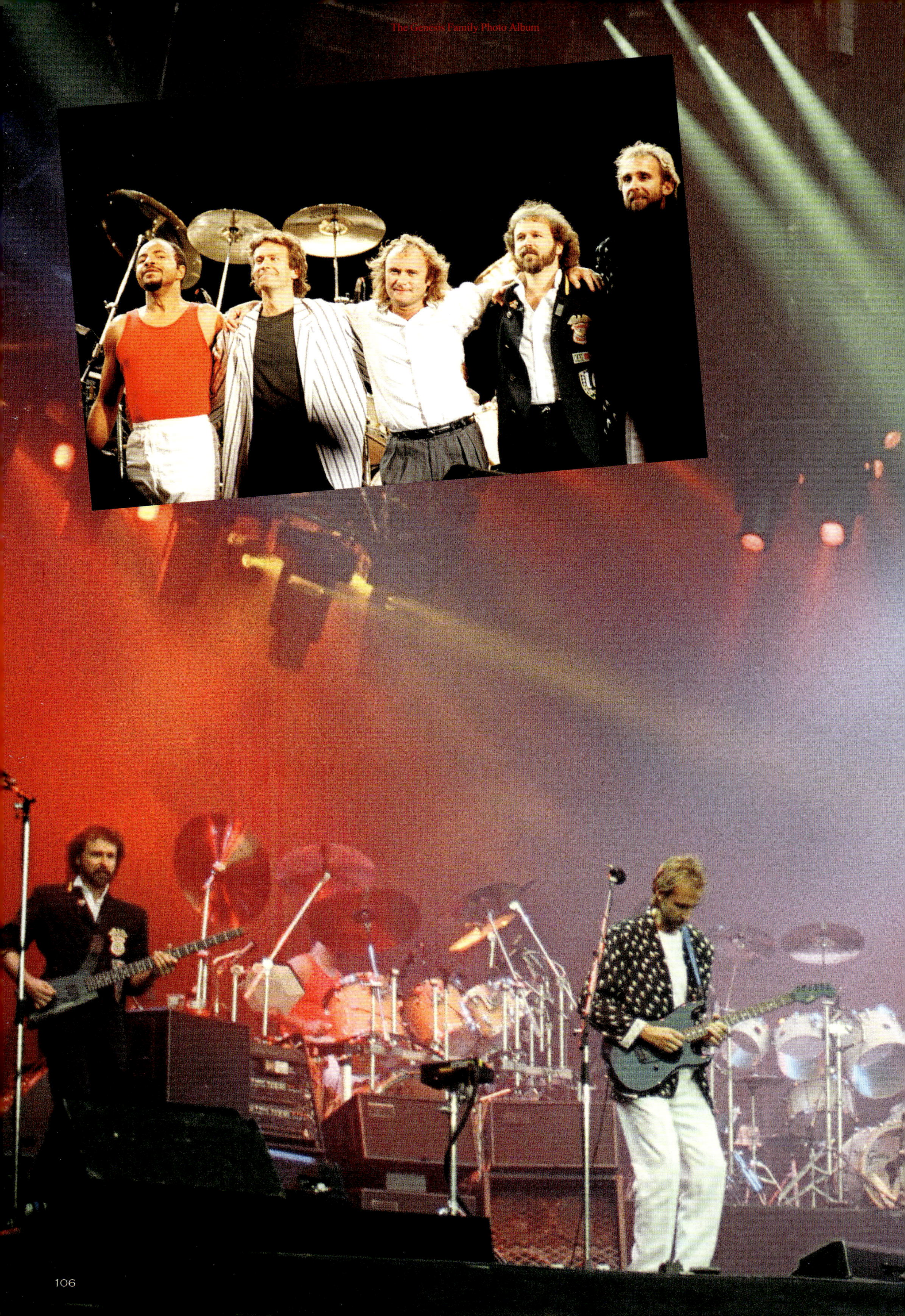

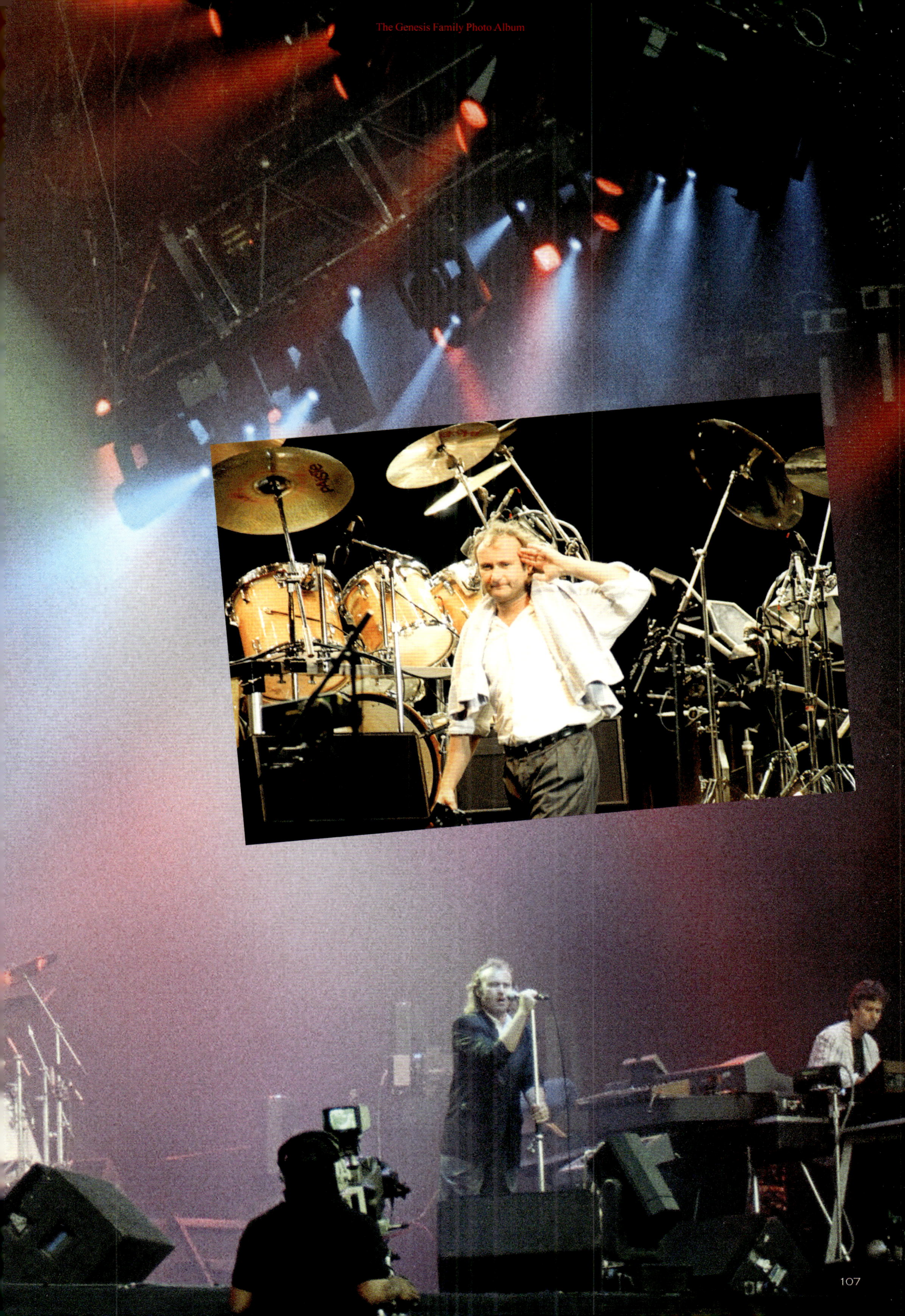

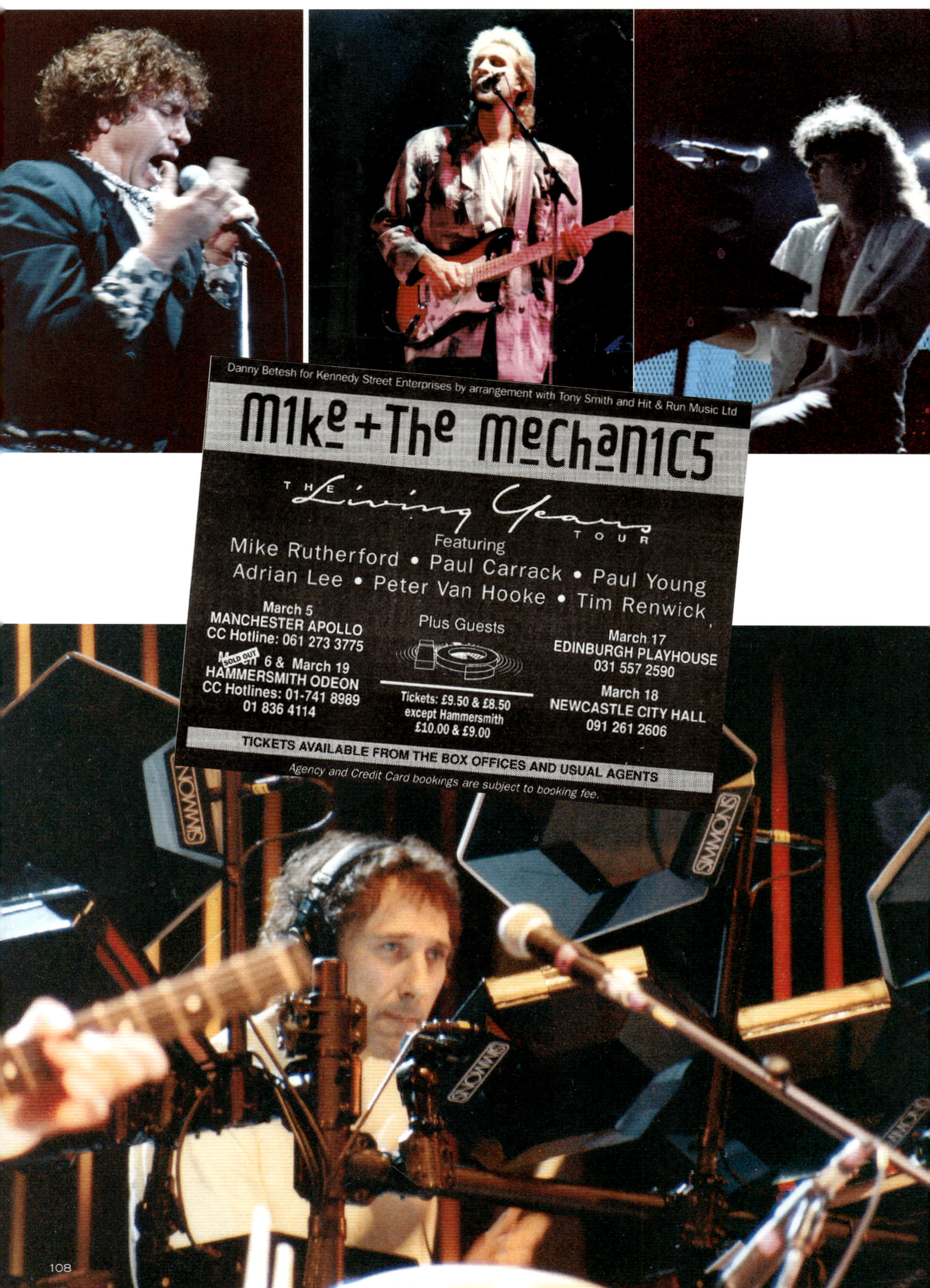
Danny Betesh for Kennedy Street Enterprises by arrangement with Tony Smith and Hit & Run Music Ltd
M1ke + The MechaN1C5
THE Living Years TOUR
Featuring
Mike Rutherford • Paul Carrack • Paul Young
Adrian Lee • Peter Van Hooke • Tim Renwick
Plus Guests
March 5
MANCHESTER APOLLO
CC Hotline: 061 273 3775
SOLD OUT
March 6 & March 19
HAMMERSMITH ODEON
CC Hotlines: 01-741 8989
01 836 4114
Tickets: £9.50 & £8.50
except Hammersmith
£10.00 & £9.00
March 17
EDINBURGH PLAYHOUSE
031 557 2590
March 18
NEWCASTLE CITY HALL
091 261 2606
TICKETS AVAILABLE FROM THE BOX OFFICES AND USUAL AGENTS
Agency and Credit Card bookings are subject to booking fee.

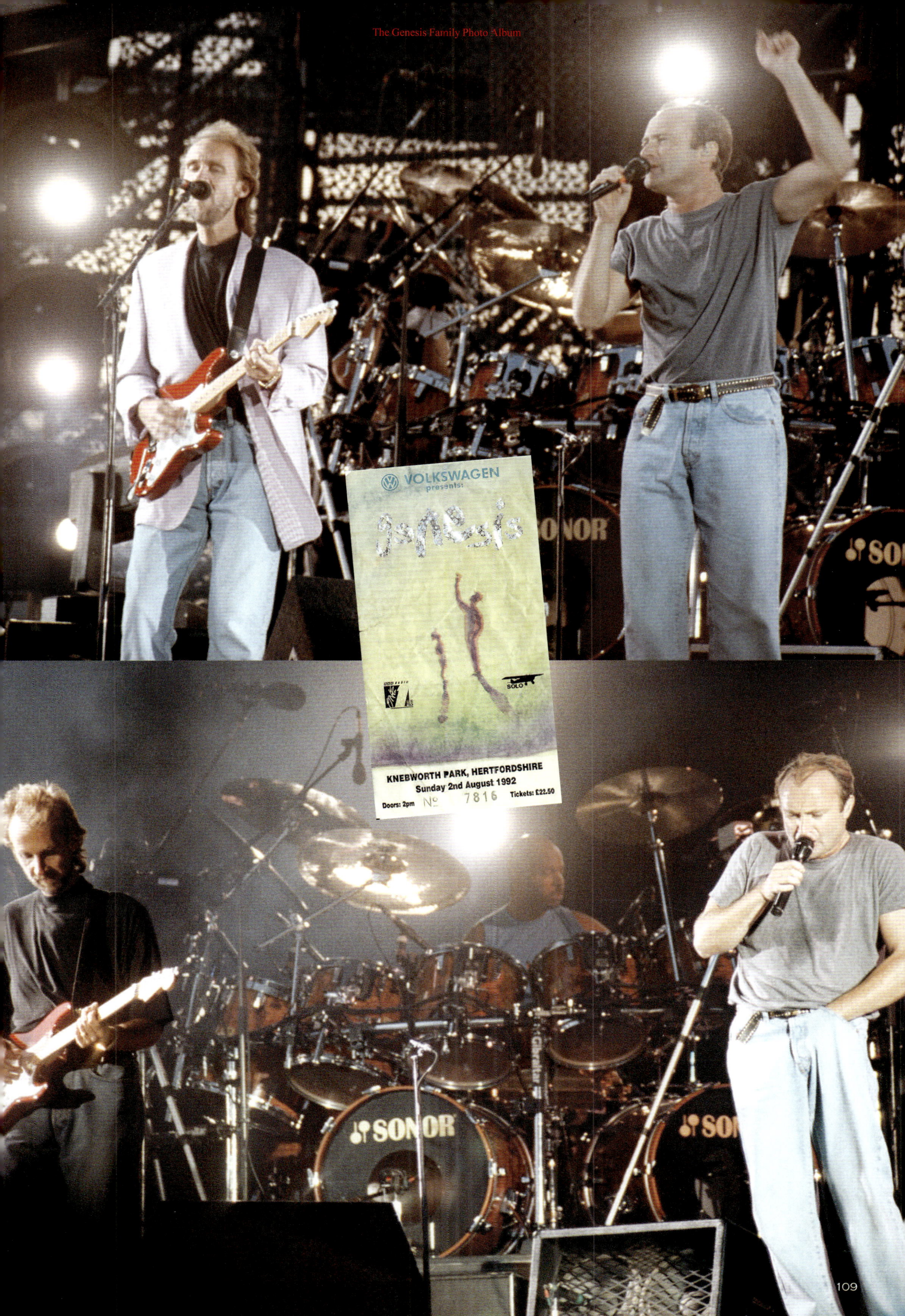
VOLKSWAGEN
presents:
Genesis
KNEBWORTH PARK, HERTFORDSHIRE
Sunday 2nd August 1992
Doors: 2pm   No 7816   Tickets: £22.50

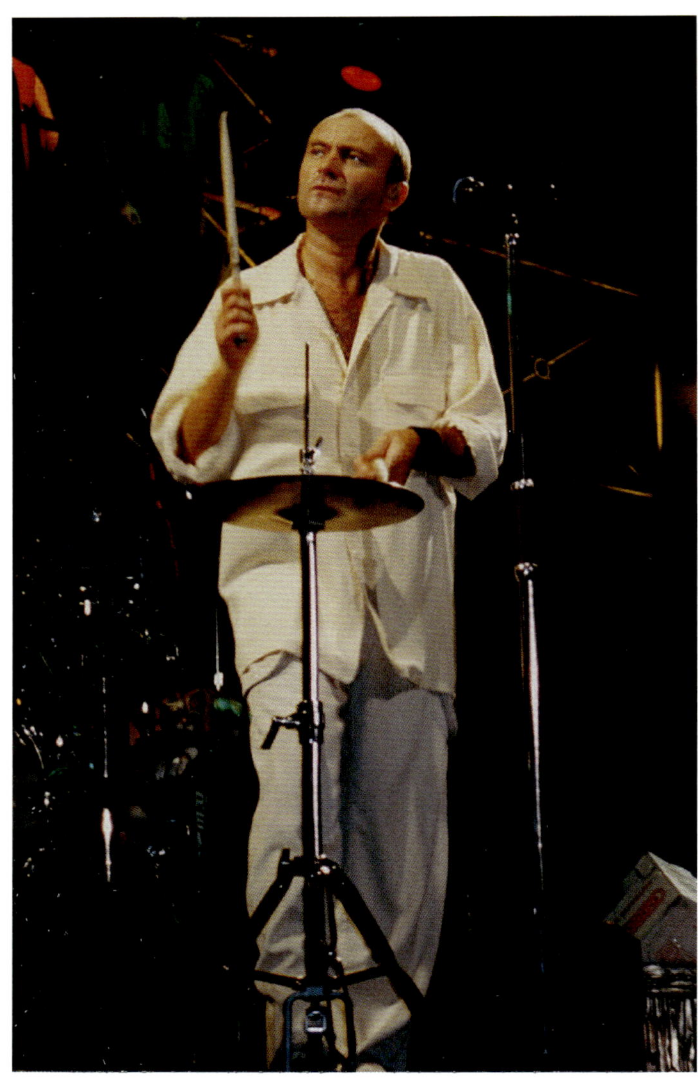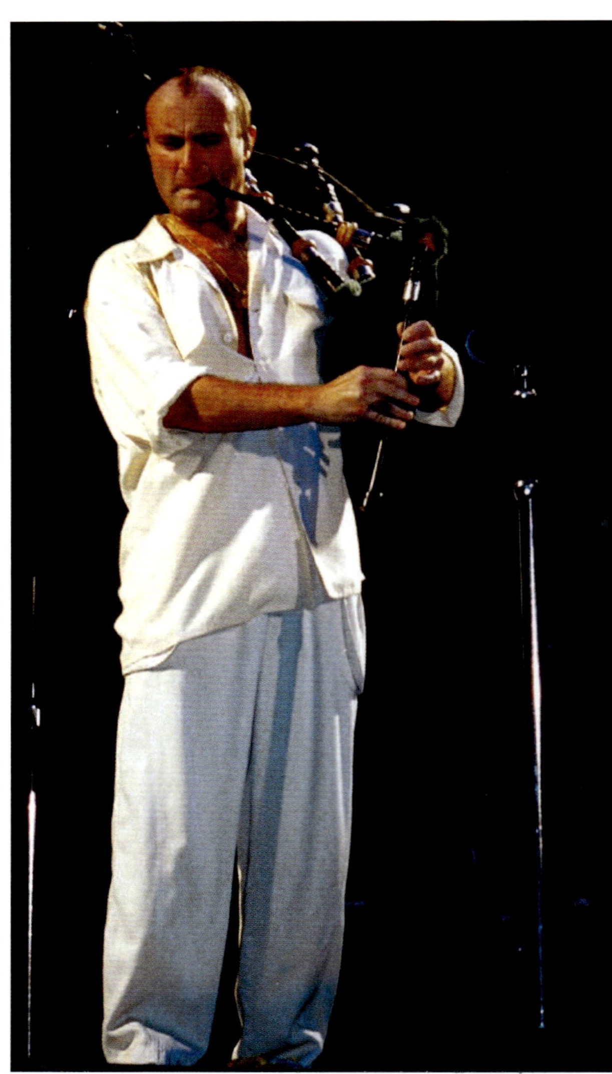

Phil on his solo tours in 1995 & (opposite page) '97, in between which times he had left Genesis.

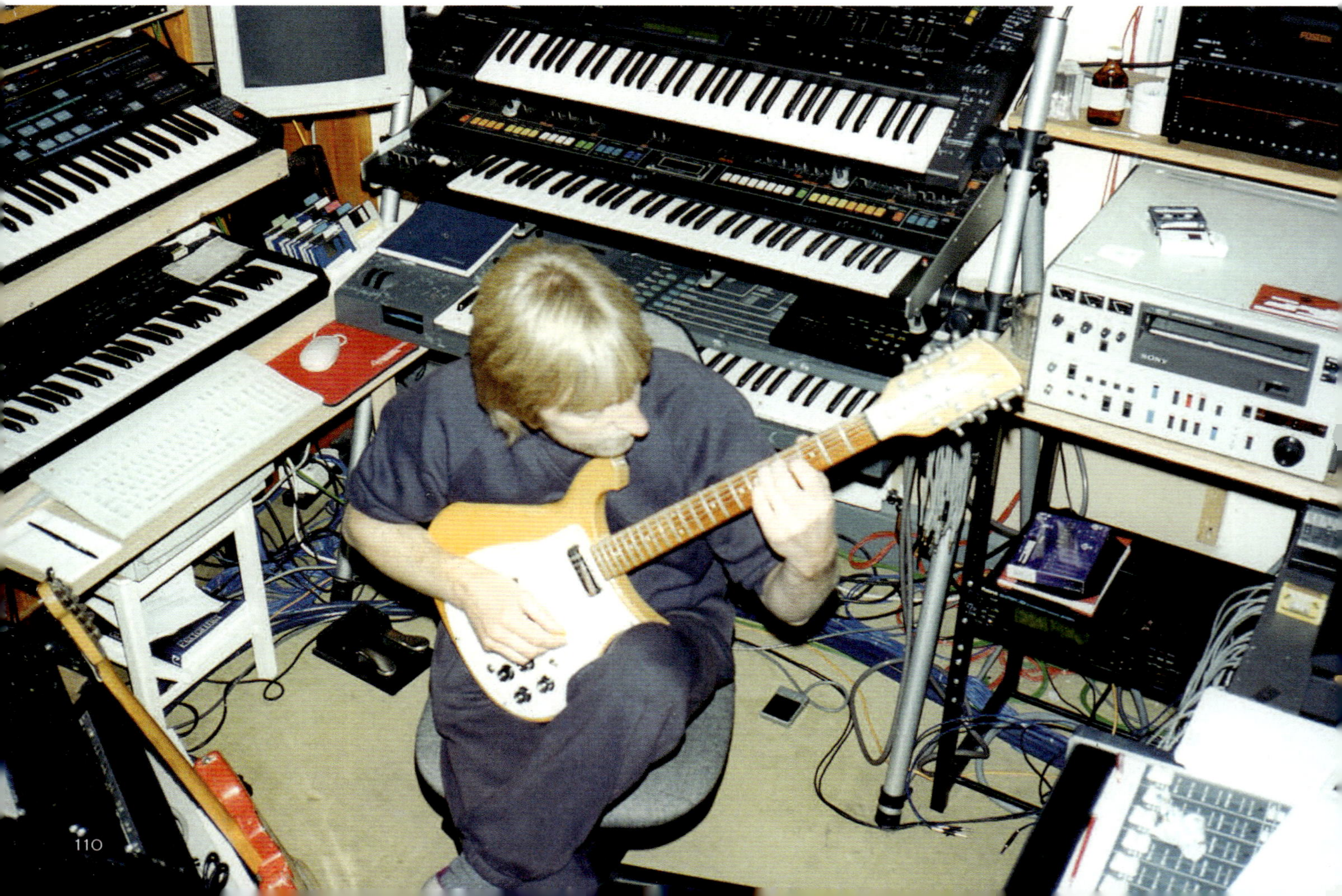

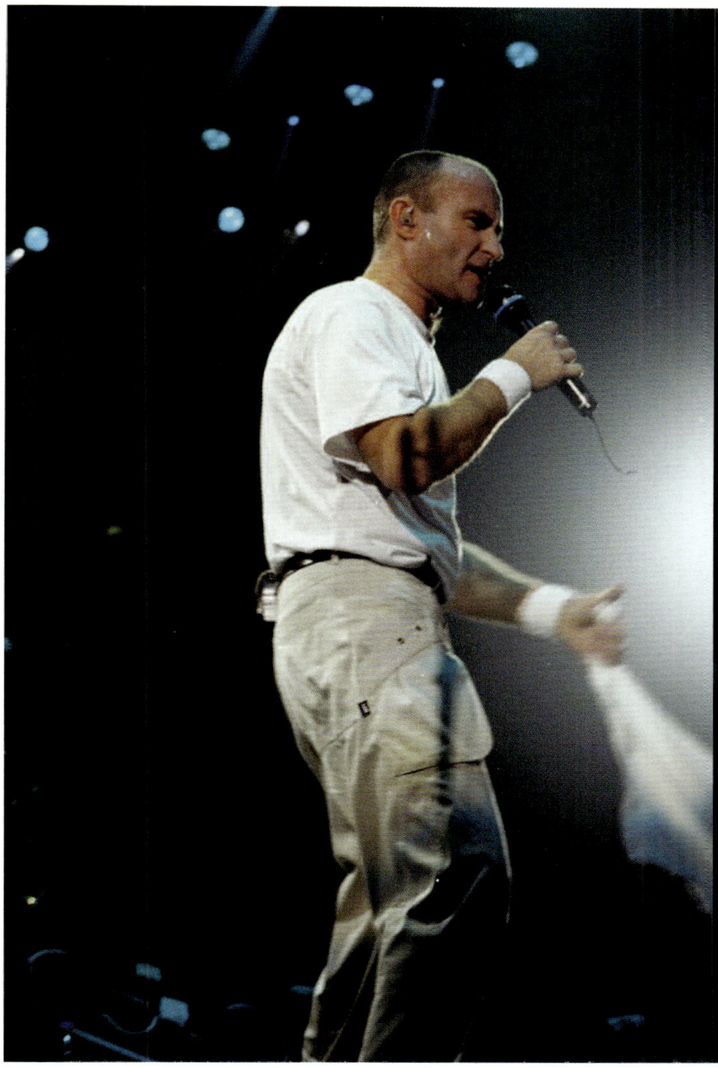

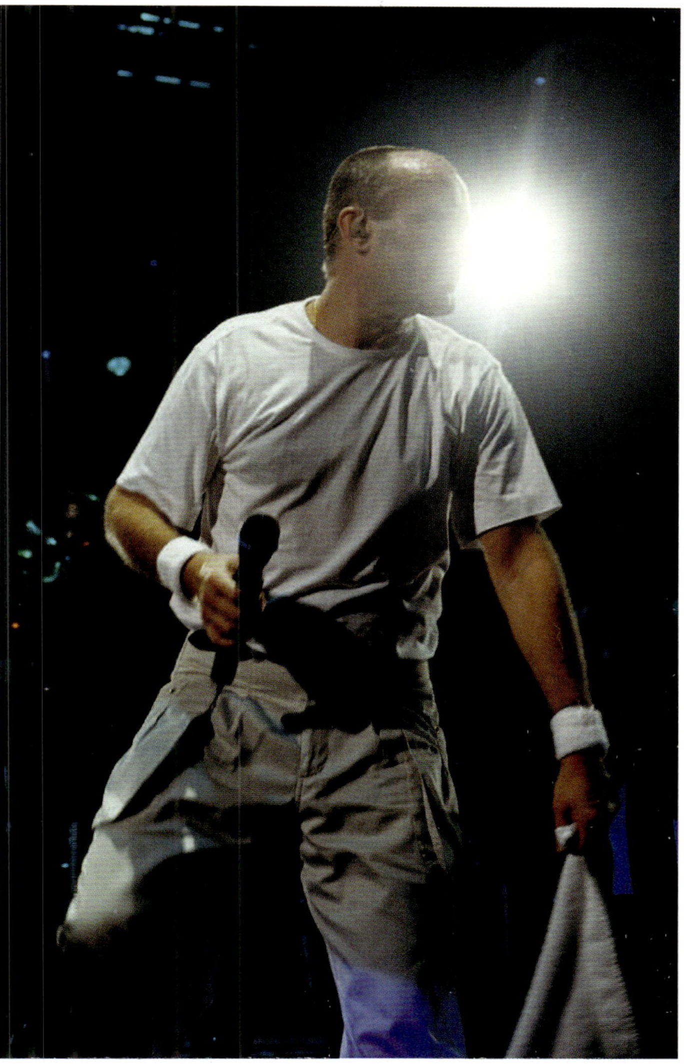

Ant in the studio in 1995.

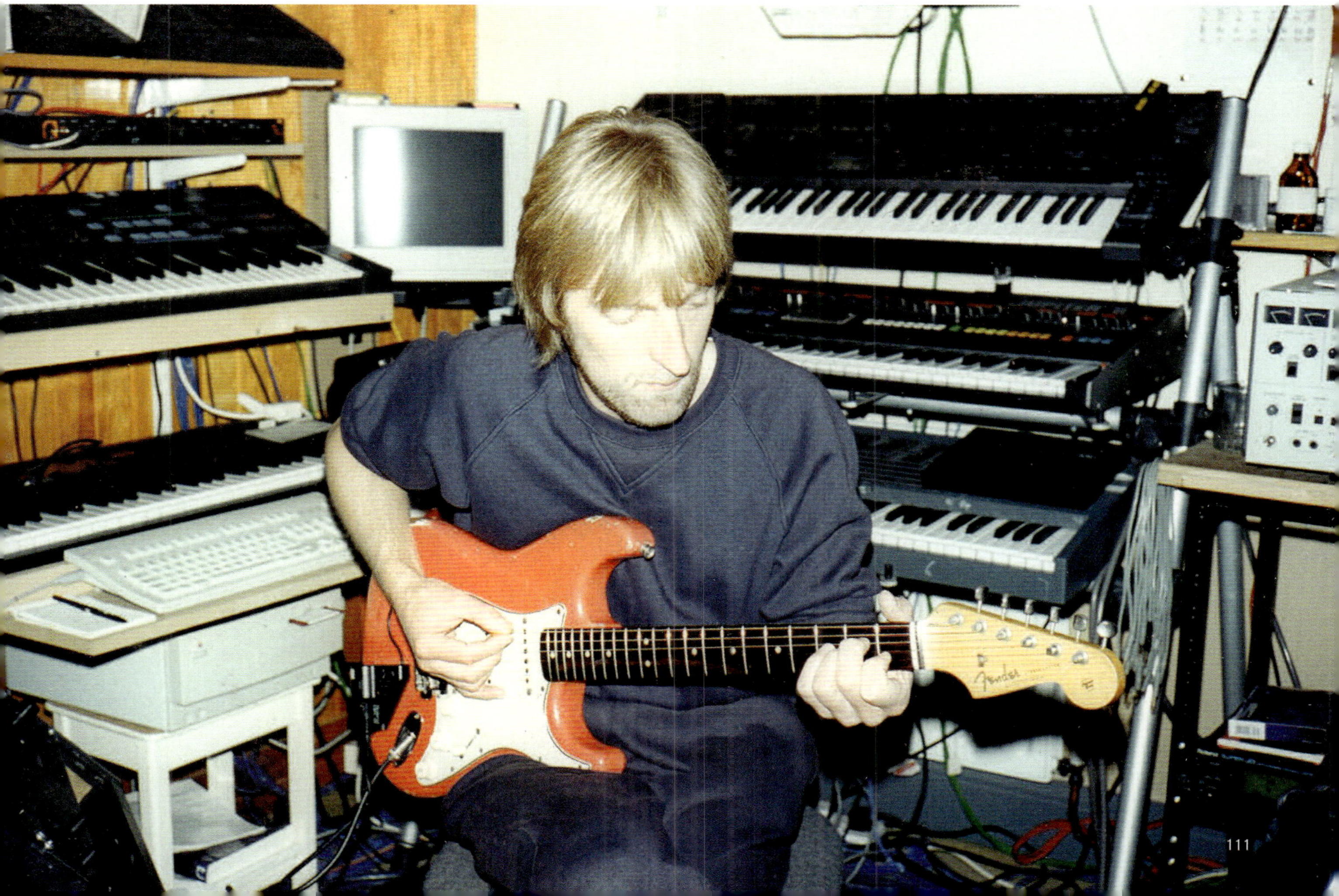

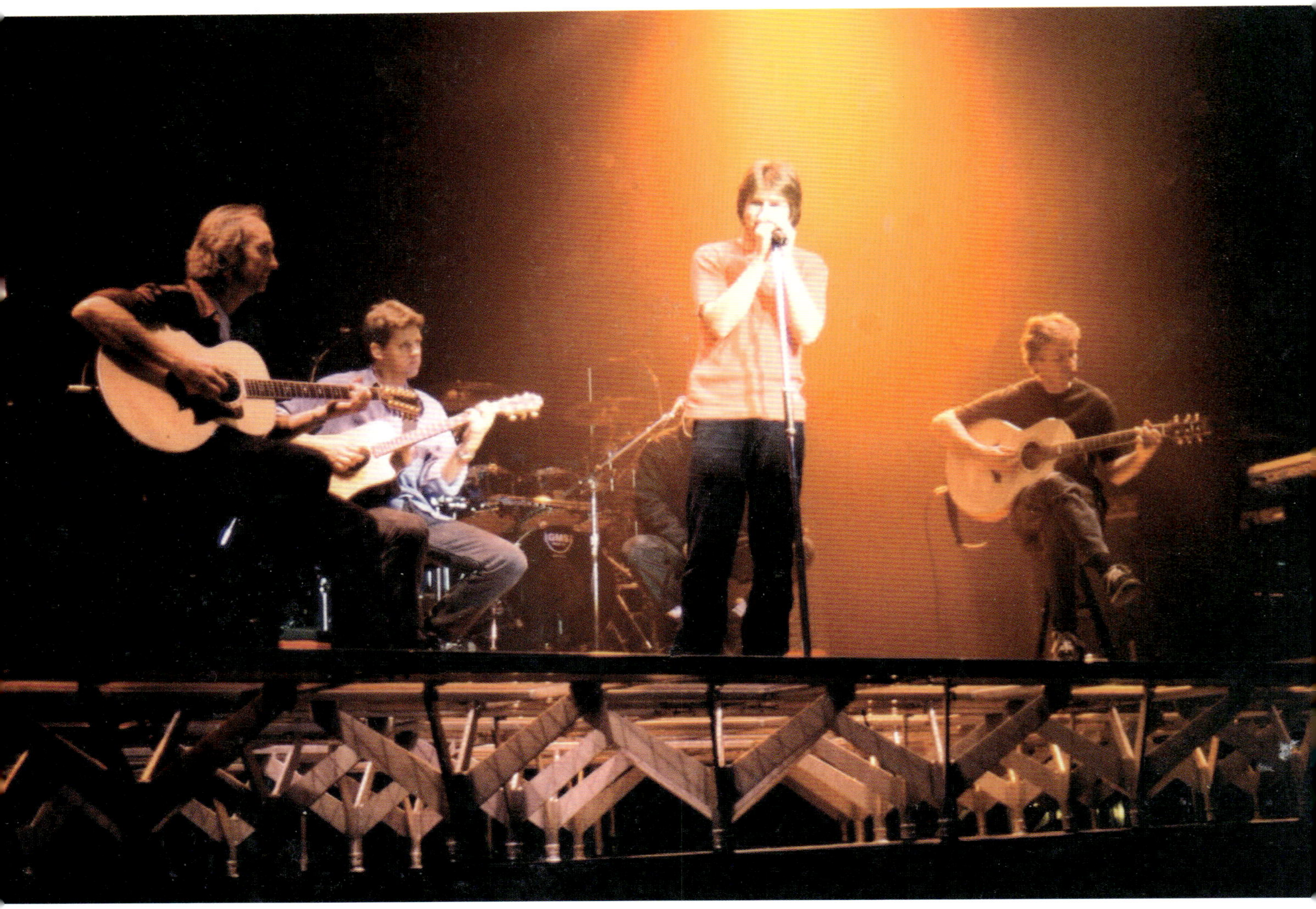

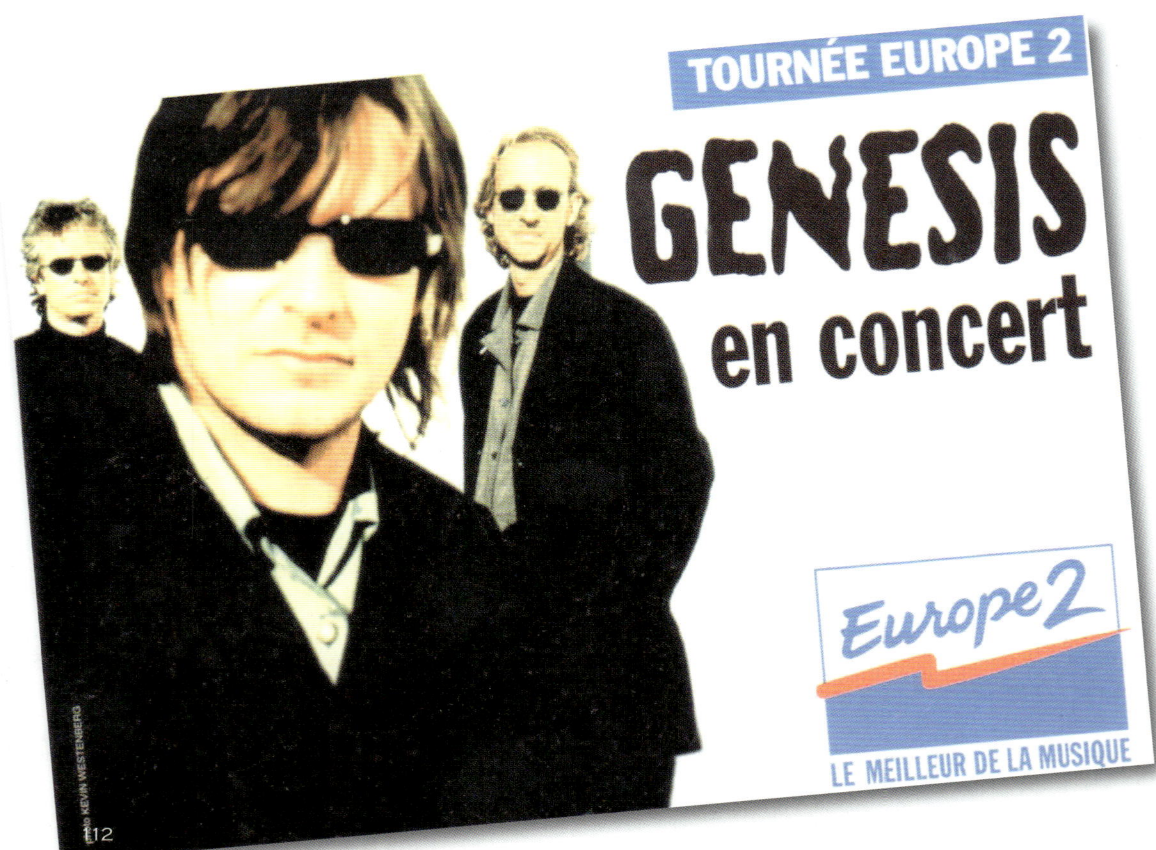

Tony and Mike rehearsing with Phil's replacement Ray Wilson along with guitarist Anthony Drennan and drummer Nir Zidkyahu who replaced Daryl Steurmer and Chester Thompson respectively.

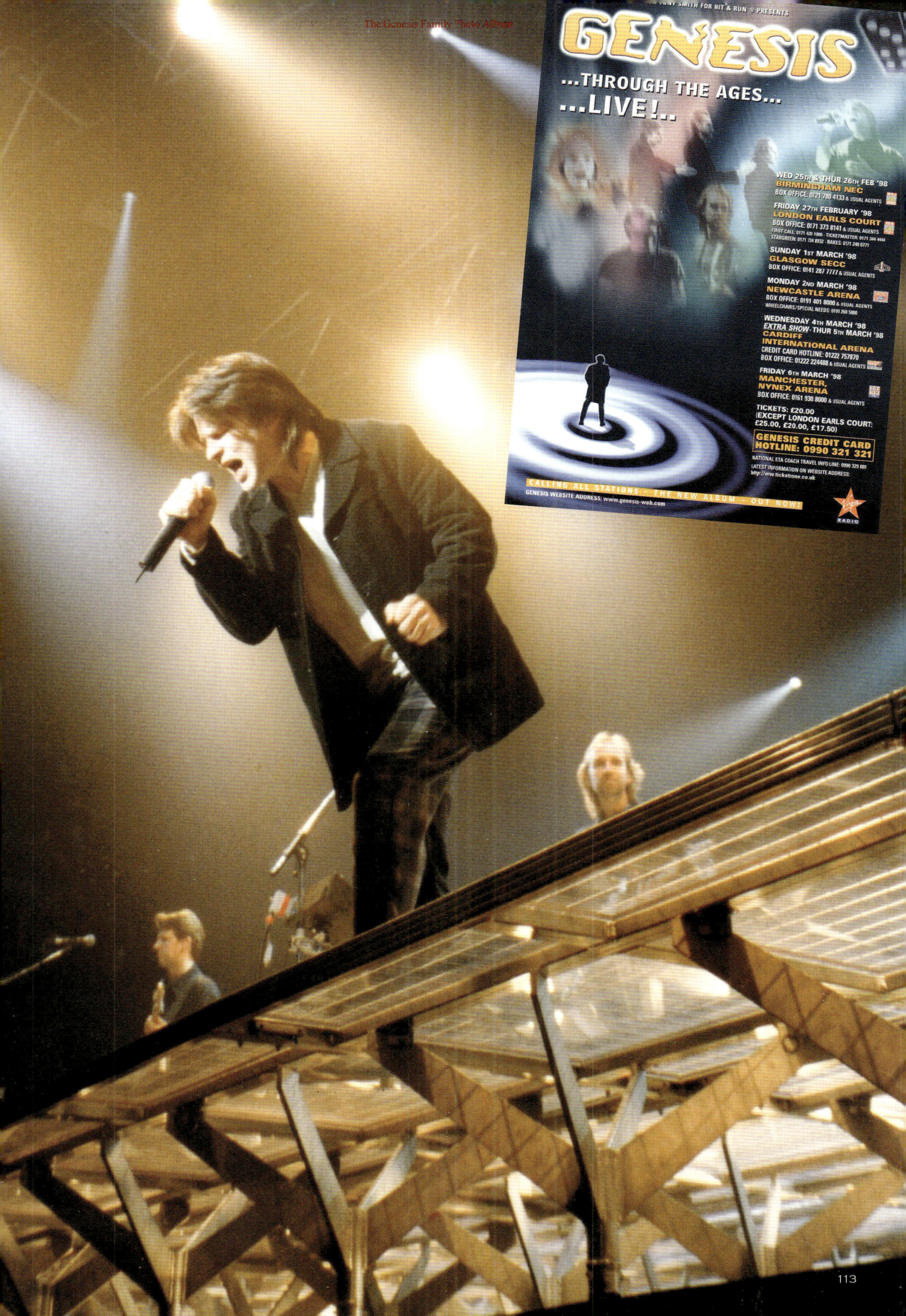
TONY SMITH FOR HIT & RUN ® PRESENTS
GENESIS
...THROUGH THE AGES...
...LIVE!..
WED 25TH & THUR 26TH FEB '98
BIRMINGHAM NEC
BOX OFFICE: 0121 780 4133 & USUAL AGENTS
FRIDAY 27TH FEBRUARY '98
LONDON EARLS COURT
BOX OFFICE: 0171 373 8141 & USUAL AGENTS
FIRST CALL: 0171 420 1000 - TICKETMASTER: 0171 344 4444
STARGREEN: 0171 734 8932 - RAKES: 0171 240 0771
SUNDAY 1ST MARCH '98
GLASGOW SECC
BOX OFFICE: 0141 287 7777 & USUAL AGENTS
MONDAY 2ND MARCH '98
NEWCASTLE ARENA
BOX OFFICE: 0191 401 8000 & USUAL AGENTS
WHEELCHAIRS/SPECIAL NEEDS: 0191 260 5000
WEDNESDAY 4TH MARCH '98
EXTRA SHOW - THUR 5TH MARCH '98
CARDIFF INTERNATIONAL ARENA
CREDIT CARD HOTLINE: 01222 757870
BOX OFFICE: 01222 224488 & USUAL AGENTS
FRIDAY 6TH MARCH '98
MANCHESTER, NYNEX ARENA
BOX OFFICE: 0161 930 8000 & USUAL AGENTS
TICKETS: £20.00
(EXCEPT LONDON EARLS COURT:
£25.00, £20.00, £17.50)
GENESIS CREDIT CARD HOTLINE: 0990 321 321
NATIONAL ETA COACH TRAVEL INFO LINE: 0990 329 885
LATEST INFORMATION ON WEBSITE ADDRESS:
http://ww.ticketzone.co.uk
CALLING ALL STATIONS - THE NEW ALBUM - OUT NOW!
GENESIS WEBSITE ADDRESS: www.genesis-web.com
Virgin RADIO

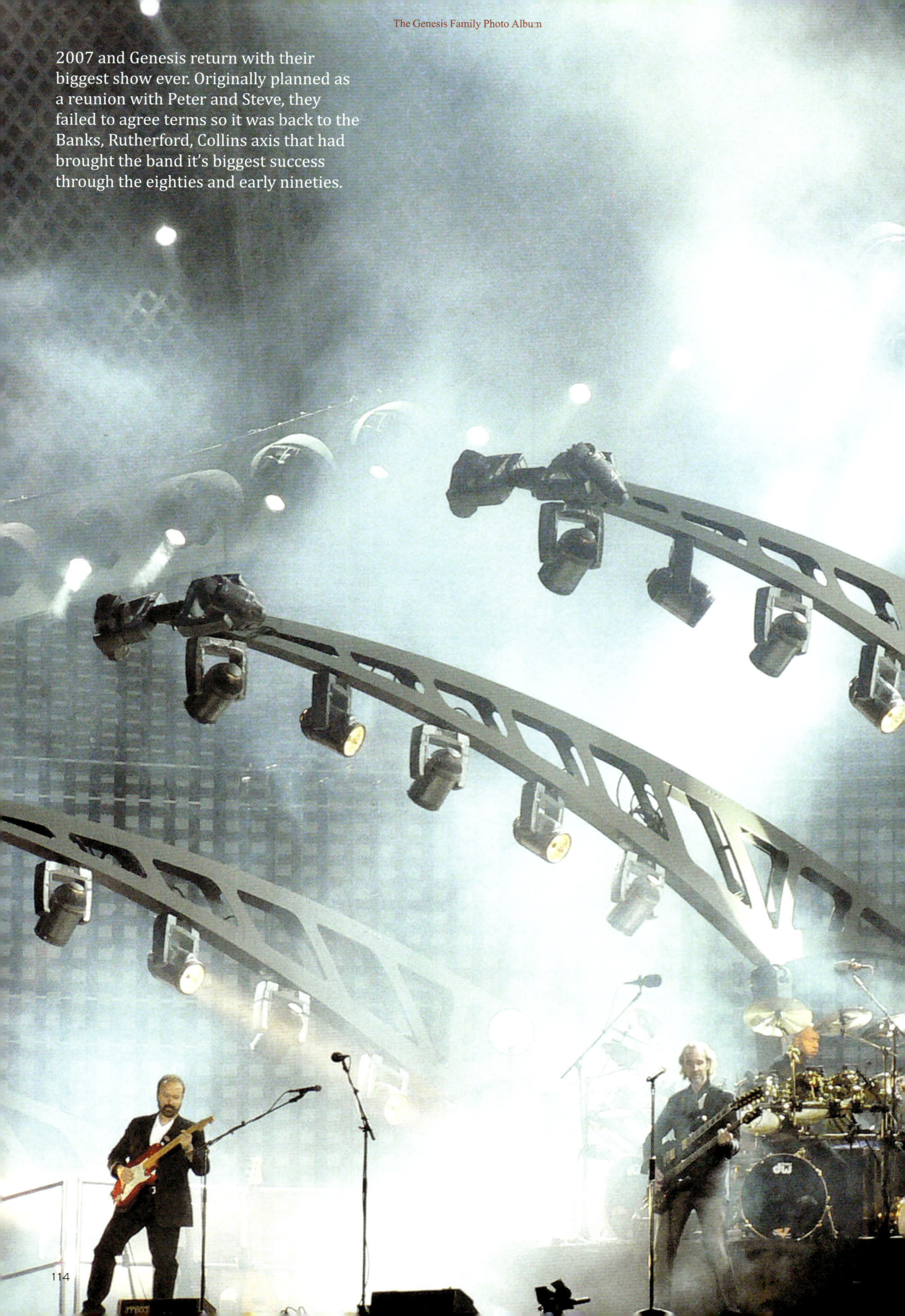

The Genesis Family Photo Album

2007 and Genesis return with their
biggest show ever. Originally planned as
a reunion with Peter and Steve, they
failed to agree terms so it was back to the
Banks, Rutherford, Collins axis that had
brought the band it's biggest success
through the eighties and early nineties.

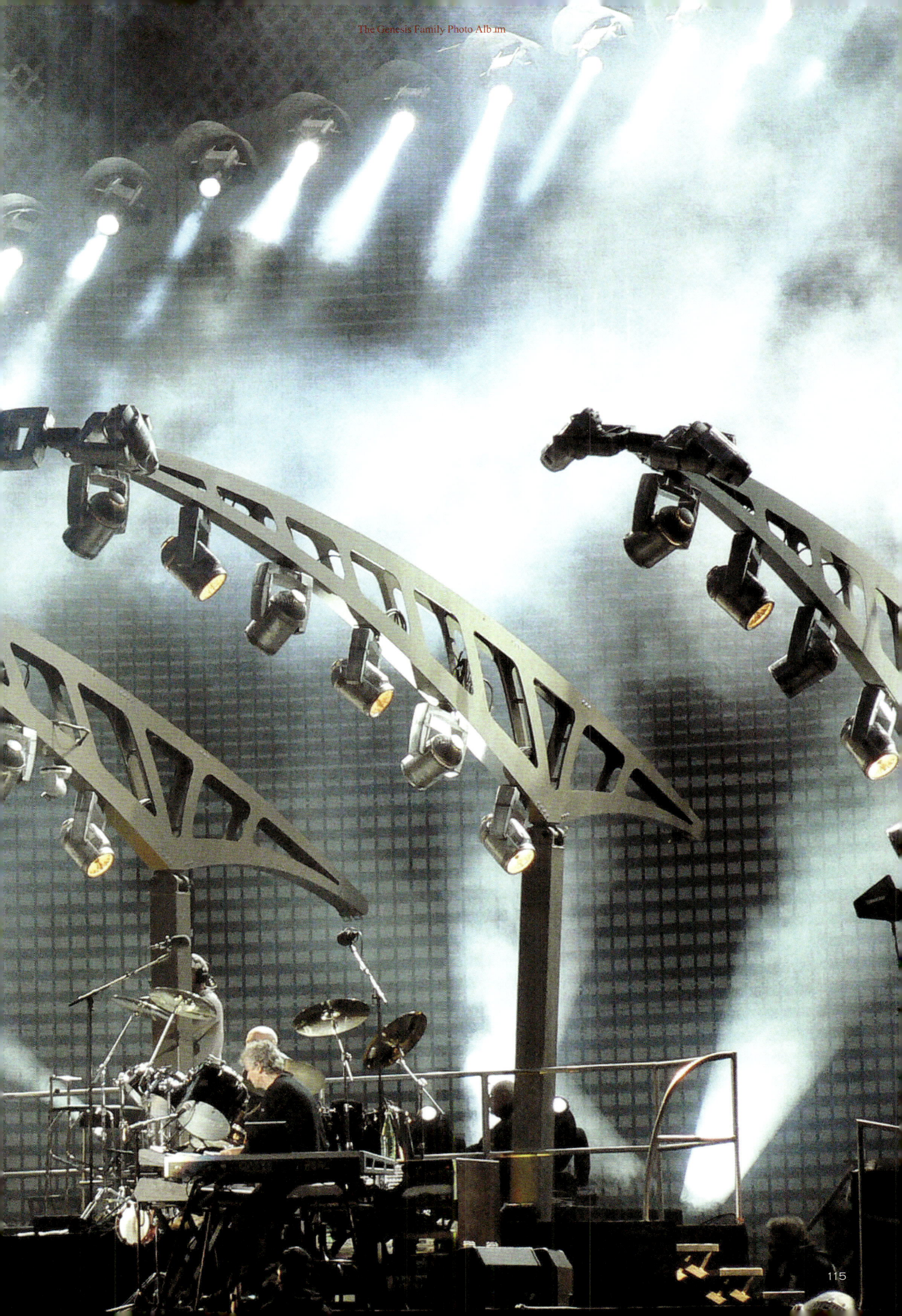

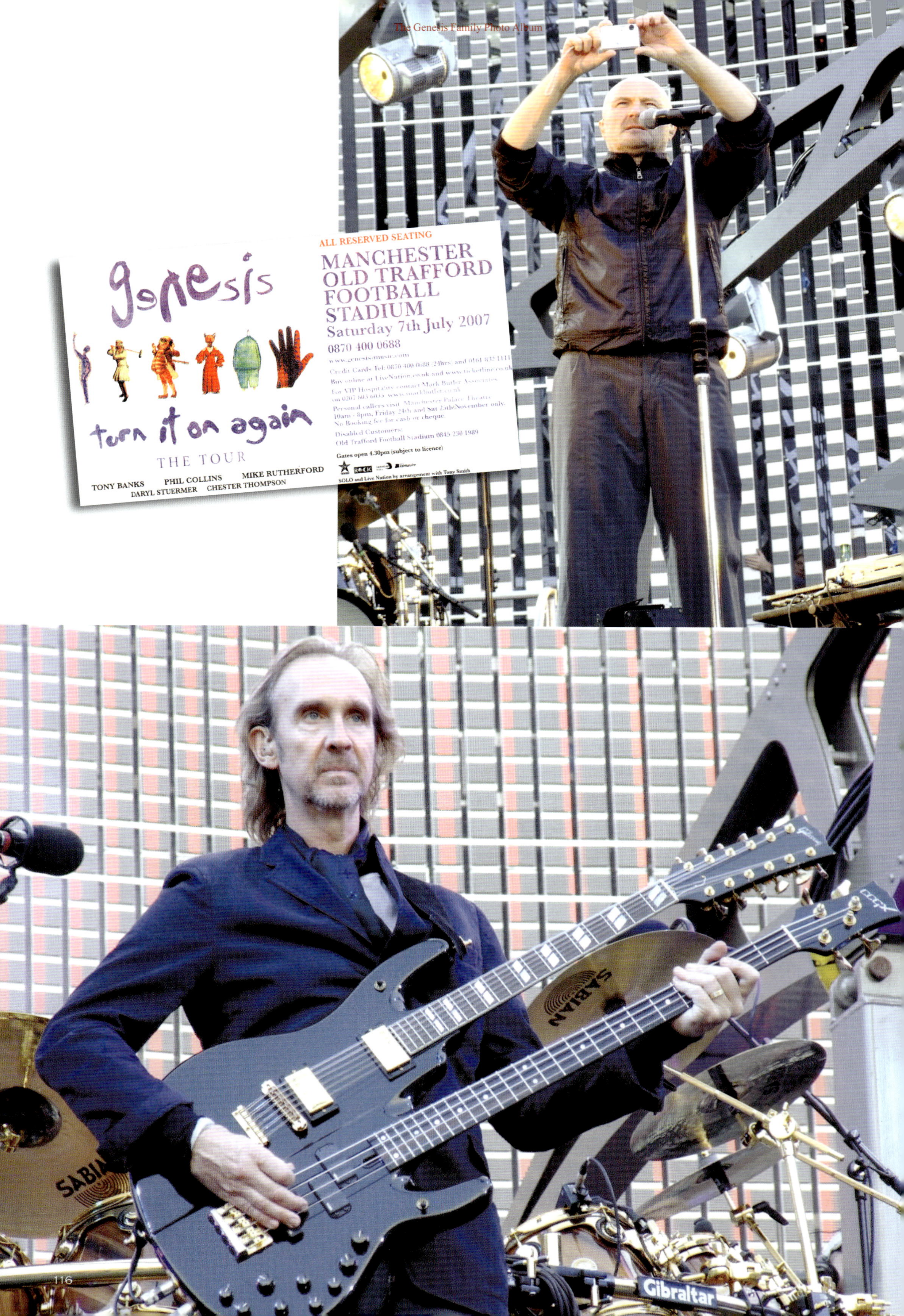
genesis
turn it on again
THE TOUR
TONY BANKS   PHIL COLLINS   MIKE RUTHERFORD
DARYL STUERMER   CHESTER THOMPSON

ALL RESERVED SEATING
MANCHESTER
OLD TRAFFORD
FOOTBALL
STADIUM
Saturday 7th July 2007
0870 400 0688
www.genesis-music.com
Credit Cards Tel: 0870 400 0688 - 24hrs. and 0161 832 1111
Buy online at Live-Nation.co.uk and www.ticketline.co.uk
For VIP Hospitality contact Mark Butler Associates
on 0207 603 6033 www.markbutler.co.uk
Personal callers visit Manchester Palace Theatre
10am - 8pm, Friday 24th and Sat 25thNovember only.
No Booking fee for cash or cheque.
Disabled Customers:
Old Trafford Football Stadium 0845 230 1989
Gates open 4.30pm (subject to licence)
SOLO and Live Nation by arrangement with Tony Smith

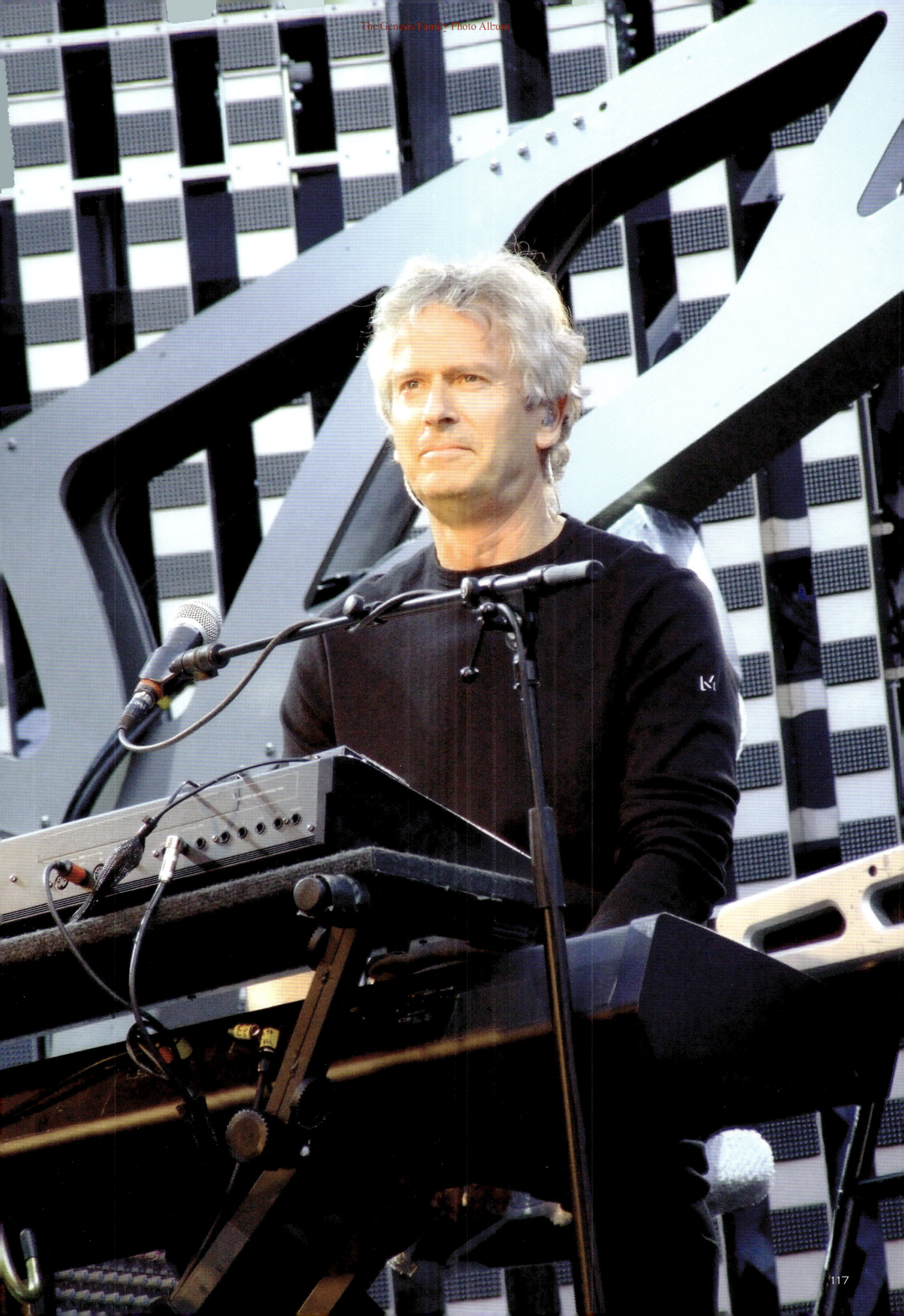

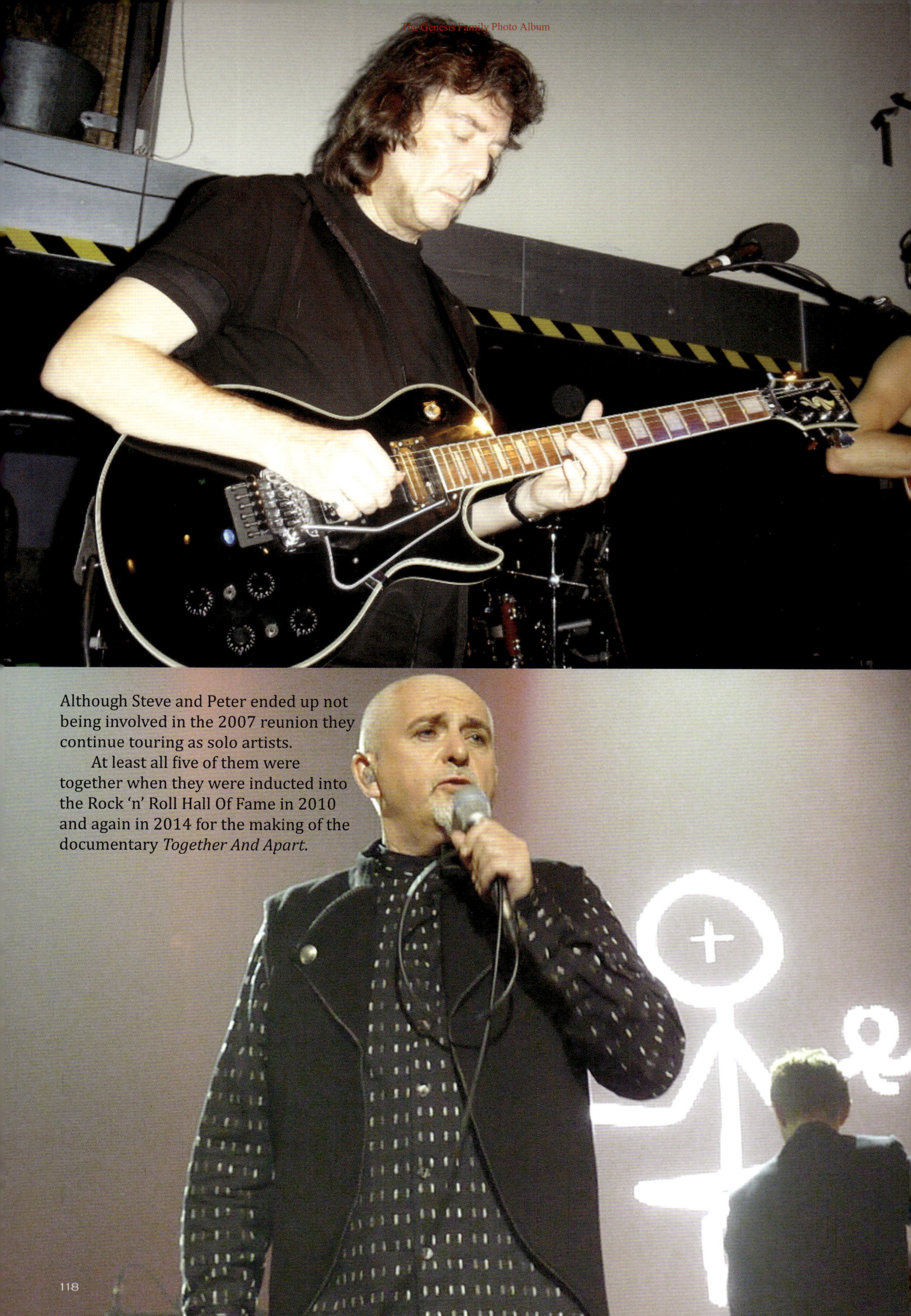

Although Steve and Peter ended up not being involved in the 2007 reunion they continue touring as solo artists.

At least all five of them were together when they were inducted into the Rock 'n' Roll Hall Of Fame in 2010 and again in 2014 for the making of the documentary *Together And Apart*.

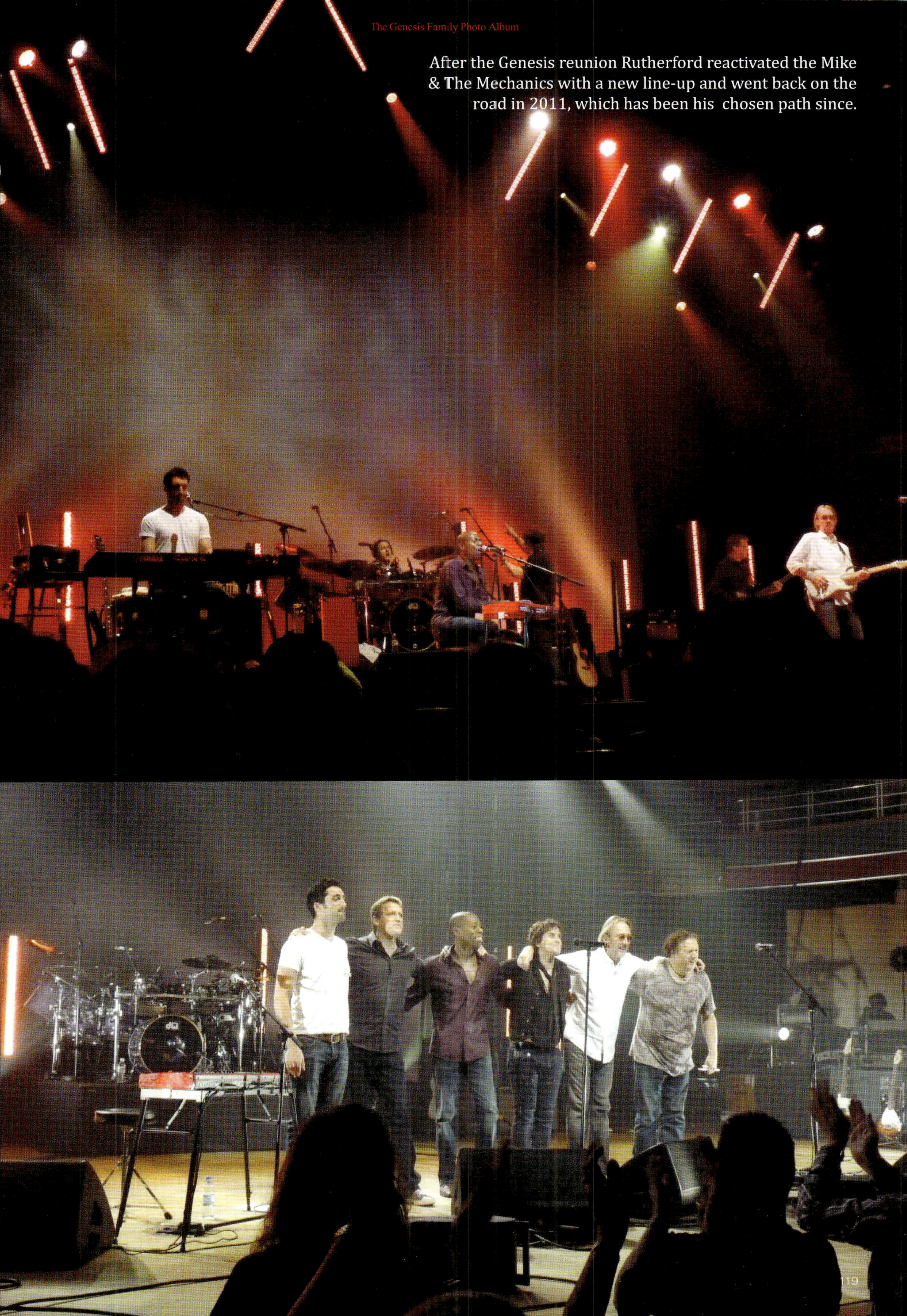

After the Genesis reunion Rutherford reactivated the Mike & The Mechanics with a new line-up and went back on the road in 2011, which has been his chosen path since.

Having released an album of reinterpretations of Genesis
songs in 1996, Steve produced a second volume in 2012
and toured on the back of it with the vast majority of the
show consisting of Genesis songs.

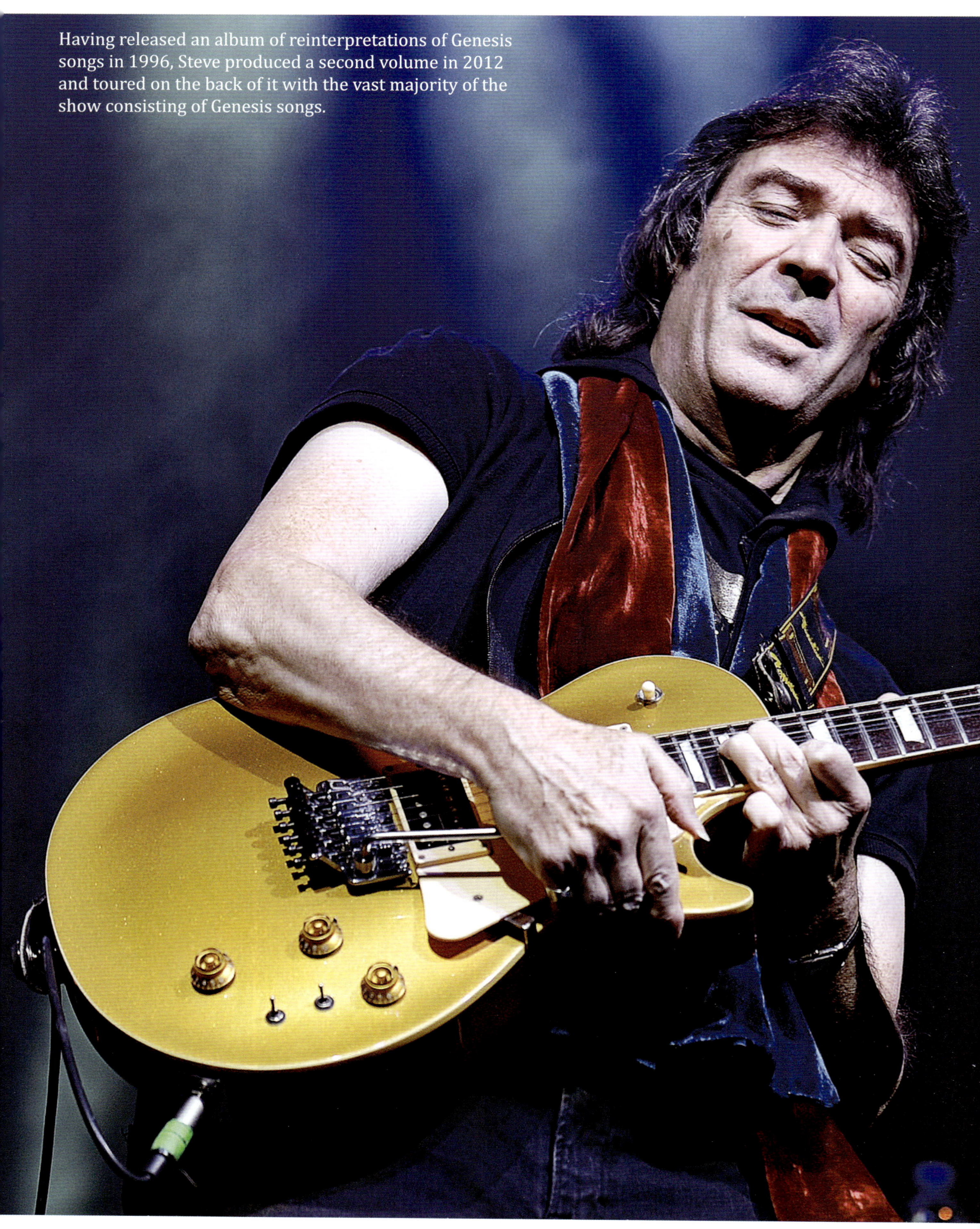

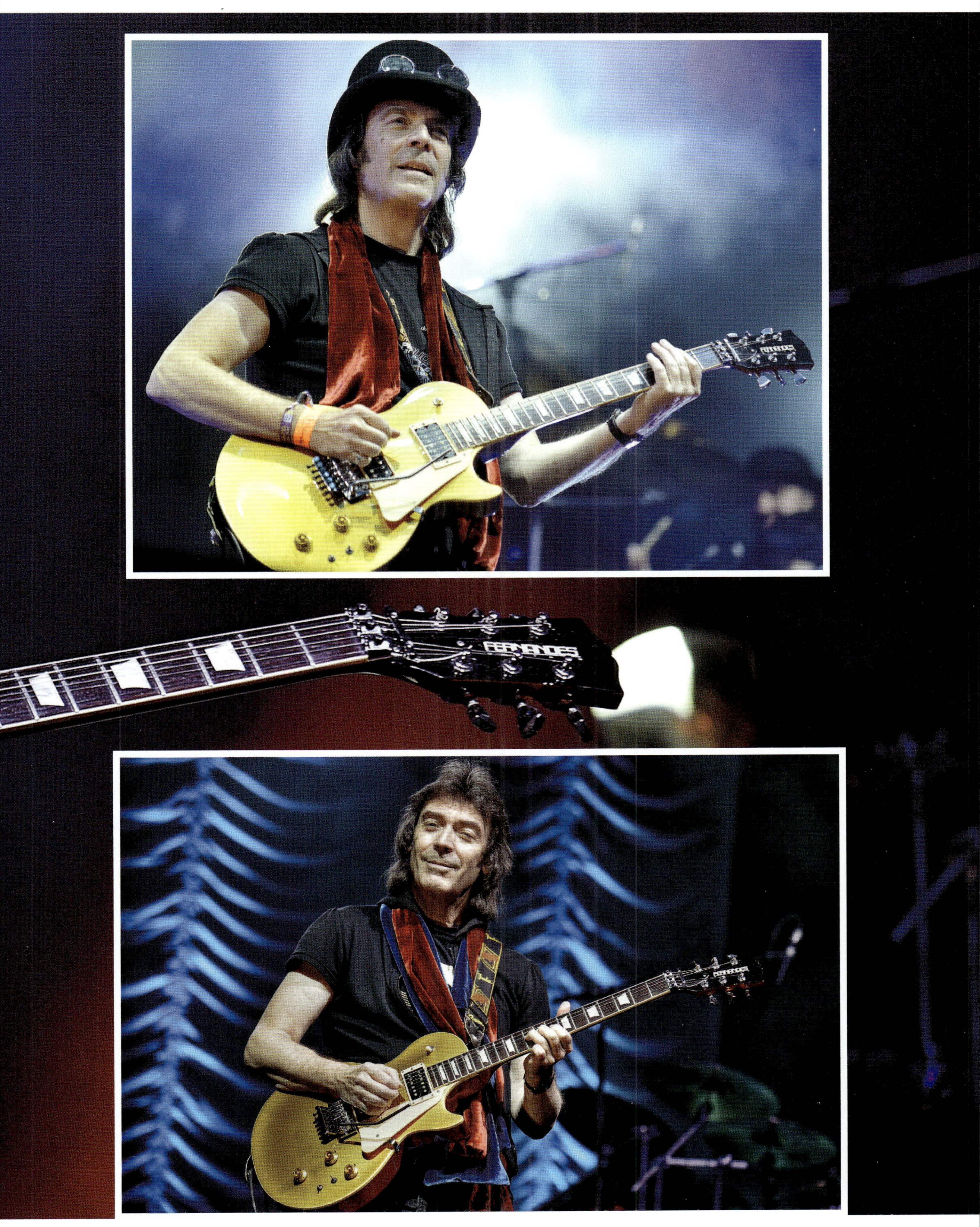

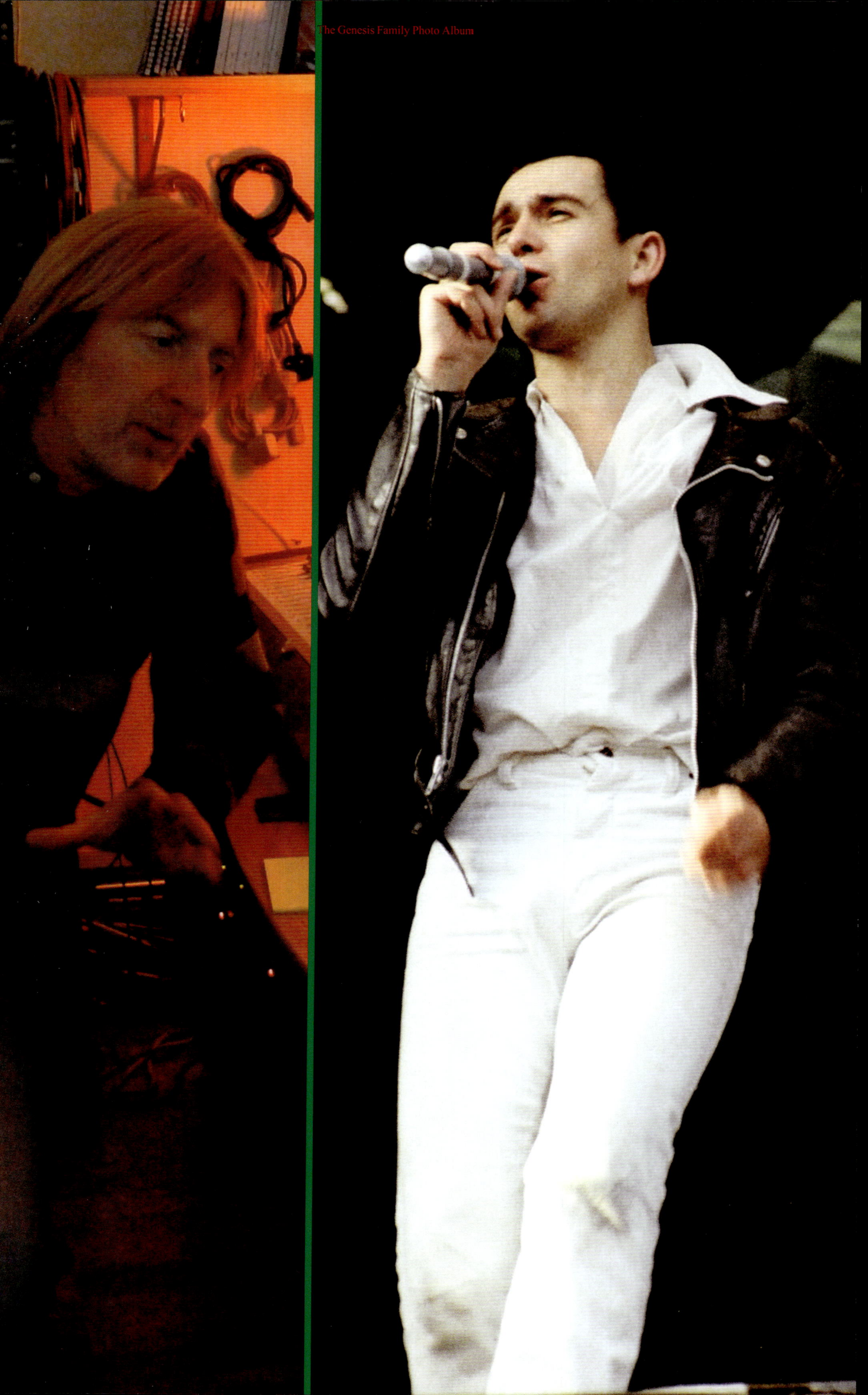

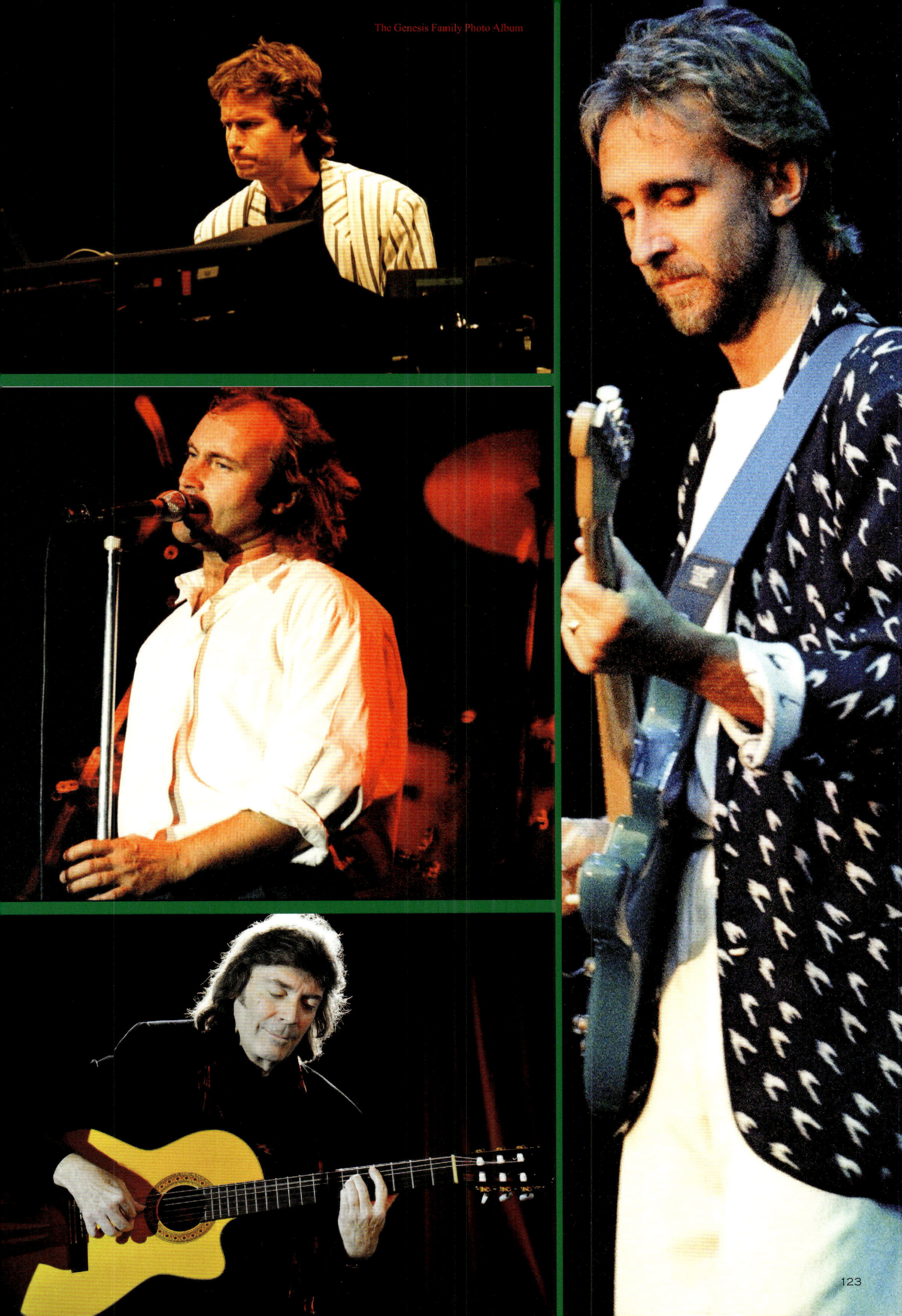

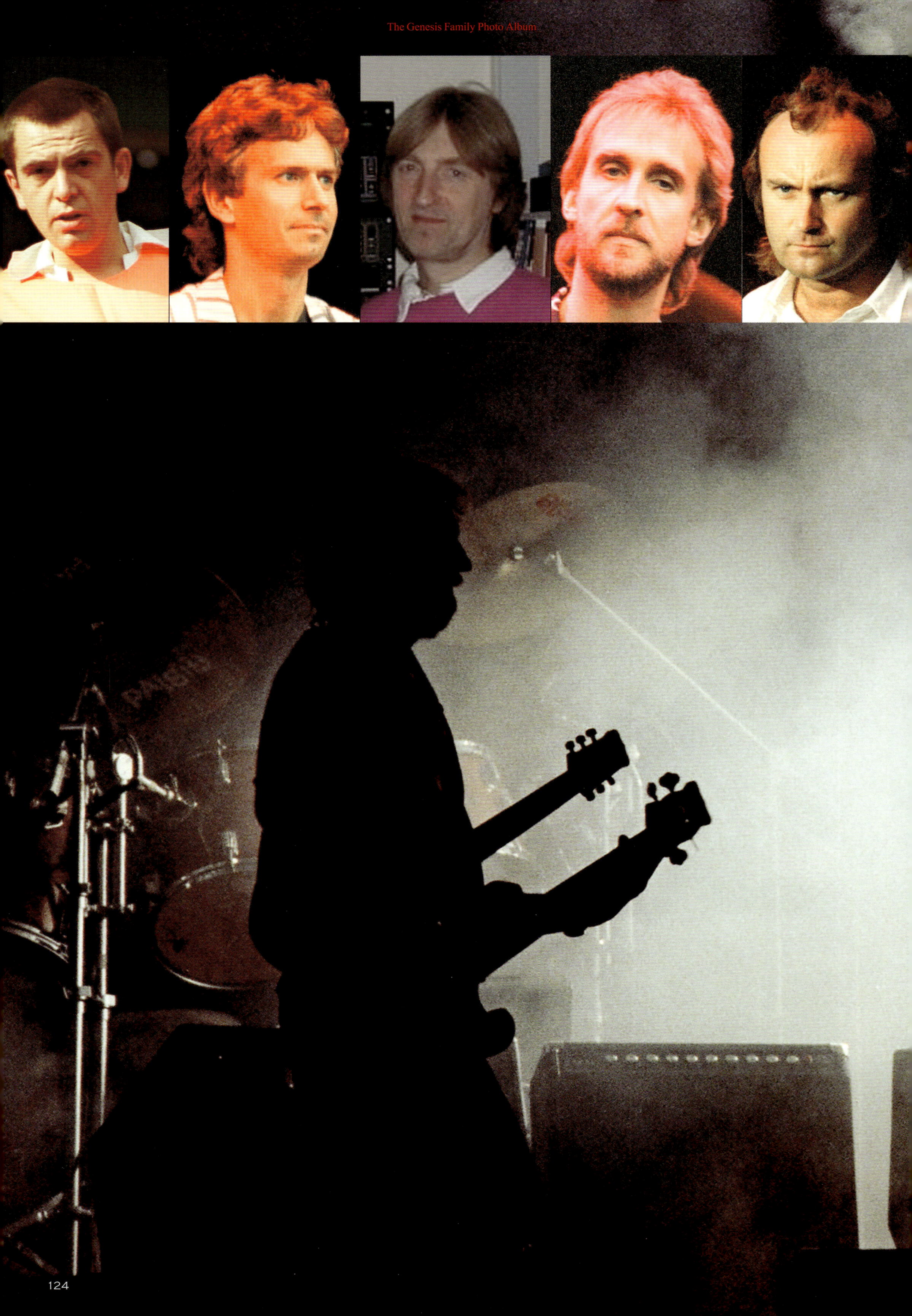

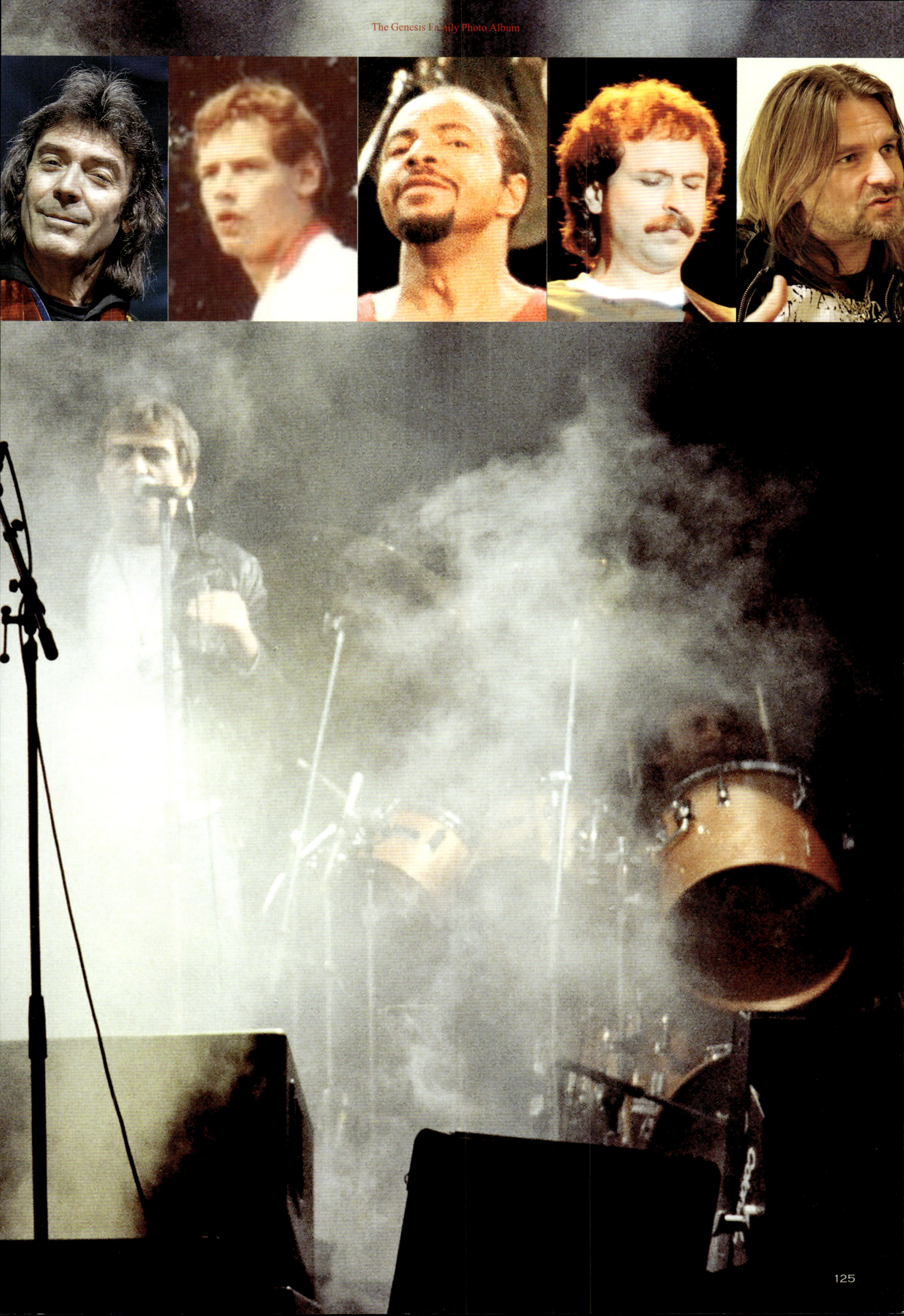

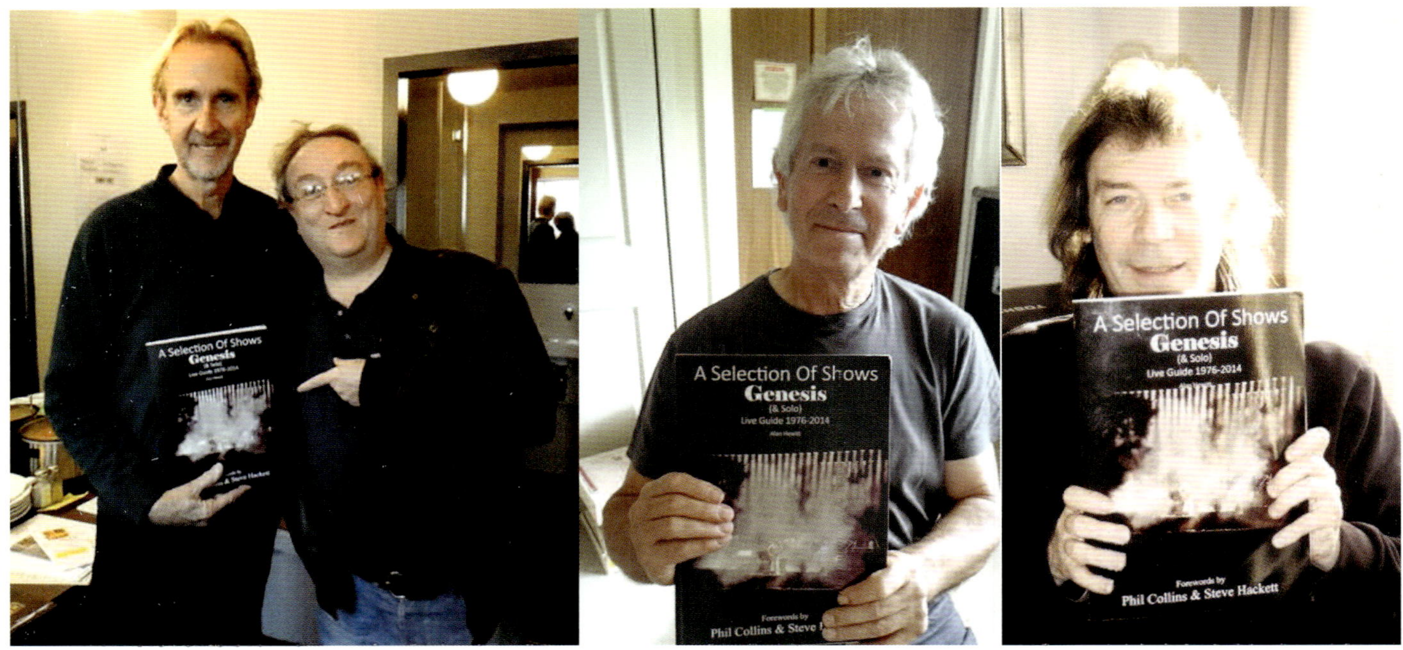

Author Alan Hewitt presenting Mike with his copy of A Selection Of Shows backstage at the Philharmonic Hall, Liverpool in 2015. Tony and Steve look suitably pleased with their copies. Steve, along with Phil wrote forewords for the book. Phil seems particularly engrossed in the contents.

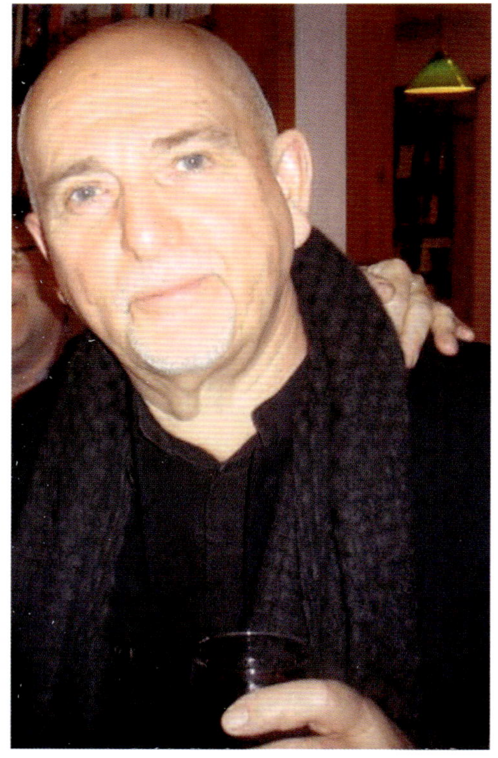

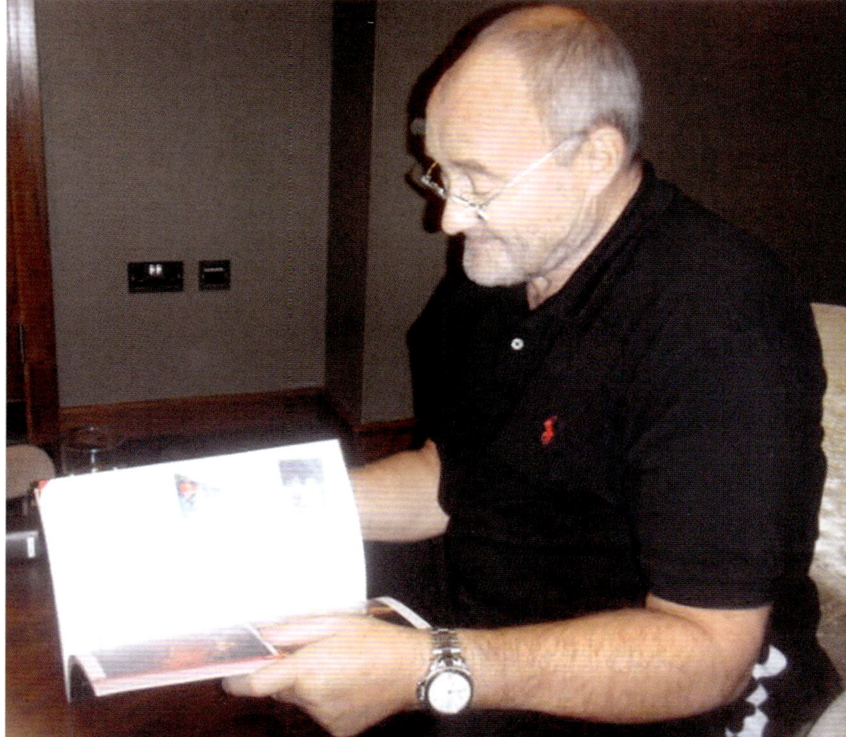

Above: Peter at Daunts Bookshop in Holland Park, London on 21st November 2017 for the launch of former road manager Richard Macphail's *My Book Of Genesis*.

Right: Steve & Ant. Steve's 2009 album release *Out of the Tunnel's Mouth* featured Ant on a couple of tracks.

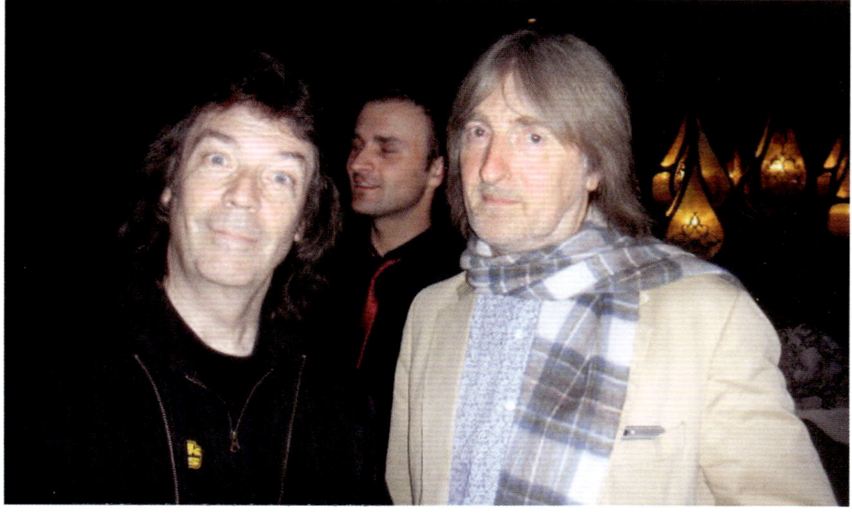

Acknowledgements

Special thanks to the following people who have helped with the production of this book:
Steve Emberton, Simon Funnell, Mario Giammetti, Norrie Gray, Richard Haines, Alan Hewitt, Richard Macphail, Colin McLeod, Lee Millward, Rene Nethtitt & Alan Perry.

Photo Credits

Colin McLeod: Lyceum, London, 24th January 1971 - p11-15.
Courtesy of Simon Funnell: Van Dike Club, Plymouth, 26th May 1972 - p16-17; Hippodrome, Birmingham, 1st May 1975 & Nuevo Pabellon Club Juventud, Badalona, 9th May 1975 - p38-41; Ekeberghallen, Oslo, 19th February 1975 - p44-45.
Richard Haines: Brighton Dome, 15th October 1973 - p18-28; Headley Grange, Hampshire, July 1974 - p30-34, 36-37.
Alan Perry: Empire Theatre, Liverpool, 18th April 1975 - p42-43; Hammersmith Odeon, 9th June 1976 - p48-49, 53 (colour inset); Empire Theatre, Liverpool, 9th January 1977 - p56, 58-61; Empire Theatre, Liverpool, 24th April 1977 - p65; Empire Theatre, Liverpool, 23rd September 1977 - p66-67; Knebworth 24th June 1978 - p70-75; Knebworth 9th September 1978 - p76-77, 122 (right); Battersea Park, 16th September 1978 - p78-79; Birmingham Odeon, 29th October 1978 - p80-81; Reading 26th August 1979 - p82-83; Empire Theatre, Liverpool, 2nd May 1980 - p4-85 (main); Empire Theatre, Liverpool, 3rd May 1980 - p88; Reading 28th August 1981 - p89; Milton Keynes Bowl, 2nd October 1982 - p6-7, 90-95, 124-125; Selhurst Park, London 9th July 1983 - p96-100; Wembley Stadium, 1st July 1877 - p102-103, 123 (top); Wembley Stadium, 2nd July 1877 - p104-105, 124 (centre & right); Wembley Stadium, 4th July 1877 - p106-107; Knebworth 2nd August 1992 - p109; National Exhibition Centre, Birmingham 5th December 1995 - p110 (top left & Right); National Exhibition Centre, Birmingham 6th November 1997 - p111 (top left & right); Old Trafford, Manchester, 7th July 2007 - p114-115; Symphony Hall, Birmingham, 29th May 2011 - p119.
Steve Emberton: Hammersmith Odeon, June 1976 - p48-52 (b/w); Rainbow Theatre, January 1977 - p54-55; Hammersmith Odeon, April 1977 - 62-64.
Courtesy of Anthony Phillips: Send Barns, Surrey, mid seventies - p57.
Roger Salem: Reading 25th August 1979 - p83 (Hackett).
Peter Ollerenshaw: Apollo, Manchester, 19th April 1980 - p84-85 (insets); St George's Hall, Bradford, 21st April 1980 p84 (left).
Unknown: Lyceum, London, 7th May 1980 - p86-87.
Phil Teague: Reading 28th August 1981 - p89 (crowd inset).
Steven Vaughan; Reading 28th August 1981 - p89 (crowd main).
Mike Ainscoe: Leisure Centre, Mansfield, 13th November 1983 - p100 (inset).
Ted Sayers: Twickenham, 1995 - p101; Apollo, Manchester, 5th March 1989 - p108; Hammersmith Odeon, 23rd March 2011 - p118 (bottom).
Lee Millward: Old Trafford, Manchester, 7th July 2007 - p116-117; Cropredy Festival, 7th August 2014 - p121 (top); Lowry, Salford, 25th October 2015 - p120, 121 (bottom); Symphony Hall, Birmingham, 1st May 2017 - p123 (bottom).
Jonathan Dann: Twickenham, 1995 - p110 (bottom).
Stuart Barnes; Twickenham, 1995 - p111 (bottom); Philharmonic Hall, Liverpool, 2015 - p126 (top left); The Farm, Surrey, 2015 (top centre).
Richard Nagy: Apollo, Manchester, 8th September 1986 - p101 (inset).
Ian Jones: Bray Film Studios, Windsor, 23rd January 1998 - p112.
Jonathan Guntrip: NYNEX Arena, Manchester, 6th March 1998 - p113.
Alan Hewitt: The Ferry, Glasgow, 19th November 2009 - p118 (top); Twickenham, 2015 (top right); London, 2015 (centre right); London, London, 2016 (bottom).
J O'Neill: Holland Park, 21st November 2017 (centre left).